Collins

Exploring Biology, Chemistry & Physics

GRADE 9

T0312468

Derek McMonagle | Series editor: Marlene Grey-Tomlinson

William Collins' dream of knowledge for all began with the publication of his first book in 1819. A self-educated mill worker, he not only enriched millions of lives, but also founded a flourishing publishing house. Today, staying true to this spirit, Collins books are packed with inspiration, innovation and practical expertise. They place you at the centre of a world of possibility and give you exactly what you need to explore it.

Collins. Freedom to teach.

Published by Collins
An imprint of HarperCollins*Publishers*
The News Building
1 London Bridge Street
London
SE1 9GF

HarperCollins*Publishers*
Macken House
39/40 Mayor Street Upper
Dublin 1
DO1 C9W8
Ireland

Browse the complete Collins catalogue at
www.collins.co.uk

10 9 8 7 6 5 4

www.collins.co.uk/caribbeanschools

ISBN 978-0-00-835335-3

British Library Cataloguing-in-Publication Data
A catalogue record for this publication is available from the British Library.

Author: Derek McMonagle
Series editor: Marlene Grey-Tomlinson
Reviewers: Bernadette Ranglin, Maxine McFarlane and Monacia Williams
Publisher: Elaine Higgleton
Commissioning editor: Tom Hardy
Content editor: Holly Woolnough
Copyeditors: David Hemsley, Sophia Ktori and Jan Schubert
Indexer: QBS Learning
Proofreader: Tony Clappison
Typesetter: QBS Learning
Illustrators: QBS Learning and Ann Paganuzzi
Cover designers: Gordon MacGilp and Kevin Robbins
Cover artwork: Blew_s/Shutterstock
Production controller: Sarah Burke
Printed and bound by Ashford Colour Press Ltd

MIX
Paper | Supporting
responsible forestry
FSC
www.fsc.org
FSC™ C007454

This book contains FSC™ certified paper and other controlled sources to ensure responsible forest management.

For more information visit: www.harpercollins.co.uk/green

The publishers gratefully acknowledge the permission granted to reproduce the copyright material in this book. Every effort has been made to trace copyright holders and to obtain their permission for the use of copyright material. The publishers will gladly receive any information enabling them to rectify any error or omission at the first opportunity.

Derek McMonagle is a leading writer of science educational materials with worldwide experience. He has developed courses at primary, secondary and advanced levels for many countries including Jamaica and the UK.

Marlene Grey-Tomlinson is a Senior teacher at Excelsior High School in Kingston, Jamaica. She has been teaching Integrated Science and Biology in Grades 7 through to 11 for over 25 years and is one of the country's leading science educationalists.

Contents

Introduction – How to use this book

Unit B1 Diffusion and osmosis

6 Diffusion

We are learning how to:

* explain how particles spread out as a result of diffusion

> This tells you what you will be learning about in this lesson.

Diffusion

Living things need to move substances around. One way by which this is done is called **diffusion**.

Sometimes when you step into your home, you know that someone has been baking or cooking. This is because when we are cooking tiny particles of food move through the air. The particles travel from the kitchen to all the other rooms in your home and our noses can detect them, even if we are not in the kitchen. We call this spreading out of particles 'diffusion'.

FIG B 1.6.1 Spicy meat, Jamaica style

> The book has plenty of good illustrations to put the science into context.

> This introduces the topic.

Activity B 1.6.1

Investigating diffusion

Your teacher will help you with this activity.

Here is what you need:

* shallow open container like a watch glass
* volatile liquid that has a characteristic smell, like a perfume
* stopwatch with a second hand

Here is what you should do:

1. Students sit or stand in rows at different distances from the teacher's table.
2. The teacher pours a small amount of perfume onto a watch glass on the table at the front of the class.
3. Each student should raise an arm and note the time when he or she first smells the perfume.
4. Note which students were first to smell the perfume.
5. Note which students were last to smell the perfume.
6. [STEAM] Suggest how this activity could be modified to investigate how easily the smell of perfume diffuses from one room to another through an open doorway.

teacher's table — perfume in watch glass
rows of students
FIG B 1.6.2

> There are often some fascinating fun facts.

> Each spread has activities to help you to investigate the topic.

> Each spread offers questions to help you to check whether you have understood the topic.

> Key terms are defined on the pages where they are used.

In Activity B 1.6.1 some of the perfume particles spread out, or diffuse, from the watch glass to all parts of the classroom. At the start, the perfume particles are at high **concentration** immediately above the watch glass and at low concentration in the rest of the classroom. The perfume particles in the air move randomly and disperse from this region of high concentration to regions of low concentration.

We say that the perfume particles diffuse across a **concentration gradient**. This is the difference in the concentration of particles between two regions.

After a while the concentration of perfume particles is the same in all parts of the room.

Substances are continually diffusing into and out of cells. However, when the concentration of a substance is higher, say outside the cell, more particles of the substance will diffuse into the cell than out of it. Conversely, if the concentration of a substance is higher inside the cell, more particles will diffuse out than diffuse in.

Substances diffuse into and out of cells across concentration gradients. For example:

* The concentration of oxygen in the blood is higher than in the cell, where it is used up during respiration, so there is a net diffusion of oxygen from the blood into the cell.
* The concentration of carbon dioxide in the cell is higher, because it is produced during respiration, so there is a net diffusion of carbon dioxide from the cell into the blood.

Activity B 1.6.2

1. Drop a crystal of potassium manganate(VII) into a beaker of water and leave it for 24 hours.
2. Sketch the appearance of the water at the start, after 15 minutes and again after 24 hours.

Check your understanding

1. Explain why the appearance of the water changed in Activity B 1.6.2.

B 1.6

Interesting fact

Diffusion also takes place through solids, but this happens much more slowly than through liquids and gases.

(a)
diffusion of oxygen
high concentration of oxygen in blood > low concentration of oxygen in cell

(b)
diffusion of carbon dioxide
low concentration of carbon dioxide in blood < high concentration of carbon dioxide in cell

FIG B 1.6.3 Diffusion of gases (a) into and (b) out of cells

Key terms

diffusion the net movement of particles from an area where they are in high concentration to an area where they are in low concentration, until the concentrations are the same

concentration the number of particles of a substance per unit volume (for example, in a solution, g/cm^3 of water)

concentration gradient the difference in the concentration of particles of a substance in one place compared to another place

43

Review of Diffusion and osmosis

- Cells are the building blocks from which all living things are made.
- A typical animal cell consists of a nucleus, cytoplasm, several small vacuoles and a cell membrane.
- A typical plant cell consists of a nucleus, cytoplasm, a single large vacuole, chloroplasts, a cell membrane and a cell wall.
- A cell membrane is a selectively permeable membrane that controls what enters and what leaves a cell.
- Diffusion is the movement of particles from a region of higher concentration to a region of lower concentration along a concentration gradient.
- Some substances can pass into and out of cells by diffusion.
- Osmosis is a special kind of diffusion that involves the movement of water particles.
- During osmosis, water molecules pass through a partially permeable membrane from a more dilute solution (region of high water concentration) to a more concentrated solution (region of low water concentration).
- Water passes into and out of cells by osmosis.
- Living tissue has membranes across which osmosis can take place.
- Diffusion involves gases and particles in solution.
- The rate of diffusion increases with increasing temperature.
- Diffusion is involved in the processes of energy storage and release during photosynthesis and respiration.
- In plants, osmosis is responsible for the absorption of water.
- In animals, osmosis is involved in the transport of substances around the body.
- Diffusion can take place in the absence of water.
- Osmosis is the movement of water.

At the end of each unit there are pages which list the key topics covered. These will be useful for revision.

At the end of each section there are special questions to help you and your teacher review your knowledge. See if you can apply this knowledge to new situations and if you can use the science skills that you have developed.

Science, Technology, Education, Arts and Mathematics (STEAM) activities are included, which present real-life problems to be investigated and resolved using your science and technology skills.

Review questions on Diffusion and osmosis

Knowledge and understanding

1. a) Listed below are some parts of cells. For each one write:

A if it is only found in animal cells

P if it is only found in plant cells

AP if it is found in both animal cells and plant cells.

   i) Chloroplast   **ii)** Cell membrane   **iii)** Small vacuole

   iv) Nucleus   **v)** Cytoplasm   **vi)** Cell wall

b) Which of the parts above controls the movement of substances into and out of a cell?

2. Mrs Livingstone is cooking a curry for dinner. The kitchen window is open. Explain how Mr Livingstone knows what is for dinner even before he enters their home.

3. State whether or not each of the following is an example of osmosis.

a) Plant roots absorb water from soil.

b) Carbon dioxide passes from the bloodstream to the air in the lungs.

c) Plants lose water vapour from their leaves into the air.

d) When soft fruit is placed in sugar syrup it gets smaller.

4. Fig B 1.RQ.1 shows different concentrations of two gases inside and outside a plant cell.

a) Name the process by which gases move into and out of cells.

b) Predict what will happen in each of the conditions, **i)** and **ii)** in Fig B 1.RQ.1.

i)   **ii)**

low concentration of carbon dioxide   high concentration of carbon dioxide   high concentration of oxygen   low concentration of oxygen

FIG B 1.RQ.1

Process skills

5. The smell of petrol diffuses across a petrol station forecourt more rapidly on a hot day than on a cold day.

a) On the basis of this observation suggest a hypothesis linking rate of diffusion and temperature.

b) Describe how you could test this hypothesis.

---

11 Estimating sugar content in a sweet potato

Sweet potatoes are a popular food in the Caribbean. They are eaten in lots of different ways including boiled, mashed, baked and as fries.

100 g of sweet potato contains about 20 g of carbohydrates, 1.6 g of protein and 0.1 g of fat. It is also a good source of vitamins A, B6, B12, C and D, and of the minerals calcium, iron and magnesium.

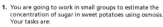

FIG STEAM B 1.11.1 Sweet potatoes

As the name 'sweet potato' suggests, a proportion of the 20 g of carbohydrates is present as sugar. This information will be useful to someone wanting to reduce their sugar intake.

1. You are going to work in small groups to estimate the concentration of sugar in sweet potatoes using osmosis. Your tasks are:

- To revise the work carried out on osmosis in this unit so that you understand the process.
- To prepare sugar solutions with different concentrations.
- To measure the mass gain or mass loss when sweet potato chips are soaked in sugar solutions with different concentrations.
- To draw a graph of mass gain/loss against concentration and use it to deduce the sugar concentration in sweet potatoes.

a) Osmosis is a special kind of diffusion involving water molecules. When solutions of different concentrations are separated by a partially permeable membrane there is a net movement of water molecules from the less concentrated solution to the more concentrated solution. Eventually the solutions will have the same concentration.

Make sure that your understanding of osmosis is clear, and read through Lesson B 1.7 to remind you of anything that you may have forgotten.

b) Make up sugar solutions of different concentrations. The percentage of sugar in sweet potato is between 0% and 10% so you should make up solutions of 0%, 1%, ... 10% by mass of sugar.

To make up each solution:

- Put a clean, dry 250 cm³ beaker on a balance
- Press the tare/zero key to zero the display

FIG STEAM B 1.11.2 Making up solutions

1 Designing an experiment

We are learning how to:

- identify a problem and formulate a hypothesis
- design an experiment
- analyse data and draw conclusions

Experiments are the one way by which scientists can gather information. They might provide qualitative observations, such as colour changes, as well as quantitative information, such as measurements of different quantities.

An experiment requires careful planning. There are several stages to consider.

Specifying the problem ▶▶▶

What is the problem you are hoping to solve? In order to be meaningful an experiment must have a specific purpose.

FIG A 1.1 Chemists carry out specific reactions

Formulating a hypothesis ▶▶▶

What do you think the solution to the problem is?

Formulating a **hypothesis** isn't the same as already knowing the answer. Scientists often have a good idea what the results of an experiment will be simply because in science things often follow patterns. Sometimes these patterns involve numbers.

We might all predict from our everyday observations that suspending weights on a spring makes the spring grow longer, but is there more to this? Is there a relationship between the length of the spring and the size of the weight?

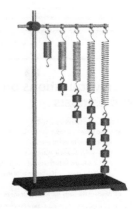

FIG A 1.2 Adding weights to a spring makes it longer

Designing the experiment ▶▶▶

How are you going to carry out the experiment? What materials and equipment will you need? Are there any safety issues that must be taken into account? How can you be sure you are carrying out a **fair test** in which one variable is allowed to change while the others are kept the same?

It is sensible to make a list of the materials and apparatus needed to carry out an experiment.

The science laboratory is no more potentially dangerous than a domestic kitchen. Provided you take sensible precautions and follow instructions, you are unlikely to

FIG A 1.3 Eye protection is essential

come to any harm. Eye protection is essential when carrying out any experiment. Laboratory coats are also useful for protecting clothing.

Analysing data ▶▶▶

What sort of data will you collect? Will you record your data in a table? How will you present your data? Sometimes the data is in the form of numbers that can be used to plot graphs.

Drawing conclusions ▶▶▶

What have you learned from carrying out your experiment? Was your hypothesis correct or not?

Negative results can be as important as positive results. They all help the scientist to understand how organisms and materials behave.

In the next three lessons you will see how this **template** can be applied to experiments in all areas of science.

Activity A 1.1

Fair testing

Abbie and Bria think that sugar dissolves more quickly in hot drinks than in cold drinks. They have designed an experiment to test their hypothesis. This is what they plan to do.

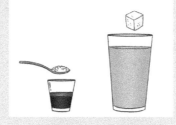

FIG A 1.4 How quickly does sugar dissolve in drinks?

After they start a stopwatch:

- Abbie is going to pour a teaspoon of sugar into a small glass of hot coffee and stir the coffee until the sugar dissolves.

- Bria is going to drop a sugar cube into a large glass of cold orange juice and observe the sugar cube until it dissolves.

Discuss within your group whether the girls are carrying out a fair test or not. Here are some things you might consider:

- Is the same volume of each drink used?

- Is the same mass of sugar used?

- Are the drinks treated in the same way?

Check your understanding

1. In which part of your plan should you include the following?

   a) A list of apparatus and materials that you will need.

   b) A table of results.

   c) A prediction about the outcome of the experiment.

   d) A statement of the problem that you are going to investigate.

   e) A discussion about whether your prediction was correct.

Key terms

hypothesis proposed explanation for something that can be tested by a suitable experiment.

fair test a test in which only one variable is allowed to change while the others are kept the same

template a pattern or way of organising

2 An experiment in biology

We are learning how to:

- apply a template to an experiment in biology

Background

Many plants reproduce by producing seeds. The seeds can remain inactive in the soil for many weeks until conditions are suitable for germination. When seeds **germinate** a root grows downwards, and a shoot that will develop leaves grows upwards.

FIG A 2.1 Germinating seeds

The problem

A student is aware that in order to germinate, seeds don't need light but they do need water and oxygen from the air. He wants to know whether temperature is also an important factor in seed germination.

His hypothesis

The student has observed that seeds in his garden at home seem to germinate more quickly in the summer when it is warmer. For this reason he thinks that the rate at which seeds germinate will increase with increasing temperature.

His experiment

- Small containers × 4
- **Seed compost**
- Cling film
- Elastic bands × 4
- Seeds × 40

Here is what he plans to do:

i) Put seed compost in four containers, each to the same depth.

ii) Water the compost in each container with 5 cm³ of distilled water.

iii) Sow 10 seeds on the compost in each container. The seeds should be spread out so they do not interfere with each other as they germinate and grow.

iv) Seal the top of each container using cling film and an elastic band to prevent the soil from drying out.

v) Leave each container in one of four locations that are at different average temperatures. The details are given in Table A 2.1.

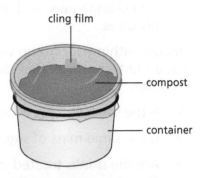

FIG A 2.2 Sealed container with compost and seeds

Seed sample	Location	Average temperature / °C
A	Refrigerator	5
B	Cool cabinet	15
C	Laboratory	25
D	Drying room	35

TABLE A 2.1

vi) Inspect the seeds each day. At the first signs of germination in any of the containers, the number of seeds that have started to germinate in each container will be recorded in a table every day for a week.

	Days after the seeds were sown						
	5	6	7	8	9	10	11
Seeds germinated in A	0	0	0	0	0	0	0
Seeds germinated in B	0	0	0	0	1	2	2
Seeds germinated in C	0	0	1	2	4	5	7
Seeds germinated in D	1	3	4	6	7	9	9

TABLE A 2.2

Data

The results that the student recorded from his experiment are shown in Table A 2.2.

Drawing conclusions

The rate at which the seeds germinated increased with increasing temperature. This supports the student's hypothesis that rate of germination is related to temperature.

Activity A 2.1

Designing an experiment

'Epsom salts' is an old name for the chemical magnesium sulphate.

Some gardeners believe that watering seed compost with a solution of 12 g of magnesium sulphate dissolved in 1 dm³ of water increases the rate at which seeds germinate. You are going to design an experiment to test whether this is true or not.

Set out your experiment plan under the headings given in the student's experiment.

FIG A 2.3 Epsom salts

Check your understanding

1. Discuss whether or not each of the following would prevent the experiment above being a fair test.

   a) Use seeds of different plants in the different containers.

   b) Water the seeds with tap water rather than with distilled water.

   c) Use soil in some containers and seed compost in the others.

   d) Put the containers in sealed polythene bags rather than cover them with cling film.

Key terms

germination process by which seeds start to grow into plants

seed compost soil containing minerals needed for germinating seeds

9

3 An experiment in chemistry

We are learning how to:

• apply a template to an experiment in chemistry

Background >>>

The food we eat passes through our **digestive system**, where it is broken down into nutrients that can be absorbed by the body. The stomach is an important organ of the digestive system.

In the stomach food is mixed with an acid as part of the digestive process. If you eat a big meal your stomach may produce too much acid.

Excess acid in the stomach may cause indigestion. Swallowing **antacid** tablets neutralises excess acid.

FIG A 3.1 Excess acid sometimes causes indigestion

The problem >>>

A student wants to know which of three types of antacid, X, Y and Z, is the most effective. She will do this by finding which of them will neutralise the most acid.

Her hypothesis >>>

From the instructions on the packaging the student thinks that type Y is the most effective.

FIG A 3.2 Antacids are used to treat indigestion

Her experiment >>>

• Beakers 250 cm³ × 3

• Dilute hydrochloric acid

• Acid–base indicator

• Mortar and pestle

Here is what she plans to do:

  i) Crush each type of antacid to form powders.

 ii) Weigh exactly 1 g of each powder and put them in separate marked beakers.

iii) Make the powders into solutions by dissolving each of the solids in 100 g of water.

 iv) Add a few drops of acid–base indicator.

  v) Add dilute hydrochloric acid from a burette to each solution in turn until a colour change indicates that the antacid has been neutralised.

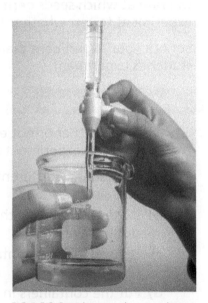

FIG A 3.3 Carrying out the experiment

vi) Record the volume of acid used each time.

vii) Repeat this process three times for each type of tablet, and for each type of tablet record the average volume of hydrochloric acid required to neutralise the antacid. For each repeated procedure she keeps the following constant:

- the size of the reaction vessel
- the mass of each tablet used
- the concentration of the dilute hydrochloric acid
- the temperature of the dilute hydrochloric acid

Data >>>

The results she obtained from her experiment are shown in Table A 3.1.

Antacid type	Average volume of dilute hydrochloric acid solution / cm³
X	18.3
Y	27.1
Z	23.8

TABLE A 3.1

Drawing conclusions >>>

The antacid that required the greatest amount of acid to neutralise it is type Y. This supports the student's hypothesis that type Y is the most effective antacid.

Activity A 3.1

Designing an experiment

You are going to determine whether tap water or river water is better for washing. Make this determination by finding out experimentally which water makes better suds.

Set out your experiment plan under the headings given in the student's experiment.

Check your understanding

1. A student wanted to compare the reactivity of two metals, zinc and magnesium, with acids by measuring the amount of hydrogen given off over time. Here is what he plans to do:
   - React zinc powder with cold dilute sulphuric acid in a boiling tube and measure the amount of hydrogen produced in 5 minutes.
   - React magnesium ribbon with cold concentrated hydrochloric acid in a round-bottomed flask and measure the amount of hydrogen gas produced in 2 minutes.
   a) Explain why the student is not carrying out a fair test.
   b) Rewrite his plan so that it will provide reliable results.

Key terms
....

digestive system part of the body where food is broken down and absorbed

antacid medication to neutralise stomach acid

4 An experiment in physics

We are learning how to:

• apply a template to an experiment in physics

Background >>>

Friction is a force that opposes the movement of one object over another.

Friction always acts in the opposite direction to the motion and only exists when objects are moving.

Friction is not limited to movement between solid surfaces. It also exists when a solid moves through a liquid or a gas. In these cases we call it **water resistance** and **air resistance**.

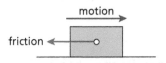

FIG A 4.1 Friction opposes motion

The problem >>>

A student has observed that although fish vary in size and colour, they often have shapes that are very similar.

Fish generally have thin elongated bodies and they do not have arms or legs. The student wants to investigate why fish have evolved in this way.

FIG A 4.2 Many fish are similar in shape

Her hypothesis >>>

From her own experience of swimming and diving she thinks that having a long and thin shape allows fish to move easily through the water.

Her experiment >>>

• Modelling clay
• Balance
• Large measuring cylinder

• Cooking oil
• Long thin stick
• Stopwatch

Here is what she plans to do:

i) Fill a measuring cylinder to near the top with cooking oil.

ii) Divide the modelling clay into four parts of equal mass. Each piece will then be made into a shape like those shown in Fig A 4.3: a, b, c and d.

iii) Hold one of the shapes on the surface of the cooking oil and then release it. At the same time start the stopwatch.

iv) Stop timing when the shape reaches the bottom of the measuring cylinder.

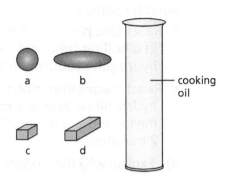

FIG A 4.3

v) Remove the shape from the oil by pushing a thin stick into it and lifting it out.

vi) Repeat the procedure for each shape.

vii) Record the results in a table.

She has chosen cooking oil rather than water because objects will take longer to fall through it. This will allow her to measure the time more accurately.

Data

The results she obtained from her experiment are shown in Table A 4.1.

Shape	Description of shape	Time taken to fall / s
a	Sphere	9
b	Sausage-shaped with pointed ends	7
c	Cube	10
d	Long rectangular prism	14

TABLE A 4.1

Drawing conclusions

The shape that fell quickest through the oil was the one that best resembled the shape of most fish. This supports the student's hypothesis that the shape of a fish aids its movement through water.

Activity A 4.1

Designing an experiment

Objects experience resistance as they move through air.

You are going to design an experiment to compare how easily objects of different shapes move through air.

Set out your experiment plan under the headings given in the student's experiment.

Check your understanding

1. In the experiment described above, the student only measured the time taken for each object to fall through the oil once.

   Explain why the student would obtain more reliable results if she timed each shape three times and then worked out the average time for each shape.

Key terms

friction force that opposes the movement of one object over another

water resistance friction an object experiences moving through water

air resistance friction an object experiences moving through air

5 Units

We are learning how to:

- express quantities in different units
- use prefixes to alter the values of units

SI base units

Scientists carry out experiments in which they often take measurements. These measurements are made in **SI units**. These are an internationally agreed set of units used by all scientists around the world. Using the same units makes it easier for scientists to communicate their work to others.

There are five SI base units used in science—see Table A 5.1.

Unit name	Unit symbol	Quantity measured	Additional information
Metre	m	Length and distance	
Kilogram	kg	Mass	
Second	s	Time	
Kelvin	K	Temperature	Degrees Celsius (°C) normally used
Ampere	A	Electric current	Unit name often abbreviated to amp

TABLE A 5.1

SI-derived units

There are a number of other units derived from the base units. One you will often use in science is the unit of volume, which is derived from the unit of length.

The volume of a regular shape like a cuboid = length × width × height. Since each of those quantities is measured in a unit of length, the volume will be given in that unit^3. The metre is the SI unit of length, therefore the cubic metre will be the SI unit of volume.

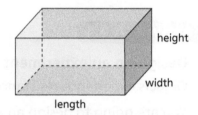

FIG A 5.1 Volume of a cuboid

Prefixes

Although the SI unit of mass is the kilogram, this unit is not suitable for expressing the mass of all objects because the values would require large numbers of zeroes. For example:

The mass of the Earth = 5 972 000 000 000 000 000 000 000 kg

The mass of one atom of carbon = 0.000 000 000 000 000 000 000 000 019 9 kg

To get around this problem scientists use a series of **prefixes** that represent different powers of 10 (see Table A 5.2).

Prefix	Symbol	Multiplying factor	Multiplying factor in scientific notation
Mega	M	1 000 000	10^6
Kilo	k	1000	10^3
Deci	d	0.1	10^{-1}
Centi	c	0.01	10^{-2}
Milli	m	0.001	10^{-3}
Micro	μ	0.000 001	10^{-6}

TABLE A 5.2

Notice that the symbol for mega is 'M' while the symbol for milli is 'm'. It is important to write all of these prefixes in upper or lower case as appropriate to avoid confusion.

You will already be familiar with some combinations of 'prefix' + 'unit'. Many of the foods we eat are sold by the kilogram.

1 kilogram = 1000 gram

The active ingredients in the medicines we take when we are not feeling well are often expressed in milligrams.

1 milligram = 0.001 gram

You probably have a ruler that measures length in centimetres, and each centimetre is divided into 10 millimetres.

1 centimetre = 0.01 metre   1 millimetre = 0.001 metre

Liquids are sold in bottles measured in litres (l) and millilitres (ml). These are not SI units but can be easily converted:

1 litre = 1 dm^3 1 millilitre = 1 cm^3

Activity A 5.1

SI units in everyday life

Look at the packaging on foods and other materials in your home. Make a note of any SI units used to show quantities.

Check your understanding

1. Write down the SI unit that is used to measure:

   a) mass   **b)** temperature   **c)** volume

2. Copy and complete the following:

   a) 1 mg = ... g   **c)** 1 cm = ... mm

   b) 1 km = ... m   **d)** 1 cm^3 = ... dm^3

FIG A 5.2 Fruits and vegetables are sold by the kilogram in the supermarket

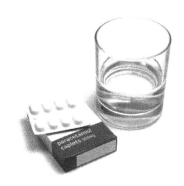

FIG A 5.3 Amounts of drugs are often expressed in milligrams

FIG A 5.4 Liquids are measured in cubic centimetres and cubic decimetres

Key terms

SI units group of internationally agreed units used in science

prefix group of letters or a short word put in front of other words to modify their meaning

6 Measurement

We are learning how to:

- use apparatus to measure physical quantities
- measure mass, volume, time and temperature

A **physical quantity** is an amount that can be measured. To obtain knowledge, scientists carry out experiments in which they make careful observations and measurements. In order to do this they may use a variety of measuring instruments and containers, which are collectively called apparatus.

The **mass** of a substance is the amount of matter it contains. The units of mass are the kilogram (kg), for large masses, and the gram (g), for small masses.

$$1 \text{ kg} = 1000 \text{ g}$$

Mass is measured on a balance. There are two types in common use in laboratories, as shown in Fig A 6.1.

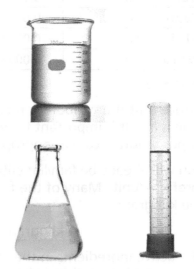

FIG A 6.2 Apparatus that show approximate volume

beam balance

electronic balance

FIG A 6.1 Balances measure mass

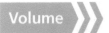

The **volume** of a substance is the amount of space that it occupies. The units of volume are the cubic decimetre (dm³) for large volumes and the cubic centimetre (cm³) for smaller volumes. For very large volumes the cubic metre (m³) may be used.

FIG A 6.3 Apparatus that show accurate volume

$$1 \text{ m}^3 = 1000 \text{ dm}^3 \qquad 1 \text{ dm}^3 = 1000 \text{ cm}^3$$

Chemical apparatus for measuring volume can conveniently be divided into two groups – apparatus that shows approximate volume (such as cylinders), and apparatus that shows accurate volume (such as burettes).

For most scientific experiments, time is measured in minutes and seconds. A wristwatch that shows seconds will provide sufficiently accurate measurements, or a digital stopwatch may be used.

FIG A 6.4 Digital stopwatch

Temperature

Temperature is a measure of the degree of hotness of a body. Although the systematic unit of temperature is the Kelvin (K), temperature is generally measured in degrees Celsius (centigrade, or °C). The relationship between degrees Celsius and Kelvin is simple.

Celsius = Kelvin – 273   Kelvin = Celsius + 273

The most common device for measuring temperature in the laboratory is the liquid-in-glass thermometer. A thermometer that has a scale from –10 °C to 110 °C is frequently used, but thermometers with different scales may also be used when lower or higher temperatures are to be measured.

FIG A 6.5 Liquid-in-glass thermometer

Activity A 6.1

Taking measurements

Here is what you need:

- tripod stand
- wire gauze
- heat source
- thermometer
- eye protection
- beaker 100 cm³
- measuring cylinder 25 cm³
- triple beam balance
- digital stopwatch

Here is what you should do:

1. Weigh a dry 100 cm³ beaker and record its mass.

2. Measure out approximately 25 cm³ of water using the measuring cylinder and pour the water into the beaker. Reweigh the beaker and water and record the total mass.

3. Calculate the mass of the water used.

4. Measure the initial temperature of the water and record it. Place the beaker on a tripod and gauze and heat it for exactly 5 minutes. Measure the final temperature of the water.

5. What was the temperature increase of the water?

Key terms

physical quantity amount that can be measured

mass amount of matter a substance contains

volume amount of space a substance occupies

temperature hotness of a body

Check your understanding

1. **a)** The mass of a beaker containing some powder is measured on an electronic balance (Fig A 6.6). What is the reading on the balance?

   b) The mass of the empty beaker is 119.87 g. What is the mass of the powder?

2. What is the volume of aqueous solution in the measuring cylinder shown in Fig A 6.7?

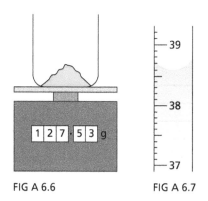

FIG A 6.6   FIG A 6.7

7 Different kinds of data

We are learning how to:
- make qualitative and quantitative observations
- present data in a table

Data is another term for information. When we carry out experiments we gather information, often by observing what happens. In everyday language **observation** usually means what you see, but in science it can mean:

- what you see
- what you smell – some gases have characteristic smells
- what you hear – sounds have different pitches and amplitudes
- what you feel – objects might feel hot or cold due to heat transfer

(a) change of colour

Qualitative observations

Many of the observations you will make don't involve numbers or measurement. These are called **qualitative** observations.

These include things like changes of colour, the release of bubbles of gas, or the emission of heat and sometimes light as well.

Quantitative observations

Some observations involve numbers and therefore measurements of some kind.

Quantitative changes include changes in mass, volume of gas produced and changes in temperature. In some experiments you might measure the quantity at the start and again at the end. This will allow you to calculate any increase or decrease.

The data in Table A 7.1 was obtained by a student who carried out a chemical reaction between granulated zinc and an excess of hydrochloric acid. This reaction produces the gas hydrogen. The total volume of gas evolved was recorded every half minute for 7 minutes.

(b) effervescence

(c) emission of heat and light

FIG A 7.1 Qualitative changes

Time / minutes	Volume of gas / cm³	Time / minutes	Volume of gas / cm³	Time / minutes	Volume of gas / cm³
0.0	0	2.5	102	5.0	154
0.5	31	3.0	115	5.5	161
1.0	54	3.5	130	6.0	165
1.5	70	4.0	138	6.5	170
2.0	85	4.5	146	7.0	174

TABLE A 7.1

Making observations

Here is what you need:

- sodium chloride crystals
- phenolphthalein
- dilute hydrochloric acid
- dilute sodium hydroxide

- calcium carbonate
- test tubes × 4
- thermometer
- copper powder
- tin lid

- balance
- heat source
- tripod
- eye protection

(a) change of mass

Here is what you should do:

Make observations on each of the following reactions and state whether the changes you observe are qualitative or quantitative.

1. Put a small amount of sodium chloride crystals in a test tube and heat them.

2. Pour some dilute sodium hydroxide into a test tube to a depth of about 1 cm. Add a few drops of phenolphthalein.

3. Put a small amount of calcium chloride in a test tube and add dilute hydrochloric acid to a depth of about 2 cm.

4. Pour some dilute hydrochloric acid into a test tube to a depth of about 3 cm. Measure the temperature of the acid. Add a similar amount of dilute sodium hydroxide. Measure the temperature of the reaction mixture.

5. Put a small amount of copper powder on a tin lid. Measure the total mass of the tin lid and copper. Put the tin lid on a tripod and heat it for a few minutes. Allow the tin lid to cool. Measure the total mass of the tin lid and product.

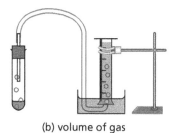

(b) volume of gas

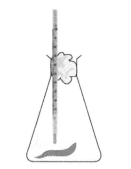

(c) change of temperature

FIG A 7.2 Quantitative changes

Check your understanding

1. State whether each of the following observations is qualitative or quantitative.

   a) The velocity of the car increased from 2.5 m/s to 3.0 m/s.

   b) When one end of the metal bar was heated the other end became warmer.

   c) The length of the plant shoot increased by 4.2 cm in one week.

   d) Effervescence was observed during the reaction.

   e) After 5 minutes the temperature of the water had fallen from 71.3 °C to 56.7 °C.

Key terms

data information

observation what you see, hear, smell or feel

qualitative to do with quality, such as colour

quantitative to do with measurement

8 Gathering data

We are learning how to:

- use a tally chart to count data
- record data in a frequency chart

Scientists often obtain data by carrying out experiments, but they may also gather data from the environment. This may be qualitative or quantitative.

If you observe the plants in a garden you will see a variety of different-shaped leaves. A biologist can group plants according to the leaf shape. Fig A 8.1 shows some of the different leaf shapes of common plants.

A biologist removed a leaf from each plant in a garden. Fig A 8.2 shows the leaves he collected.

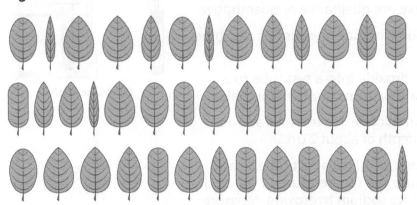

FIG A 8.2

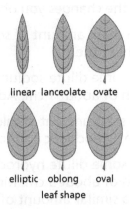

FIG A 8.1 Different shapes of leaves

This is called **raw data**. He organised the data into a **tally chart**, shown in Table A 8.1. This allowed him to see the number, or **frequency**, of each leaf shape.

Leaf shape	Tally	Frequency
Linear	IIII	4
Lanceolate	III	3
Ovate	HHH HHH II	12
Elliptic	HHH II	7
Oblong	HHH IIII	9
Oval	HHH	5
	Total	40

TABLE A 8.1

A simple way of making sure you have not missed a reading is to make sure the frequencies collectively add up to the number in the sample.

Collecting data may involve measurement of quantities such as length, mass and volume.

Interesting fact

A tally is a quick way of counting in sets of five using only straight lines, so: one (I), two (II), three (III), four (IIII) and for five we cross the gate (HHH). For example, a tally of HHH HHH II equals 5 + 5 + 2 = 12.

Here is an example of how a biologist gathered information about dog whelks. These animals live on rocky sea shores, and their shells come in a range of sizes. By gathering information on the sizes of dog whelk shells in different locations, it is possible to come to conclusions about the conditions that best suit these animals.

Comparing the sizes of single dog whelk shells in different locations would not provide useful information because an individual dog whelk might not be representative of a typical animal for that location.

To obtain meaningful information the biologist measured the shell lengths of 25 dog whelks at each location. After the shell of each animal had been measured, it was replaced where it had been found. Here are the measurements she took at location A, correct to the nearest millimetre:

27, 22, 21, 25, 24, 22, 26, 25, 23, 26, 25, 23, 28, 24, 26, 27, 26, 27, 26, 24, 25, 28, 24, 26, 25

Once again the raw data is used to construct a tally chart (see Table A 8.2). This allows the biologist to see the frequency of each shell length.

FIG A 8.3 A dog whelk shell

Shell length / mm	Tally	Frequency
21	I	1
22	II	2
23	II	2
24	IIII	4
25	HHH	5
26	HHH I	6
27	III	3
28	II	2
	Total	25

TABLE A 8.2

Activity A 8.1

Collecting data

Here is what you need:

- 30 cm ruler

Here is what you should do:

1. Go outside into the school field or into an undeveloped area near to where you live.

2. Find a population of living things that you might measure. This could be snails, but could equally well be leaves, flower stems, flowers, etc.

3. Take the same measurement for a sample of 25.

4. Record your raw data.

5. Use your raw data to compile a tally chart.

Check your understanding

1. Here is a second set of measurements that the biologist took at a different location, B.

   24, 20, 19, 22, 22, 20, 23, 23, 21, 24, 22, 21, 26, 22, 23, 24, 23, 23, 23, 22, 22, 25, 21, 23, 24

   Construct a tally chart from these readings.

Key terms

raw data scores or information before it is organised in any way

tally chart means of adding the numbers of items at different values

frequency the number of items of a particular value

9 Displaying data

We are learning how to:

- present data as a bar chart
- present data as a histogram

In the previous lesson you learned how to organise raw data into a tally chart. The frequencies give information about the distribution of data but this can be seen more easily if the data is presented in certain ways. In this lesson you are going to learn about **bar charts** and **histograms**. In the following lesson you will look at graphs.

Bar charts

Bar charts are used to display qualitative data. They consist of a series of bars. The length of each bar is determined by the frequency of the data it represents.

Leaf shape provides qualitative data and so it can be displayed as a bar chart. The data from Table A 9.1 has been used to draw the bar chart in Fig A 9.1.

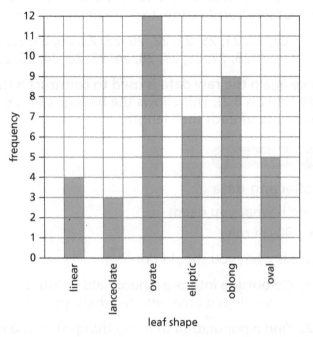

FIG A 9.1 Bar chart showing leaf shape of plants in a garden

Leaf shape	Tally	Frequency
Linear	IIII	4
Lanceolate	III	3
Ovate	HHT HHT II	12
Elliptic	HHT II	7
Oblong	HHT IIII	9
Oval	HHT	5
	Total	40

TABLE A 9.1

The height of each bar shows the total number of plants with that particular leaf shape. It is much easier to see the distribution of plants with different-shaped leaves from the bar chart than from the tally chart.

Notice that in a bar chart, spaces are often left between the bars. This can make it easier to read the height of each bar.

Histograms

A bar chart is a good way of displaying qualitative data. However, it is not used to display quantitative data. A histogram is used to do this.

The data in Table A 9.2 relates to the length of dog whelk shells. It is quantitative data because it has been obtained by measurement. The data has been used to draw the histogram in Fig A 9.2. The height of each bar corresponds to the frequency of each measurement.

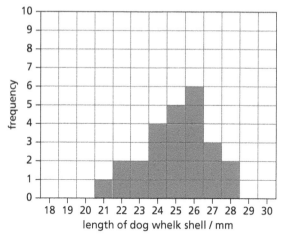

Shell length / mm	Tally	Frequency
21	I	1
22	II	2
23	II	2
24	IIII	4
25	HHI	5
26	HHI I	6
27	III	3
28	II	2
	Total	25

TABLE A 9.2

FIG A 9.2 Histogram showing lengths of dog whelk shells at location A

Notice that the histogram looks very similar to a bar chart but gaps are not left between the bars. There are other differences that you will learn about later in your course.

Activity A 9.1

Displaying data

Here is what you should do:

1. Present the data you gathered in Activity A 8.1 as a bar chart if it is qualitative data, or a histogram if it is quantitative data.

2. a) Draw a histogram of the data relating to the dog whelk population in location B (Lesson 1.8 Check your understanding).

   b) Compare the histograms for the two locations and comment on the sizes of the dog whelk shells at each one.

Key terms

bar chart method of displaying qualitative data

histogram method of displaying quantitative data

Check your understanding

1. There are four blood groups: O, A, B and AB. Everyone's blood is in one of these groups.

   Table A 9.3 gives the blood groups of all the students in a science class.

   a) Why should this data be presented as a bar chart and not a histogram?

   b) Draw a bar chart to illustrate this information.

Blood group	Number of students who have blood in that group
O	14
A	9
B	7
AB	2
Total	32

TABLE A 9.3

10 Plotting graphs

We are learning how to:

- present data in the form of a graph
- interpret information from a graph

In Lesson 1.7 the data in Table A 7.1 relates to the volume of hydrogen gas given off at different times during a chemical reaction.

The pattern is easier to see if the data is presented in the form of a graph.

Here are some important points about the graph in Fig A 10.1 that you should bear in mind when plotting your own graphs:

- The scales for the axes have been chosen to make use of most of the graph paper.

- The axes are labelled with the quantity and the unit used.

- Each point is plotted with a small 'x' drawn with thin lines. Using large dots leads to inaccuracy.

- A smooth **'line of best fit'** is drawn through the points. This line is not meant to pass through every point but to show the general pattern between volume of gas and time.

- The graph has a meaningful title that describes the nature of the data.

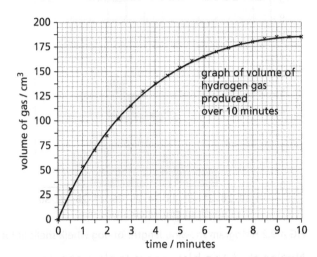

FIG A 10.1 A graph of the volume of hydrogen gas against time

Interpreting a graph ▶▶▶

A graph shows a pattern between two quantities. It can provide useful information.

The slope of a graph is called the **gradient**. In the graph in Fig A 10.2 the gradient is steep at the start but becomes shallower over time. At the end, the graph is horizontal. Since the hydrogen gas is one of the products of the chemical reaction, the graph shows that the rate of this reaction gradually decreases until the reaction stops.

Interpolation is finding values between the plotted points. This is possible because the graph shows the general pattern between volume of hydrogen gas produced and time.

- If we want to know how long it took to produce 100 cm³ of hydrogen gas, we draw a horizontal line from 100 cm³ to the curve, and then a vertical line from the curve to the time axis. The answer is 2.4 minutes.

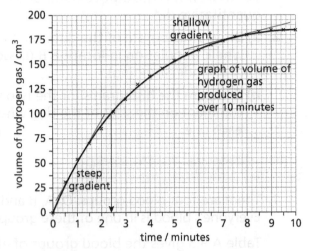

FIG A 10.2 A graph can provide information about the relationship between measurements

Activity A 10.1

Investigate the reaction between calcium carbonate and hydrochloric acid

Here is what you need:

- electronic balance
- beaker 250 cm³
- measuring cylinder 100 cm³

- calcium carbonate chippings
- dilute hydrochloric acid
- eye protection

Here is what you should do:

1. Weigh about 2 g of calcium carbonate chippings and put them in a 250 cm³ beaker.
2. Measure 100 cm³ of dilute hydrochloric acid in a measuring cylinder.
3. Place the beaker and the measuring cylinder on a balance and record their total mass.
4. Add the hydrochloric acid to the beaker, replace the empty measuring cylinder on the balance and at the same time start timing.
5. Record the total mass of apparatus and reaction mixture every 30 seconds until the reaction is complete. How can you tell when the reaction is complete?
6. Present your results in the form of a table.
7. Use your results to plot a graph of loss of mass against time for this reaction.
8. Measure the gradient of your graph at three different points and use your results to describe how the gradient changes over time.

Key terms

line of best fit line which best shows the pattern between two quantities on a graph

gradient slope of a graph

interpolate estimate values between data points

Check your understanding

1. A sample of calcium carbonate was reacted with an excess of hydrochloric acid. The volume of carbon dioxide gas produced by the reaction was recorded every half minute for 8 minutes. The results are shown in the graph in Fig A 10.3.

   a) What was the total volume of carbon dioxide collected by the end of the reaction?

   b) After how many minutes was the reaction complete?

   c) After how many minutes had half of the calcium carbonate reacted?

   d) Measure the gradient of the graph at 1, 2 and 3 minutes. Comment on your values.

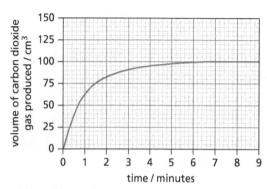

FIG A 10.3

11 Information from graphs

We are learning how to:

- obtain information from distance–time and displacement–time graphs
- obtain information from velocity–time graphs

A graph is a method of presenting the pattern between two variables in a way that is easily seen. However, some graphs can also provide quantitative information about the variables. This is the case for graphs associated with motion.

Distance–time graphs »

You can represent the movement of an object as a graph by plotting the distance it has travelled at different times on its journey.

The shape of a **distance–time graph** depends on how the object moves. If an object moves at a constant speed the distance–time graph will be a straight line, (see Fig A 11.1). The speed of an object moving at constant speed is given by the gradient of the graph (See Fig A 11.2).

If an object is moving in a particular direction we call the distance the **displacement**, and the speed in that direction becomes the **velocity**.

The velocity of an object moving at constant velocity is given by the gradient of the **displacement–time graph**.

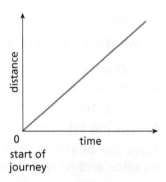

FIG A 11.1 Distance–time graph of an object moving at constant speed

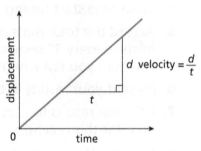

FIG A 11.2 Velocity is equal to the gradient of a displacement–time graph

$velocity = \frac{d}{t}$

Velocity–time graphs »

A **velocity–time graph** shows the velocity of an object at different times. When the displacement is measured in metres and the time in seconds, the velocity is expressed in metres per second.

The shape of the graph indicates how the velocity of the object is changing (see Fig A 11.3).

- When the graph is sloping upwards the velocity of the object is increasing. The object is **accelerating**.

- When the graph is horizontal the velocity of the object is constant.

- When the graph is sloping downwards the velocity of the object is decreasing. The object is decelerating.

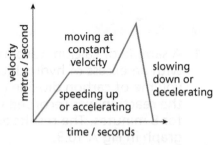

FIG A 11.3 A velocity–time graph

The acceleration of the object is given by the gradient of the graph over a given period of time.

- When the object is accelerating the gradient is positive.
- When the object is moving at constant velocity the gradient is zero.
- When the object is decelerating the gradient is negative.

Activity A 11.1

Velocity–time graph

Discuss the following worked example in your group.

Fig A 11.4 shows the velocity of an object over a period of 10 s.

What is the acceleration of the object between these times?

a) 0–4 s   **b)** 4–8 s   **c)** 8–10 s

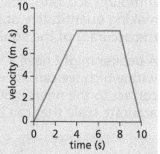

FIG A 11.4

Solution

The acceleration is given by the gradient of the graph for each time period.

a) acceleration $= \dfrac{8-0}{4} = 2$ m/s^2

b) acceleration $= \dfrac{8-8}{4} = 0$ m/s^2, so the object is at constant velocity

c) acceleration $= \dfrac{0-8}{2} = -2$ m/s^2; negative acceleration is deceleration

Key terms

distance–time graph graph that shows how the distance travelled varies with time

displacement the distance travelled in a particular direction

velocity the speed in a particular direction

displacement–time graph graph that shows how displacement varies with time

velocity–time graph graph that shows how velocity varies with time

acceleration rate of change of increase in velocity with respect to time

Check your understanding

1. On a distance–time graph:
   a) What information is given by the gradient of the graph?
   b) How can you tell whether an object is stationary?

2. On a velocity–time graph:
   a) What information is given by the gradient of the graph?
   b) Describe the motion of the object when the graph is horizontal.
   c) How can you tell whether an object is accelerating or decelerating?

12 Accuracy and scientific measurement

We are learning how to:

- express answers to different degrees of accuracy
- express numbers in scientific notation

Although accurate measurement is an essential part of making quantitative observations, we are often limited by the accuracy of the equipment we use.

A beaker might have a scale down the side, but the accuracy with which we can use it to measure out liquid is perhaps correct to the nearest 50 cm³. A burette has a much more accurate scale that can be read to the nearest 0.05 cm³.

beaker

burette

FIG A 12.1 Reading the level of liquid

Significant figures

You may sometimes be told to express values to a certain number of significant figures.

In a large number like 123456 the digit '1' is the most significant because it represents 100 000. The digit '2' is next in significance because it represents 20 000, and so on.

The same is true of a very small number. For example, in the number 0.009 876 543 the digit '9' is the most significant because it represents nine 1000ths. The digit '8' is next in significance because it represents eight 10 000ths and so on.

In any number, therefore, the most significant digit is the one that appears on the left, provided it is not zero. However, any zeroes to the right of this will be significant. The term 'significant figures' is often shortened to 'sig figs' or 'sf'.

The rules for rounding to the nth significant figure are:

- if the (n + 1)th significant figure is 5 or more you round up the nth figure;
- if the (n + 1)th significant figure is 4 or less leave the nth figure unchanged.

For example: The mass of a beaker containing water is 129.65 g. Give this value to three significant figures. The fourth significant figure is 6 so we round up the third significant figure. The mass of the beaker and water is 130 g (correct to 3 sf).

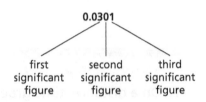

FIG A 12.2 Significant figures

Scientific notation

You may have noticed in Table A 5.2 that as well as listing prefixes for use with SI units, the multiplying factors were also given in **scientific notation**, which is also called **standard form**.

Scientific notation is a format for writing numbers in which there is a single digit between 1 and 9 to the left of the decimal point, and then numbers to the right of the decimal point, and this is multiplied by a power of 10. For example, the number of atoms in 12 g of carbon is 6.02×10^{23}.

Scientific notation is also used to express very small values. The only difference is that the powers of 10 are negative. For example, the diameter of a carbon atom in metres is 1.54×10^{-10}, which is the same as $1.54 \times \dfrac{1}{10^{10}}$.

Any number can be expressed in scientific notation. To do this:

- write the number with a single digit to the left of the decimal point;
- multiply by 10 to the power needed to generate the number when expanded.

For example, to write 234.56 in scientific notation:

$$234.56 = 2.3456 \times 10^{n}$$

This would be equal to 234.56 if $n = 2$, therefore 234.56 in scientific notation is 2.3456×10^{2}.

Activity A 12.1

Here is what you need:

- beaker 250 cm³ marked every 50 cm³
- measuring cylinder 100 cm³
- syringe 100 cm³
- conical flask 250 cm³ marked every 50 cm³

Here is what you should do:

1. Weigh the beaker dry and empty.
2. Use the beaker to measure out 50 cm³ of water as accurately as you can. Reweigh the beaker and water and calculate the mass of the water.
3. Write your result in a table.
4. Repeat steps 1 to 3 for the other three pieces of apparatus.
5. The mass of 50 cm³ of water is 50.00 g. Which piece of apparatus measured the water: a) most accurately; b) least accurately?

FIG A 12.3 Measuring apparatus

Key terms

scientific notation method of writing numbers as a decimal between 1 and 10 multiplied by a power of 10

standard form same as scientific notation

Check your understanding

1. Express each of the following to the stated number of significant figures.

   a) 21.43 cm³ (1 sf) b) 129 s (2 sf)   c) 1.919 g (2 sf)

2. Rewrite the following in scientific notation.

   a) 29.6 g   b) 129 s   c) 814 °C

Review of Working like a scientist

- Carrying out an experiment involves the following stages:
  - specifying the problem
  - formulating a hypothesis
  - designing the experiment
  - analysing data
  - drawing conclusions.
- Scientists express quantities in SI units.
- There are a small number of base units and many other units derived from them.
- Prefixes are used in front of units to denote different powers of ten.
- Prefixes commonly used are mega, kilo, deci, centi, milli and micro.
- Many everyday substances are measured in SI units.
- Mass is the amount of matter a substance contains and is measured using a balance.
- Volume is the amount of space a substance occupies and can be measured using different apparatus including measuring cylinders and burettes.
- Time is measured in seconds, or sometimes in minutes, using a digital watch.
- Temperature is measured in Kelvin or degrees Celsius using a thermometer.
- Data is another word for information and it can be displayed in different ways.
- Qualitative data doesn't involve numbers.
- Quantitative data involves numbers and is sometimes displayed in the form of a graph.
- A graph shows how the value of one variable changes as the value of another is varied.
- The gradient of a graph is its slope at a point.
- Interpolation of a graph involves finding values between the plotted points.
- Values are sometimes expressed to a certain number of significant figures.
- Values may be expressed in scientific notation (which is also called standard form).

Review questions on Working like a scientist

Knowledge and understanding

1. What is the SI unit used to measure:

   a) length   **b)** time   **c)** mass   **d)** temperature?

2. Express each of the following in the unit indicated.

   a) 12 mm in cm   **c)** 100 mg in g   **e)** 150 µg in mg   **g)** 0.25 dm^3 in cm^3

   b) 5 kg in g   **d)** 50 cm^3 in dm^3 **f)** 25 cm in m   **h)** 0.75 kg in g

3. **a)** Express the following temperatures in units of Kelvin: **i)** 0 °C and **ii)** 85 °C.

   b) Express the following temperatures in degrees Celsius: **i)** 373 K and **ii)** 450 K.

4. State whether each of the following observations is qualitative or quantitative.

   a) The volume of hydrogen increased from 10.3 cm^3 to 18.9 cm^3.

   b) The blue colour of the copper(II) sulphate solution became paler.

   c) The magnesium burned with a bright flame and formed a white powder.

   d) The seeds germinated more slowly at a lower temperature.

Process skills

5. The graph in Fig A RQ.1 shows the mass lost during a chemical reaction.

   a) At which point in the reaction was the gradient largest?

   b) At what time was the reaction complete? Explain how you know this.

   c) Estimate: **i)** the mass loss after 1.5 minutes; **ii)** the time when the mass loss was 0.5 g.

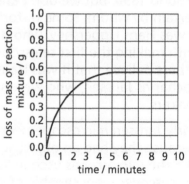

FIG A RQ.1

6. Express each of the following to the stated number of significant figures.

   a) 37.21 dm^3 (1 sf)   **c)** 12.19 s (3 sf)   **e)** 3.409 kg (3 sf)

   b) 0.0846 g (2 sf)   **d)** 747.25 °C (3 sf)   **f)** 0.1649 kg (2 sf)

7. Rewrite the following in scientific notation.

   a) 187.06 g   **b)** 0.016 s   **c)** 2390 cm^3 **d)** 0.0000103 g

8. When solutions of compound A and compound B are mixed, a chemical reaction takes place and heat is given out. Plan an experiment in which you could measure the temperature change of the reaction mixture. Your plan should:

   - list the apparatus you would use

   - describe how you would measure the temperature change

   - describe how you would present your results.

1 Development of biology I

We are learning how to:

- understand some important contributions to the development of biology

There have been many important developments and discoveries that have helped scientists to increase their knowledge of biology. In this and the next three spreads, we are going to look at four examples.

Invention of the microscope

Today we take it for granted that the world is full of organisms so small that we cannot see them with the unaided eye, but this wasn't always the case. Prior to the invention of the microscope scientists had no notion of a world of tiny creatures.

The microscope was invented in Holland around 1590, but we don't know for certain by whom. Some historians believe it was Hans Lippershey, who is credited with making the first telescope, and others believe that it was Hans and Zacharias Janssen, who were spectacle makers.

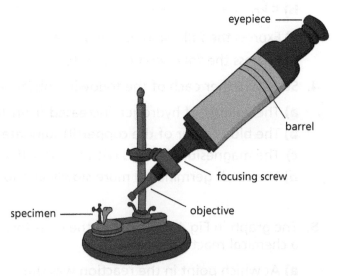

FIG B 0.1.1 Microscope from around 1670

Early Janssen microscopes were compound microscopes because they had an objective lens and an eyepiece, just like the microscopes used in laboratories today. These microscopes were capable of magnifying between 3 times and 9 times the true size.

People were quick to see the opportunities provided by the microscope and a number of famous scientists like Galileo Galilei and Robert Hooke contributed to their development.

Compound microscopes gave greater magnification than single lenses but the early versions produced a distorted image. The Dutch scientist van Leeuwenhoek designed a high-power single lens microscope around 1670 that could magnify up to 270 times the actual size. He used it to examine many things, including yeast, red blood cells, bacteria and protozoa.

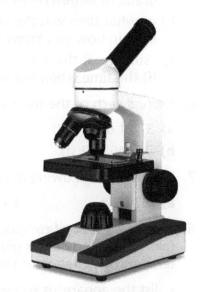

FIG B 0.1.2 A modern laboratory microscope with three different objective lenses

Despite the early problems with compound microscopes they prevailed and, as instrument makers became more skilled at producing lenses, the power of these microscopes increased. In 1882 the German physician Robert Koch devised methods of staining specimens, which allowed him to identify the bacilli bacteria that are responsible for tuberculosis and for cholera.

By the start of the 20th century optical microscopes had reached the limit of what could be achieved in terms of magnification.

The year 1931 witnessed the first of a new generation of electron microscopes. These instruments use beams of electrons rather than light, and are capable of magnifications up to 1 000 000 times actual size. Electron microscopes allowed biologists to see the structure of objects like cells, bacteria and viruses in great detail.

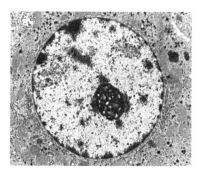

FIG B 0.1.3 Cross section of a cell viewed using an electron microscope at magnification x4040

Activity B 0.1.1

Here is what you need:

- microscope
- microscope slide

Here is what you should do:

1. Look at the microscope and identify the parts.

2. Turn the knob that adjusts the focus, and observe how this moves the tube up and down.

3. Put a small specimen in the middle of the microscope slide. For example, you might want to look at a hair.

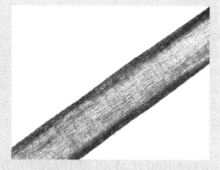

FIG B 0.1.4 A human hair as seen under a microscope at magnification x400

4. Adjust the microscope until the object comes into focus.

5. If your microscope has more than one objective lens, look at the object through low power first and then through high power.

6. Practise drawing what you can see.

Check your understanding

1. When and where was the first microscope made?

2. What names are given to the two lenses in a compound microscope?

3. Why was van Leeuwenhoek's single lens microscope initially more effective than a compound microscope?

4. Why was the development of the microscope important for understanding the causes of many diseases?

5. What advantage does an electron microscope have over an optical microscope?

2 Development of biology I (continued)

Natural selection

In the great days of exploration, sailing ships undertook trips sometimes lasting several years in search of previously undiscovered lands that might provide important materials and opportunities for trade. These ships usually took a scientist, called a naturalist in those days, to record new animals and plants.

In 1831 Charles Darwin signed up as the naturalist for a five year voyage of exploration on HMS Beagle. Darwin visited many places and saw many interesting things during the voyage, but his visit to the Galapagos Islands was to be of greatest significance.

FIG B 0.2.1 Charles Darwin

The Galapagos Islands are far enough away from each other, and from the mainland, to ensure that animals can't easily travel from one to another. Darwin noticed that there were many similarities between the animals found on the different islands, but that there were also some important differences. For example, Darwin noticed that the finches on the different islands were generally similar, but had different-shaped beaks.

He realised that all of these finches were likely to be descendants of a flock of identical finches that had perhaps been carried from the mainland by the wind and colonised the islands. If the ancestors were identical, why were their descendants different?

FIG B 0.2.2 The Galapagos Islands are in the Pacific Ocean off the coast of Ecuador

Darwin reasoned that:

• In each generation of finches there would be some small differences. Perhaps some had slightly longer beaks or slightly fatter beaks than others.

• On each of the islands the sources of food for the finches would be different.

• On any particular island the finches with beaks best suited to eating the food would survive to breed again, while finches with beaks that weren't as well suited to the food types available would not.

• Over time the whole population of finches on the island would have this favourable feature.

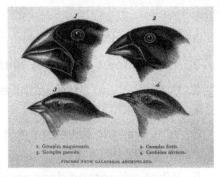

FIG B 0.2.3 Darwin's finches

Darwin coined the phrase 'natural selection' to describe the process by which those animals best suited to their environment would survive, while others would not. This is sometimes described as the 'survival of the fittest'.

Activity B 0.2.1

Evolution of parrots in the Caribbean

The Caribbean Islands are not so different from the Galapagos Islands in that they are a group of islands that are geographically close but have different environments.

Find out what you can about the parrots on the different Caribbean Islands.

In your group, discuss what factors may have determined how parrots evolved and why the distribution of parrots is not the same on all of the islands.

FIG B 0.2.4 Caribbean parrots

Check your understanding

1. Darwin noticed that the giant tortoises on different islands had different-shaped shells.

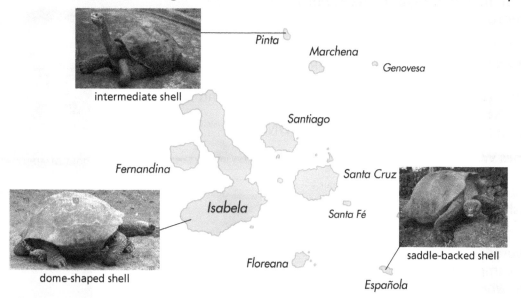

Pinta

Marchena

Genovesa

intermediate shell

Santiago

Fernandina

Santa Cruz

Isabela

Santa Fé

saddle-backed shell

Floreana

dome-shaped shell

Española

FIG B 0.2.5 Galapagos tortoises

When the Galapagos Islands were still part of the mainland all the tortoises that roamed the land would have been the same. Explain why the tortoises have evolved differently on the different islands.

3 Development of biology II

We are learning how to:

- understand some important contributions to the development of biology

The structure of DNA »

DNA is short for deoxyribonucleic acid. This molecule is sometimes described as the molecular basis of all life. It was first discovered by the Swiss chemist Friedrich Miescher in the 1860s. He called the substance 'nuclein' and observed that it had different properties to other proteins with which he was familiar.

In 1881 the German biochemist Albrecht Kossel established that nuclein was, in fact, one of a group of chemicals called nucleic acids, and he renamed the substance DNA. He was also able to isolate five nucleotide bases, which are the building blocks from which DNA is formed, but he had no idea about the structure of the DNA molecule.

Over the next fifty years it was established that DNA was somehow involved in the transfer of characteristics from one generation of an organism to the next, but scientists were still no closer to establishing its actual structure.

In 1952 the physical chemist Rosalind Franklin used a technique called X-ray crystallography to produce two sets of high-resolution photographs of DNA strands. From these she was able to calculate the dimensions of the strands and deduce that DNA probably had a double-helix structure.

In 1953 James Watson and Francis Crick were able to build on the work of Rosalind Franklin and establish the double-helix structure of DNA.

They discovered that there were two helices composed of sugar phosphates, which are joined by pairs of bases rather like the rungs on a ladder.

FIG B 0.3.1 Albrecht Kossel

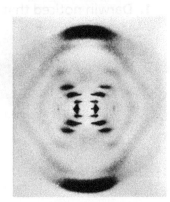

FIG B 0.3.2 One of Rosalind Franklin's photographs

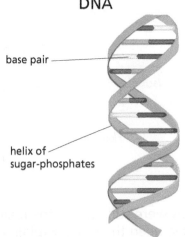

DNA

base pair

helix of sugar-phosphates

FIG B 0.3.3 DNA double-helix structure established by Watson and Crick

Activity B 0.3.1

Building a model of DNA

Build a model to show the structure of DNA using whatever materials are available.

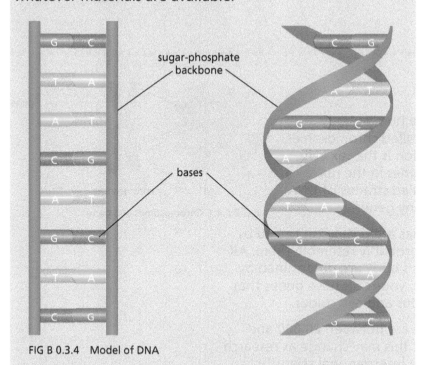

sugar-phosphate backbone

bases

FIG B 0.3.4   Model of DNA

Fig B 0.3.4 shows a model built from strips of coloured card. It was built flat and then twisted to form the helix structure.

Check your understanding

1. Why was Miescher particularly interested in the compound he called 'nuclein'?

2. **a)** What is 'DNA' short for?

   b) Why did Kossel rename the compound originally discovered by Miescher DNA?

3. What process did Rosalind Franklin use to obtain photographs of a DNA molecule?

4. What structure did Watson and Crick propose for DNA?

4 Development of biology II (continued)

We are learning how to:

- understand some important contributions to the development of biology

Human Genome project

In the nucleus of every cell in the human body there are 23 pairs of structures called chromosomes, giving a total of 46. (The exception is the sex cells, which contain only 23 chromosomes in the nucleus). Each chromosome consists of coiled strands of DNA. Each strand of DNA contains many genes.

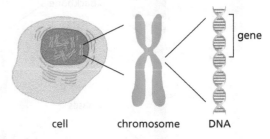

FIG B 0.4.1 Chromosomes and genes

A gene is a unit of heredity. Genes are passed on to you by your parents, which is why you probably resemble them. All of the characteristics of a person's body are determined by one or more genes. For example, your cells have genes that determine features like hair colour and eye colour.

Scientists currently believe there are between 20 000 and 25 000 genes in human DNA but this may change as research in this area continues. In 1990 an international scientific research project started with the aim of identifying and mapping all of the genes in human DNA. The project was completed in April 2003.

human

chimpanzee

gorilla

FIG B 0.4.2 Bands of similar genes provide evidence of evolution

Scientists can now identify the location of genes and the distances between them. This is particularly useful in a number of ways. Here are some examples of what is now possible.

- By comparing the genes of individuals, scientists can determine whether they are related or not.

- By comparing the genes of races in different parts of the world scientists can see how populations have migrated at different times in prehistory.

- Comparing the genes of different organisms provides scientists with evidence of how organisms evolved.

FIG B 0.4.3 Logo of the Sickle Cell Support Foundation of Jamaica

Scientists estimate that there are up to 10 000 diseases affecting humans that are caused by mutations in a single gene.

In Jamaica sickle-cell disease, a genetic blood disorder, affects 1 in every 150 babies born. Scientists are able to use the information provided by the Human Genome Project to locate the specific genes responsible for diseases as part of devising new treatments for them.

Activity B 0.4.1

DNA paternity testing

It is now possible to say with 99.99% accuracy whether a man is the father of a child or not by comparing the DNA of the child with that of the father and the mother.

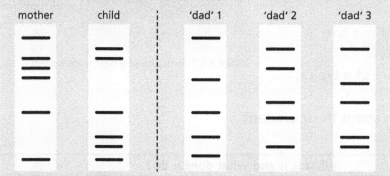

mother   child   'dad' 1   'dad' 2   'dad' 3

FIG B 0.4.4 Paternity testing

1. Use the example above to explain how paternity testing works.

2. Discuss in your group what social implications paternity testing might have.

Check your understanding

1. What is the relationship between a chromosome, DNA and genes?

2. What was the goal of the Human Genome Project, and how long did it take?

3. Give three examples of how comparing the genes of individuals, or of races, and of different organisms can be useful.

4. A person might carry the gene for a particular disease but may not develop the disease. How could scientists check whether the person is carrying the gene or not?

5 Functions of parts of a cell

We are learning how to:

- identify cells as the building blocks from which all living things are made
- describe the structure of a simple animal cell
- describe the structure of a simple plant cell

The cell is the building block from which all organisms are composed. Most organisms contain large numbers of cells. The cells of animals and plants have some similarities but they also have some important differences.

FIG B 1.5.1 Structure of a typical animal cell

Structure of a simple animal cell >>

Fig B 1.5.1 shows the basic structure of a typical animal cell.

Table B 1.5.1 contains information about the important structures in the cell.

Part of animal cell	What is it and what does it do?
Nucleus	This controls the different processes that take place in the cell. It also contains structures called **chromosomes** that are made of DNA. Each chromosome contains information in the form of genes. These determine many of the features of an animal and allow it to pass those features on to the next generation.
Cytoplasm	This is a jelly-like substance that almost fills the cell. Many chemical reactions take place here and materials that the cell needs are continually being made and broken down.
Vacuoles	These are tiny, water-filled bubbles in the cytoplasm. They contain soluble food like sugars to provide the cell with energy, and waste materials produced by the cell. In animal cells there are generally lots of small vacuoles.
Cell membrane	This is a thin, partially permeable layer that surrounds the cell. It has a very important function of controlling what substances can pass into and out of the cell.

TABLE B 1.5.1 Parts of a typical animal cell

Plant cells >>

Fig B 1.5.2 shows the structure of a typical plant cell.

Plant cells have the same three main parts as animal cells: a nucleus, cytoplasm and a cell membrane. They also have some additional parts.

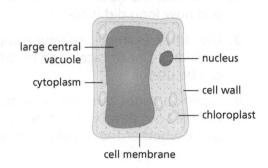

FIG B 1.5.2 Structure of a typical plant cell

Part of plant cell	What is it and what does it do?
Nucleus	Same as in an animal cell
Cytoplasm	Same as in an animal cell
Vacuole	A plant cell generally has a single large vacuole that occupies much of the cell. It contains cell sap, which is a solution of sugars and minerals needed by the cell. The cell sap keeps the plant cell firm and prevents it from collapsing in on itself.
Cell membrane	Same as in an animal cell
Chloroplasts	Many types of plant cells have these. They contain the green pigment chlorophyll, which traps light energy for photosynthesis. This is the process by which plant cells make food.
Cell wall	In addition to a cell membrane, plant cells have a cell wall. This is a strong structure made of **cellulose**. It helps the cell to retain its shape and to support the plant.

TABLE B 1.5.2 Parts of a typical plant cell

Activity B 1.5.1

Observing animal cells and plant cells

Here is what you need:

- microscope
- prepared slide of animal cells
- prepared slide of plant cells

Here is what you should do:

1. Look at the animal cells under low magnification and find a well-detailed cell.
2. Look at that cell under higher power and identify the nucleus, the cytoplasm and the cell membrane.
3. Draw a labelled diagram of the animal cell.
4. Repeat this with a slide showing plant cells. In addition to the parts identified on the animal cell, identify chloroplasts, the cell wall and any large vacuoles that may be present.
5. Draw a labelled diagram of the plant cell.
6. The average diameter of a human cheek cell is 60 mm and the average length of an onion cell is 0.25 mm. Express both these values in metres using standard form.

Check your understanding

1. Fig B 1.5.3 shows a typical plant cell.

   a) Name the parts (i) to (vi).

   b) Which of these parts would you not see in a typical animal cell?

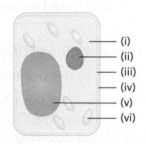

FIG B 1.5.3

Key terms

nucleus part of the cell that controls the reactions and processes that take place in the cell

chromosomes structures in the nucleus that carry genetic material in DNA to pass features on to new generations

cytoplasm jelly-like substance that surrounds the nucleus and in which many chemical reactions and processes are carried out

vacuole a fluid-filled structure inside a cell

cell membrane a selectively permeable membrane that surrounds and controls what enters and leaves the cell

chloroplast structure in a plant cell containing the green pigment chlorophyll, which traps the energy needed for photosynthesis

cell wall the rigid outer layer of a plant cell

6 Diffusion

We are learning how to:

- explain how particles spread out as a result of diffusion

Diffusion >>>

Living things need to move substances around. One way by which this is done is called **diffusion**.

Sometimes when you step into your home, you know that someone has been baking or cooking. This is because when we are cooking tiny particles of food move through the air. The particles travel from the kitchen to all the other rooms in your home and our noses can detect them, even if we are not in the kitchen. We call this spreading out of particles 'diffusion'.

FIG B 1.6.1 Spicy meat, Jamaica style

Activity B 1.6.1

Investigating diffusion

Your teacher will help you with this activity.
Here is what you need:

- shallow open container like a watch glass
- volatile liquid that has a characteristic smell, like a perfume
- stopwatch with a second hand

Here is what you should do:

1. Students sit or stand in rows at different distances from the teacher's table.

2. The teacher pours a small amount of perfume onto a watch glass on the table at the front of the class.

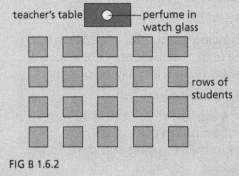

FIG B 1.6.2

3. Each student should raise an arm and note the time when he or she first smells the perfume.

4. Note which students were first to smell the perfume.

5. Note which students were last to smell the perfume.

6. [STEAM] Suggest how this activity could be modified to investigate how easily the smell of perfume diffuses from one room to another through an open doorway.

In Activity B 1.6.1 some of the perfume particles spread out, or diffuse, from the watch glass to all parts of the classroom. At the start, the perfume particles are at high **concentration** immediately above the watch glass and at low concentration in the rest of the classroom. The perfume particles in the air move randomly and disperse from this region of high concentration to regions of low concentration.

We say that the perfume particles diffuse across a **concentration gradient**. This is the difference in the concentration of particles between two regions.

After a while the concentration of perfume particles is the same in all parts of the room.

Substances are continually diffusing into and out of cells. However, when the concentration of a substance is higher, say outside the cell, more particles of the substance will diffuse into the cell than out of it. Conversely, if the concentration of a substance is higher inside the cell, more particles will diffuse out than diffuse in.

Substances diffuse into and out of cells across concentration gradients. For example:

- The concentration of oxygen in the blood is higher than in the cell, where it is used up during respiration, so there is a net diffusion of oxygen from the blood into the cell.

- The concentration of carbon dioxide in the cell is higher, because it is produced during respiration, so there is a net diffusion of carbon dioxide from the cell into the blood.

Activity B 1.6.2

1. Drop a crystal of potassium manganate(VII) into a beaker of water and leave it for 24 hours.

2. Sketch the appearance of the water at the start, after 15 minutes and again after 24 hours.

Check your understanding

1. Explain why the appearance of the water changed in Activity B 1.6.2.

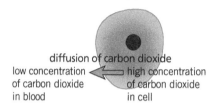

FIG B 1.6.3 Diffusion of gases (a) into and (b) out of cells

Key terms

diffusion the net movement of particles from an area where they are in high concentration to an area where they are in low concentration, until the concentrations are the same

concentration the number of particles of a substance per unit volume (for example, in a solution, g/cm^3 of water)

concentration gradient the difference in the concentration of particles of a substance in one place compared to another place

7 Osmosis

We are learning how to:

- explain why water molecules move between regions of different concentration during osmosis

Osmosis

Osmosis is a special kind of diffusion that is concerned only with the movement of water molecules. Like other substances, water diffuses down a concentration gradient from a place where water is in high concentration to a place where it is in low concentration.

This can be a little confusing because water is in a higher concentration in a dilute solution and in a lower concentration in a concentrated solution. What we are saying, therefore, is that under suitable conditions water will move from a dilute solution to a concentrated solution.

A **partially** or **selectively permeable membrane** is a membrane with holes that are large enough to allow small molecules like water to pass through, but small enough to prevent the movement of large molecules.

Fig B 1.7.1 shows what happens if we separate pure water from a solution of a compound by a differentially permeable membrane. Notice that the water molecules move in both directions through the differentially permeable membrane. However, to start with more water molecules pass from the dilute solution to the concentrated solution than pass in the other direction. Eventually the concentration of the solution reaches **equilibrium**, and equal numbers of water molecules pass in each direction.

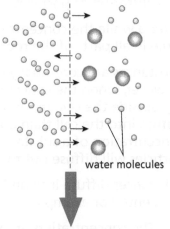

partially or selectively permeable membrane

water molecules

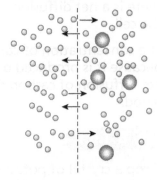

partially or selectively permeable membrane

FIG B 1.7.1 Movement of particles across a partially or selectively permeable membrane

Activity B 1.7.1

Investigating osmosis

Here is what you need:

- fresh fruit – mango or paw-paw
- knife
- shallow dish
- sugar

Here is what you should do:

1. Peel the fruit with a knife and cut it in half. If you are using a mango or a paw-paw, remove the seeds to make a well in the flesh of the fruit.

Interesting fact

- A dilute solution is made up of a little solute in lots of solvent.

- A concentrated solution is made up of lots of solute in a little solvent.

2. Cut the outside of each half to make a flat surface for it to stand on.

sugar

distilled water

FIG B 1.7.2

3. Stand the two halves of the fruit on their flat parts in a shallow bowl of distilled water so that the well is at the top. Add a layer of sugar to just cover the bottom of one of the wells, as shown in Fig B 1.7.2

4. Do not put any sugar in the well of the other half of the fruit.

5. Leave the halves of fruit in the water for 30 minutes.

6. After 30 minutes record your observations.

7. Explain your observations in terms of osmosis.

8. [STEAM] Design an activity to compare the rate at which osmosis takes place in two different fruits.

In Activity B 1.7.1 the sugar dissolves in one half of the fruit, forming a sugar solution. The concentration of water in the dish is higher than the concentration of water in the sugar solution, so water passes from the dish into the fruit, through the fruit cells, by osmosis.

Water passes into and out of all living cells by osmosis. The process of osmosis controls the concentration of substances in the cells.

Key terms

osmosis the movement of water from an area of high concentration to an area of low concentration passing through a partially or selectively permeable membrane

differentially or **selectively permeable membrane** a membrane that allows some particles but not others to pass through it

equilibrium a situation in which the movement of particles in one direction is equal to the movement of particles in the opposite direction

Check your understanding

1. Visking tubing is a partially or selectively permeable membrane. Fig B 1.7.3 shows a bag made of Visking tubing filled with 20% sugar solution and then suspended in a beaker of distilled water.

a) Predict what will happen to the level of liquid in the glass tube if the apparatus is left to stand for 30 minutes.

b) Explain your answer to **a)**.

c) Predict what will happen if the same apparatus is used, but distilled water is placed in the Visking bag and sugar solution in the beaker.

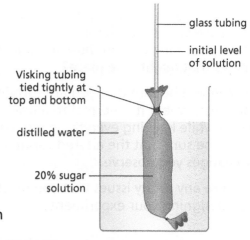

glass tubing

initial level of solution

Visking tubing tied tightly at top and bottom

distilled water

20% sugar solution

FIG B 1.7.3

8 Planning an experiment on osmosis

We are learning how to:

* plan an experiment on osmosis

An egg is covered by a hard shell composed of calcium carbonate. Immediately under the shell there is a thin membrane that holds the contents of the egg. If an egg is left in some weak acid for a few days, the shell reacts with the acid and the egg is deshelled, while the membrane remains undamaged.

The membrane surrounding the egg will allow water to pass into and out of the egg. Your teacher will provide you with two deshelled eggs, some pure water and a strong sugar solution. You need to design an experiment in which you use these materials to investigate osmosis. Here are the stages you should follow.

FIG B 1.8.1 The membrane surrounding the egg

1. Identify what is being investigated

What is the purpose of the experiment? What do you hope to find out about osmosis?

2. Formulate a **hypothesis**

Apply what you already know about osmosis and predict what you think the outcome of your experiment might be.

3. Design the experiment

How are you going to carry out your experiment? What materials and equipment will you need in addition to the deshelled eggs, the water and the sugar solution?

What will you do? You might decide to put the deshelled eggs in the water and the sugar solution. If that is what you do, how long do you think it would take to see any changes that might take place?

How can you be sure that you are carrying out a **fair test**? In any experiment it is normal to allow one variable to change while keeping everything else constant. In this way you can be sure that the altered variable is responsible for any changes you observe.

FIG B 1.8.2 Deshelled eggs in sugar solution and in distilled water

Are there any safety issues that you must take into account when designing your experiment?

4. Analysing data

What changes do you think might take place? For example, do you think that the masses of the eggs might change? Do you think that the circumferences of the eggs might change? Do you think that the volume of the eggs might change? Are there other things that might change? How can these changes be measured?

How will you record any data that you collect? Do you need to construct a table? In what units will you make your measurements? How accurate can you hope to be?

Can you think of an interesting way to present your data?

5. Drawing conclusions

What conclusions are you hoping to draw from this experiment? How do you think the data you gather will support your conclusions?

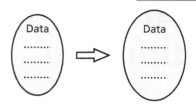

FIG B 1.8.3 An egg before and after

Key terms

hypothesis proposed explanation

fair test test that gives valid results

Check your understanding

1. In an experiment on osmosis, 30 chips of similar size were cut from one potato. They were divided into six batches of five chips and each batch was weighed.

Each batch of chips was put in a sugar solution of a different concentration to the others and left for five hours. At the end of this time the batches were removed from their solutions, and the chips in each batch were wiped and then reweighed. The results of the experiment are given in Table B 1.8.1.

Batch	Sugar concentration	Mass of chips at start / g	Mass of chips at end / g	Mass gain (+) or loss (–) / g
A	Low	51.3	52.6	+1.3
B		49.8	50.7	
C		50.2	50.7	
D		51.6	51.4	
E		48.9	48.3	
F	High	50.7	49.7	–1.0

TABLE B 1.8.1

a) i) Copy and complete the table by calculating the missing changes in mass.
ii) What substance is being gained or lost by the potato chips?
iii) Predict what would have happened if another batch of potato chips had been left in a sugar solution that was even less concentrated than the solution for Batch A.

b) For which batch was the concentration of the sugar solution closest to that of the concentration of the solution in the cells of the potato chips? Explain your answer.

c) Explain why:
i) batches of five chips and not single chips were used.
ii) the experiment was left for five hours and not five minutes.

9 Comparing osmosis and diffusion

We are learning how to:

- compare the processes of diffusion and osmosis
- determine in what ways diffusion and osmosis are similar and in what ways they are different

Diffusion is the spontaneous net movement of particles from an area of higher concentration to one of lower concentration.

When you make a cup of tea the coloured substances contained in the tea leaves diffuse out into the hot water. We can speed up the process by stirring the water.

Diffusion is the result of the random motion of particles. As the temperature increases the particles move more quickly. Diffusion therefore takes place more rapidly at higher temperatures.

Osmosis is the spontaneous net movement of water molecules across a partially permeable, or selectively permeable, membrane.

When plant cells or animal cells are left in a solution, water molecules continually move into and out of the cells. Eventually the concentration of the solution inside a cell is equal to the concentration of the solution outside the cell.

FIG B 1.9.1 Coloured substances in tea leaves diffuse out into hot water

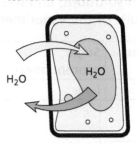

FIG B 1.9.2 Water moves into and out of cells

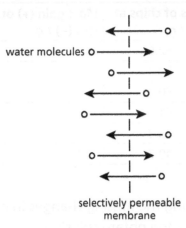

FIG B 1.9.3 Equal numbers of water molecules pass each way across the membrane

When the concentrations of the solutions on both sides of a membrane are the same, water molecules continue to move in each direction through the membrane (see Fig B 1.9.3). They move at the same rate, so the concentrations remain unchanged. This is called **dynamic equilibrium**.

Diffusion and osmosis look to be very similar in that they are both means by which substances enter and leave cells.

However, there are some important differences between these processes.

	Diffusion	Osmosis
When does it occur?	Diffusion occurs in the gaseous state or with particles in solutions. (It can take place in solids, but very slowly.)	Osmosis occurs when there is a difference in the concentrations of solutions on either side of a selectively permeable membrane.
Why is it important?	Diffusion is associated with storing and releasing energy in photosynthesis and respiration.	In animals osmosis allows the distribution of substances. In plants osmosis is responsible for the absorption of water from soil by the plant roots.
Concentration gradient	Diffusion takes place from a region of high concentration to a region of low concentration.	Osmosis takes place from a less concentrated solution to a more concentrated solution.
Requirement for water	Diffusion can take place in the absence of water.	Osmosis is the movement of water.

TABLE B 1.9.1

Check your understanding

1. Decide whether each of the following is the result of diffusion or of osmosis.

    a) In the lungs oxygen gas passes from the air into the bloodstream.

    b) Water passes into red blood cells.

    c) Carbon dioxide passes from the air into plant cells.

    d) When a raw potato chip is placed in strong sugar solution it shrinks.

    e) You can smell the petrol vapour as you get close to a petrol station. You do not need to be standing near the pumps.

    f) When one segment of a grapefruit is left in sugar in a sealed bag, the sugar forms a syrup after a short time.

Interesting fact

Tea is correctly described as an infusion. This is an extract obtained by soaking leaves or whole plants in water.

Interesting fact

Diffusion takes place quickly through gases and less quickly through liquids.

Key term

dynamic equilibrium a system that is continually changing but remains in balance

Review of Diffusion and osmosis

- Cells are the building blocks from which all living things are made.
- A typical animal cell consists of a nucleus, cytoplasm, several small vacuoles and a cell membrane.
- A typical plant cell consists of a nucleus, cytoplasm, a single large vacuole, chloroplasts, a cell membrane and a cell wall.
- A cell membrane is a selectively permeable membrane that controls what enters and what leaves a cell.
- Diffusion is the movement of particles from a region of higher concentration to a region of lower concentration along a concentration gradient.
- Some substances can pass into and out of cells by diffusion.
- Osmosis is a special kind of diffusion that involves the movement of water particles.
- During osmosis, water molecules pass through a partially permeable membrane from a more dilute solution (region of high water concentration) to a more concentrated solution (region of low water concentration).
- Water passes into and out of cells by osmosis.
- Living tissue has membranes across which osmosis can take place.
- Diffusion involves gases and particles in solution.
- The rate of diffusion increases with increasing temperature.
- Diffusion is involved in the processes of energy storage and release during photosynthesis and respiration.
- In plants, osmosis is responsible for the absorption of water.
- In animals, osmosis is involved in the transport of substances around the body.
- Diffusion can take place in the absence of water.
- Osmosis is the movement of water.

Review questions on Diffusion and osmosis

1. a) Listed below are some parts of cells. For each one write:

A if it is only found in animal cells

P if it is only found in plant cells

AP if it is found in both animal cells and plant cells.

    i) Chloroplast   **ii)** Cell membrane   **iii)** Small vacuole

    iv) Nucleus   **v)** Cytoplasm   **vi)** Cell wall

b) Which of the parts above controls the movement of substances into and out of a cell?

2. Mrs Livingstone is cooking a curry for dinner. The kitchen window is open. Explain how Mr Livingstone knows what is for dinner even before he enters their home.

3. State whether or not each of the following is an example of osmosis.

a) Plant roots absorb water from soil.

b) Carbon dioxide passes from the bloodstream to the air in the lungs.

c) Plants lose water vapour from their leaves into the air.

d) When soft fruit is placed in sugar syrup it gets smaller.

4. Fig B 1.RQ.1 shows different concentrations of two gases inside and outside a plant cell.

a) Name the process by which gases move into and out of cells.

b) Predict what will happen in each of the conditions, **i)** and **ii)** in Fig B 1.RQ.1.

i)

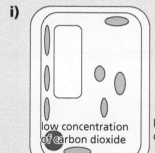

low concentration of carbon dioxide | high concentration of carbon dioxide

ii)

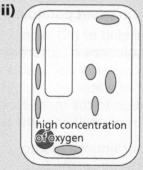

high concentration of oxygen | low concentration of oxygen

FIG B 1.RQ.1

5. The smell of petrol diffuses across a petrol station forecourt more rapidly on a hot day than on a cold day.

a) On the basis of this observation suggest a hypothesis linking rate of diffusion and temperature.

b) Describe how you could test this hypothesis.

11 Estimating sugar content in a sweet potato

Sweet potatoes are a popular food in the Caribbean. They are eaten in lots of different ways including boiled, mashed, baked and as fries.

100 g of sweet potato contains about 20 g of carbohydrates, 1.6 g of protein and 0.1 g of fat. It is also a good source of vitamins A, B6, B12, C and D, and of the minerals calcium, iron and magnesium.

As the name 'sweet potato' suggests, a proportion of the 20 g of carbohydrates is present as sugar. This information will be useful to someone wanting to reduce their sugar intake.

FIG STEAM B 1.11.1 Sweet potatoes

1. You are going to work in small groups to estimate the concentration of sugar in sweet potatoes using osmosis. Your tasks are:

   - To revise the work carried out on osmosis in this unit so that you understand the process.

   - To prepare sugar solutions with different concentrations.

   - To measure the mass gain or mass loss when sweet potato chips are soaked in sugar solutions with different concentrations.

   - To draw a graph of mass gain/loss against concentration and use it to deduce the sugar concentration in sweet potatoes.

a) Osmosis is a special kind of diffusion involving water molecules. When solutions of different concentrations are separated by a partially permeable membrane there is a net movement of water molecules from the less concentrated solution to the more concentrated solution. Eventually the solutions will have the same concentration.

   Make sure that your understanding of osmosis is clear, and read through Lesson B 1.7 to remind you of anything that you may have forgotten.

b) Make up sugar solutions of different concentrations. The percentage of sugar in sweet potato is between 0% and 10% so you should make up solutions of 0%, 1%, ... 10% by mass of sugar.

   To make up each solution:

   - Put a clean, dry 250 cm³ beaker on a balance
   - Press the tare/zero key to zero the display

FIG STEAM B 1.11.2 Making up solutions

- Add sugar to the required mass
- Top up with distilled water until the display reads 100 g

Wrap some cling film over the top of the beaker to prevent water evaporating or being absorbed from the air before you use the solution. Make sure you label each beaker with the concentration of sugar solution it contains.

c) From one or more peeled sweet potatoes cut 55 chips of similar thickness.

The chips should not be too thick. This shape provides a large surface area for osmosis to take place.

d) Use a spreadsheet to record the following data.

Weigh a batch of five chips and record their mass. Put them in 0% sugar solution. Repeat this for each concentration up to 10% sugar solution.

Leave the chips in their solutions overnight. The following day remove each batch of five chips from each solution, wipe them to remove surface solution and then reweigh them. Record their mass.

Use the spreadsheet to calculate the change in mass and the percentage change in mass for each batch.

e) Use the data you have collected to plot a graph of percentage mass gained or lost on the *y*-axis against concentration of sugar in the solution on the *x*-axis.

Draw the straight line of best fit through your points and find the concentration at which there would be no increase or decrease in the mass of sweet potato chips. This will be your estimate of the concentration of sugar in sweet potatoes.

f) Prepare a PowerPoint presentation in which you should focus on the results you obtained, and make suggestions as to how people might use your results. You might ask questions such as:

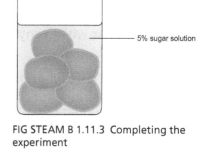

FIG STEAM B 1.11.3 Completing the experiment

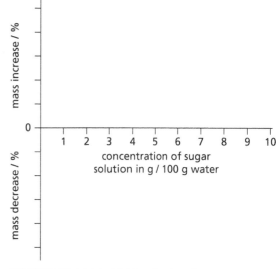

FIG STEAM B 1.11.4 Grid for plotting data

- What is the daily recommended intake of sugar?
- How many spoonfuls of sugar does a typical sweet potato contain?
- Should sweet potato be something you eat every day?

As part of your presentation you could hold up a sweet potato and then measure out and hold up the amount of sugar that the sweet potato contains.

12 Role of a transport system

We are learning how to:

- describe the importance of a transport system in a living organism

What do transport systems do? »

We are familiar with many different **transport** systems in our everyday lives.

Buses transport people from one place to another. People travelling to a place outside the country might be transported by boat or by aeroplane.

FIG B 2.12.1 Buses transport people

Trucks transport materials or goods between factories and shopping outlets.

In all but the simplest organisms, there is also a need for a transport system to carry substances around the body.

There are thousands of different chemical reactions taking place inside the cells of the body. These reactions are collectively called the body **metabolism**. They are driven by fuel, in the form of foods, and provide heat energy to maintain the body temperature and also mechanical energy to do work.

FIG B 2.12.2 Trucks transport materials and goods

In any organism there is a need to:

- transport substances taken from outside the body to all of the cells

- transport waste substances from the cells to be expelled from the body

- transport substances from one part of the body to another

In some organisms substances may be transported by diffusion.

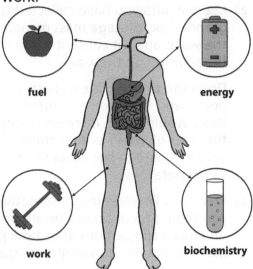

FIG B 2.12.3 Metabolism

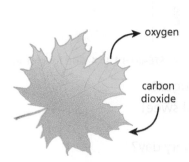

FIG B 2.12.4 Gases diffuse into and out of leaves

For example, plants produce the sugar glucose by a process called photosynthesis. The carbon dioxide needed for this process diffuses into the leaf through tiny pores. The oxygen that is also produced by photosynthesis diffuses out of the leaf in the same way.

In some organisms, like humans, substances dissolve in the blood and are pumped around the body by the heart.

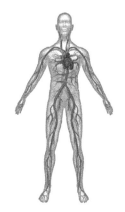

FIG B 2.12.5 Substances are transported in the blood

Activity B 2.12.1

Transporting things around the home

Here is what you should do:

1. Imagine that your home is an organism. In a group discuss how things are transported at your home.

2. Identify things that are transported into your home.

3. Identify things that are transported out of your home.

4. Identify things that are transported within your home.

5. Draw a simple diagram to illustrate home transport.

Interesting fact

Many different chemical reactions take place at the same time inside a cell. If we tried to carry out lots of different chemical reactions in a test tube we would end up with a mess. It is possible in a cell because reactions are controlled by special chemicals called enzymes. Each reaction has its own particular enzyme.

Check your understanding

1. Fig B 2.12.6 illustrates human metabolism.

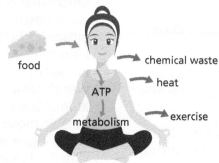

FIG B 2.12.6

a) What is shown being taken in by the body?

b) What forms of energy result from metabolism?

c) What is shown being removed from the body?

Key terms

transport moving from place to place

metabolism the many chemical reactions that take place inside the cells of an organism

13 Transport in unicellular and multicellular organisms

We are learning how to:

- identify unicellular organisms
- identify multicellular organisms

The ways in which substances move into and out of an organism depend on its structure. In this lesson we are going to consider transport in unicellular and in multicellular organisms.

Unicellular organisms >>>

Some organisms consist of only a single cell. These are called **unicellular** organisms and they live in water. There are many different types of unicellular organism, but they are not a feature of our everyday lives because they are very small and the vast majority can only be seen with the help of a microscope.

  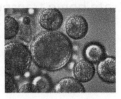

FIG B 2.13.1 Examples of unicellular organisms

The outer cell membrane or cell wall (if present) of a unicellular organism controls what enters and what leaves the cell.

- Passing into the cell are oxygen, which is needed for respiration, and nutrients to provide energy and sustain growth.
- Passing out of the cell are waste products which, if they were allowed to build up, would poison the organism.

Since these organisms consist of only a single cell, it is easy for substances to diffuse into and out of the cell. There is no need for any form of transport system to carry substances inside the cell.

Unicellular organisms are no longer classified as animals or plants but are placed in other kingdoms.

> **Interesting fact**
>
> At one time all organisms, including unicellular organisms, were classified as being either in the animal kingdom or the plant kingdom. The amoeba was classified as an animal because it was able to move about, while algae were classified as plants because they contained chlorophyll. However, problems arose when classifying organisms like euglena, which is both able to move about and contains chlorophyll.

Observing unicellular organisms

Here is what you need:

- microscope
- microscope slide and coverslip
- sample of pond water containing unicellular organisms

Here is what you should do:

1. Put one drop of pond water on a microscope slide and cover it with a cover slip.

2. Using low magnification, look carefully at the water and find a unicellular organism.

3. Use higher magnification to examine the organism in more detail.

4. All living things, including unicellular organisms, have seven characteristics: nutrition, growth, respiration, excretion, sensitivity, movement and reproduction. As you examine your unicellular organism think about how these characteristics apply to it.

Multicellular organisms 》》》

Multicellular organisms contain more than one cell, and often many millions of cells.

The plants and animals we see in everyday life are multicellular organisms. In multicellular organisms not all of the cells are the same. Different types of cells are specialised to carry out different jobs within the organism. For example, the cells in the leaves of a plant are different to those in the plant roots.

The body of a multicellular organism is many cells thick. Diffusion would allow the movement of substances to and from the cells at the surface but not those inside the organism. In order to supply all of the cells with oxygen and nutrients, and to remove waste materials from them, some sort of transport system is needed.

FIG B 2.13.2 Examples of multicellular organisms

Check your understanding

1. **a)** State the difference between a unicellular organism and a multicellular organism.

   b) Explain why a unicellular organism doesn't need a transport system.

Key terms
....

unicellular describes organisms that consist of only a single cell

multicellular describes organisms that consist of many cells

14 Substances transported in animals

We are learning how to:

• identify substances transported in animals

The substances that are transported in animals can be divided into three groups according to whether they are taken into or removed from the body, or simply transported between places within the body.

Substances taken into the body

Respiration is the process by which an organism produces the energy needed to drive metabolic processes. For respiration to take place, cells must be provided with glucose and oxygen.

When an animal eats, the food is transported along the **alimentary canal** where it is broken down into nutrients. These are absorbed and transported around the body in the blood. They include **glucose**, for use in respiration, **amino acids**, for growth and repair of tissues, and other nutrients including vitamins and minerals.

The **oxygen** needed for respiration is absorbed by the lungs. It is also transported around the body in the blood.

Substances expelled by the body

The metabolic processes that take place in the body produce waste substances. If concentrations of these substances were allowed to build up they might poison the animal, so they must be expelled from the body.

The waste products of respiration are **carbon dioxide** and water. Carbon dioxide is transported, in the blood, from the cells back to the lungs. The water passes into the blood making it more dilute.

FIG B 2.14.1 Exhaled air is saturated with water vapour

Some water is lost as water vapour when the blood passes through the lungs. The air you breathe out is always saturated with water vapour, which is why it condenses into mist on a cold day.

Water is also lost through sweating and when the blood passes through the kidneys. This water collects in the bladder and is transported out of the body as urine.

Urea is another waste product that is transported in the blood. It is formed in the liver during the breakdown of amino acids that are not required by the body.

Urea passes into the blood from the liver and is transported around the body. Some is lost through the skin in sweat and the remainder is removed by the kidneys to pass out of the body in urine.

Substances that move within the body

Hormones are chemical messengers that are released by one part of the body to trigger changes in another part. They are transported in the blood.

For example, the amount of water removed from the blood in the kidneys is controlled by a hormone released by part of the brain. You will learn more about hormones in a later unit.

Activity B 2.14.1

The lymphatic system

The lymphatic system operates alongside the blood system in the body. It consists of a series of vessels through which a fluid called lymph flows.

Here is what you should do:

1. Use the resources available to you to find out what substances are transported around the body by the lymphatic system.

Check your understanding

1. Describe how the materials needed for respiration are transported to the cells of the body.

2. Describe how the waste product of converting unwanted amino acids into glucose is transported out of the body.

FIG B 2.14.2 Sweating removes water and urea from the body

Interesting fact

Pathogens are microorganisms that cause diseases. When they enter the body they are transported in the blood to different parts.

Key terms

respiration process by which organisms obtain energy to drive their metabolism

alimentary canal part of the body where digestion takes place

glucose obtained from the digestion of carbohydrates and used in respiration

amino acids obtained from the digestion of proteins

oxygen gas needed for respiration

carbon dioxide waste gas formed during respiration

urea waste product of the breakdown of amino acids in the liver

15 The circulatory system

We are learning how to:

- identify the components of the circulatory system

The **circulatory system** is a complex network of blood vessels that delivers blood to every cell in the body. At the centre of the network is the **heart**. The role of the heart is to pump blood around the blood vessels.

The human circulatory system can be described as a **double circulatory system** because it has two circuits, or parts, to it.

In one circuit blood passes between the heart and the lungs. As it passes through the lungs, blood absorbs oxygen and releases carbon dioxide and water vapour.

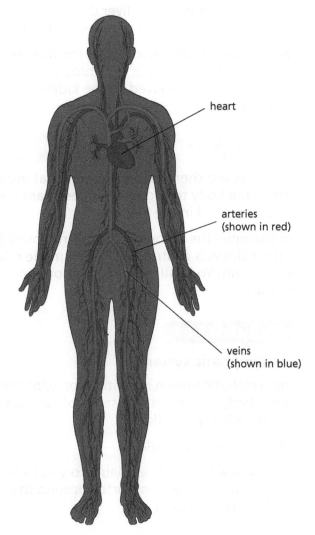

FIG B 2.15.1 Human circulatory system

heart

arteries (shown in red)

veins (shown in blue)

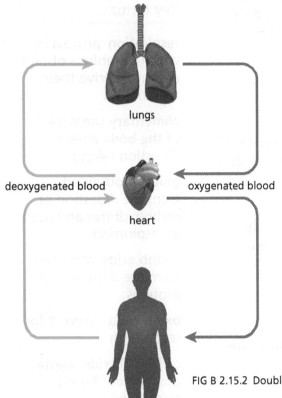

lungs

deoxygenated blood

oxygenated blood

heart

body

FIG B 2.15.2 Double circulatory system

In the other circuit, blood passes between the heart and the rest of the body. Essential substances such as oxygen and glucose are carried to the cells of the body, and waste products such as carbon dioxide and urea are removed.

The advantage of this double system is that blood being transported to the rest of the body after receiving fresh oxygen in the lungs is pumped by the heart, and so is at a much higher pressure than would otherwise be possible. This ensures that oxygenated blood reaches all parts of the body.

Activity B 2.15.1

Finding your way around the circulatory system

Your teacher will help you to organise this activity. It involves making a large map of the human circulatory system.

Here is what you need:

- pegs
- string
- large labels for the different parts of the circulatory system fixed on sticks or rods

Here is what you should do:

1. On the school field or any hard area, mark out the parts of the circulatory system using the pegs. You should include the heart, the lungs and any other major organs that you know. Write labels inside the organs.

2. Connect the organs using string. You can use different coloured string to represent arteries and to represent veins.

3. Take a walk around the circulatory system and make a note of what is happening at each place you visit.

4. Afterwards, discuss your 'trip' with other students in your class.

Check your understanding

1. Copy and complete the following sentences.

   a) Blood is pumped around the body by the
   _____ .

   b) Blood delivers oxygen to the _____ .

2. What happens in the lungs?

3. What is the advantage of the double circulatory system?

Interesting fact

In diagrams of the circulatory system the arteries are traditionally shown in red and the veins in blue. This does not mean that the blood changes colour from red to blue passing through the body.

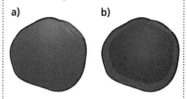

a)   b)

FIG B 2.15.3 Samples of:
a) oxygenated blood
b) deoxygenated blood

Blood that carries oxygen is described as oxygenated blood and is bright red. Blood that has lost its oxygen is called deoxygenated blood and is dark red.

Key terms

circulatory system system that carries blood around the body

heart muscular four-chambered organ that is at the centre of the circulatory system and pumps blood around the body

double circulatory system a circulatory system in which one circuit is from the heart to the lungs and back, and the other is from the heart to the rest of the body and back

16 The heart

We are learning how to:

- draw and identify the four chambers of the heart
- describe how blood passes through the heart

The heart »

The heart is a muscular organ that pumps blood around the body.

The heart has four chambers. The terms 'right' and 'left' are used as if you are viewing a person's heart from the front of their body. There are two upper chambers – **atria** – and two lower chambers – **ventricles**.

The two sides of the heart are separated by a thick muscular wall – the **septum**. This prevents the **oxygenated** blood in the left side from mixing with the **deoxygenated** blood in the right side.

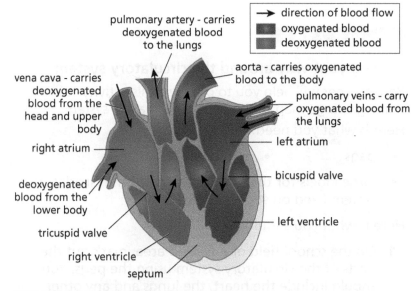

FIG B 2.16.1 The four chambers of the heart

The flow of blood through the heart is as follows:

body → right atrium → right ventricle → lungs → left atrium → left ventricle → body

Deoxygenated blood returns to the right atrium of the heart from all parts of the body. The blood passes into the right ventricle and is then pumped to the lungs, where it absorbs oxygen and releases carbon dioxide.

The oxygenated blood flows from the lungs into the left atrium. In the heart the blood passes into the left ventricle from where it is pumped to all parts of the body.

Diastole and systole

The heart continues to pump by repeatedly contracting and relaxing every second that you are alive. Heart muscle does not become exhausted and stop as other muscles might.

The moment when the heart muscle relaxes is called the **diastole**. During this time:

- deoxygenated blood from the body enters the right atrium
- oxygenated blood from the lungs enters the left atrium.

The moment when the heart muscle contracts is called the **systole**. During this time:

- the atria contract first, forcing blood into the ventricles
- then, when full, the ventricles contract, forcing blood out of the heart.

There are valves in the heart to make sure that the blood only flows in one direction and cannot flow backwards.

Activity B 2.16.1

Examining an animal's heart

Here is what you need:
- pig, cow or goat heart
- scissors
- scalpel
- dissecting pins

Here is what you should do:

1. Carefully examine the outside of the heart. Can you see the coronary blood vessels that supply the heart muscle with blood?
2. Observe where the blood vessels attached to the heart are connected.
3. Cut into the heart and identify the four chambers.
4. Look for the valves that prevent blood flowing backwards.

Check your understanding

1. **a)** In what order does blood pass through the chambers of the heart?

   b) Which chambers of the heart contain:

      i) oxygenated blood?
      ii) deoxygenated blood?

Interesting fact

Some people are born with a congenital defect – a hole in their heart. This means that there is a hole in the septum. This allows deoxygenated blood to pass from the right side of the heart to the left side without passing through the lungs.

As a result, the person's blood does not carry sufficient oxygen around the body so they lack energy and are often tired. This condition can be corrected by surgery to seal the hole.

Key terms

atria upper chambers of the heart

ventricles lower chambers of the heart

septum thick muscular wall that separates the two sides of the heart

oxygenated contains oxygen

deoxygenated does not contain oxygen

diastole the moment when the heart muscle relaxes

systole the moment when the heart muscle contracts

17 Arteries, veins and capillaries

We are learning how to:

- describe the structures of arteries, veins and capillaries
- explain the roles of arteries, veins and capillaries

Arteries and veins

Arteries	Veins
carry blood away from the heart	carry blood to the heart
most carry oxygenated blood (exception is pulmonary artery)	most carry deoxygenated blood (exception is pulmonary vein)
 FIG B 2.17.1 Cross section through an artery	 FIG B 2.17.2 Cross section through a vein
have thick walls that include a thick layer of muscle to withstand the high pressure of blood leaving the heart	have thinner walls and contain less muscle, because the blood pressure inside a vein is much lower than the blood pressure in an artery
the inside diameter of space, or **lumen**, of an artery is relatively small	the inside diameter of space, or lumen, is greater than that of an artery
the blood flow is at high pressure so valves are not needed because there is no chance of backflow	the blood flowing through veins does not have the benefit of high pressure created by the pumping heart. Instead, it relies on being squeezed through the veins as our body muscles contract. In order to prevent blood flowing backwards, long veins, such as those in the arms and legs, have non-return valves that allow the blood to flow in one direction only. FIG B 2.17.3 Long veins contain non-return valves

Arteries and veins are ideal for transporting blood from one part of the body to another, but their walls are far too thick for substances to diffuse into and out of them.

Arteries sub-divide many times, first forming **arterioles** and finally a network of blood **capillaries**, so that every cell is supplied with blood.

Blood capillaries are much thinner than a human hair and their walls are only one cell thick. This allows substances such as oxygen and glucose to diffuse out of the capillaries into the cells. At the same time, waste products such as carbon dioxide and urea diffuse out of the cells and into the capillaries.

As blood flows through the capillaries, it provides cells with the substances that they require. The capillaries leaving the cells join together to form slightly larger blood vessels called **venules**, which then combine to become veins, carrying the blood back to the heart.

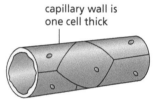
capillary wall is one cell thick

FIG B 2.17.4 A blood capillary

Interesting fact

The artery that connects the heart with the lungs is the only artery in the body that carries deoxygenated blood. It is called the pulmonary artery.

Activity B 2.17.1

Cross sections of blood vessels

Here is what you need:

- plain paper
- paints or coloured pens/pencils

Here is what you should do:

1. Here are typical values for the inside diameters of blood vessels: artery = 5 mm, vein = 20 mm and capillary = 7.5 mm. Convert these values to metres in standard form and use them to draw the blood vessels to scale.

2. Draw a cross section of an artery, a vein and a capillary next to each other.

3. Use a different colour for each of the materials in the blood vessel walls.

4. Label your blood vessels.

Check your understanding

1. Explain why:

   a) the walls of an artery need to be thicker than the walls of a vein

   b) long veins have valves but long arteries do not

   c) the walls of blood capillaries are much thinner than the walls of arteries or veins.

Key terms

arteries vessels that are part of the circulatory system that carries blood away from the heart

veins vessels that are part of the circulatory system that carries blood to the heart

lumen the inside space of an artery or vein

arterioles smaller sub-divisions of arteries that transport blood to the body cells

capillaries vessels that are part of the circulatory system; they are very thin, have walls one cell thick and allow substances to diffuse out into cells

venules blood vessels formed by capillaries joining together, which join up with veins taking blood back to the heart

18 Components of blood

We are learning how to:

- identify different components of blood
- describe the roles of different components of blood

Blood »

Blood consists of a liquid part – plasma – and a solid part that is made up mostly of blood cells. Plasma is about 90 per cent water but also contains some important substances, including:

- nutrients obtained by the digestion of food, which are being taken to the cells of the body

- waste products such as urea, which will eventually be excreted from the body

- blood proteins such as antibodies, which help to protect the body from disease, and fibrinogen, which helps blood to clot

- hormones that coordinate different functions within the body.

red blood cells   phagocyte   lymphocyte

white blood cells

FIG B 2.18.1 Red and white blood cells

The mass of blood cells contains a mixture of both **red blood cells** and **white blood cells**, each with vital roles in our wellbeing. Blood also contains **platelets** – these look like fragments of red blood cells. They are essential for the clotting process.

Activity B 2.18.1

Observing blood cells

Here is what you need:

- microscope
- prepared slides showing different blood cells

Here is what you should do:

1. Place the prepared slides under a microscope and observe them first under low power and then under high power.
2. Draw examples of the blood cells you observe.
3. A typical red blood cell has a diameter of 7.2 mm, and a typical white blood cell has a diameter of 15 mm:

   a) Give the diameter of a red blood vessel correct to one significant figure.

   b) Approximately how many times greater is the diameter of a white blood cell compared to a red blood cell?

Interesting fact

Every year thousands of people in Jamaica donate blood to help others.

FIG B 2.18.2 Blood donation

The blood is given to patients who have lost blood as a result of an accident or during surgery.

4. **[STEAM]** Sickle cell disease affects about 1 in 150 persons in Jamaica. Research how observing red blood cells could help a doctor to identify this disease in a patient.

Red blood cells	White blood cells
• transport oxygen around the body	• fight any infection that might enter the body
• contain a protein called haemoglobin, which is responsible for the red colour and contains iron	• there are two types – **phagocytes** and **lymphocytes**, which fight infection in different ways
• a shortage of red blood cells causes anaemia – a condition that may be due to insufficient iron in the diet	• phagocytes engulf bacteria or parts of bacteria into the cell and then kill them and digest them
	• lymphocytes release chemicals – antibodies – that destroy bacteria

Check your understanding

1. Fig B 2.18.3 shows a sample of blood viewed through a microscope.

   Which of the following are indicated by A, B, C and D?

   a) Platelets

   b) Lymphocyte

   c) Red blood cell

   d) Phagocyte

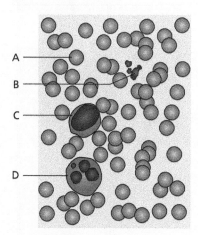

FIG B 2.18.3

Key terms

red blood cells cells that transport oxygen around the body

white blood cells blood cells that fight any infection that might enter the body

platelets small blood particles that are essential for the clotting process

phagocytes white blood cells that engulf bacteria or parts of bacteria into the cell and then kill and digest them

lymphocytes white blood cells that release chemicals called antibodies that destroy bacteria

19 Modelling the circulatory system

We are learning how to:
• model the circulatory system

You are going to contribute to a display of models relating to the circulatory system. You will be working in a group with other students. Your teacher will lead a class discussion on what sort of models the class might make.

It is up to you and the students in your group to decide what materials to use and how to build your model. Here are some ideas that might help you.

You could use modelling clay or buttons of different sizes and colours to model the components of blood. You will need to devise some way of representing the two different types of white blood cells. How will you represent blood platelets?

FIG B 2.19.2 Modelling arteries and veins

You could use half of a length of pipe to represent a section along an artery. Different coloured modelling clay can be used to build up the outer wall and the thick layer of muscle and elastic fibres. How will the model of a vein differ from that of an artery? Can you think of a way of showing valves in your model of a vein?

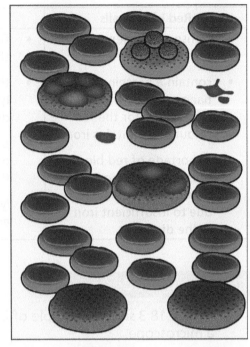

FIG B 2.19.1 Modelling components of the blood

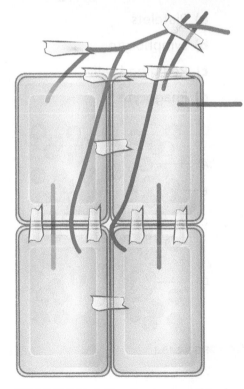

FIG B 2.19.3 Modelling the structure of the heart

The heart has four chambers. You could represent each chamber using a thick polythene bag. The arteries and veins that carry blood to and from the heart could be represented by coloured string.

If you want to be a little more ambitious you can try to model the pumping action of the heart using plastic water bottles. How will you control the movement of liquid between the different parts of your heart?

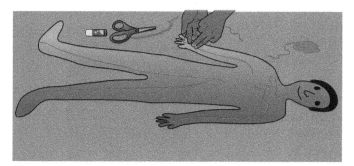

FIG B 2.19.5 Modelling the circulatory system

You could model the main arteries and veins that carry blood around the body. How will you represent the arteries and veins? You could just paint them on but the model would look better if they were three-dimensional. How about something like different coloured tubing or knitting wool?

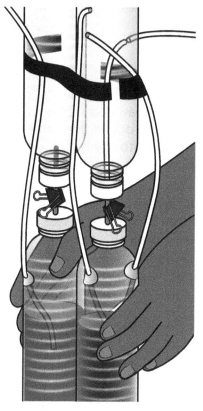

FIG B 2.19.4 Modelling the action of the heart

Activity B 2.19.1

Modelling some aspects of the circulatory system

Here is what you need:

- materials for modelling
- tools

Here is what you should do:

1. Discuss as a group what you are hoping to show with your model.

2. Decide the best way to achieve this.

3. Determine within the group who is going to be responsible for the different tasks in making your model.

4. Carry out your plan but be prepared to modify it if things don't work out quite as you planned or if someone has a good idea you would like to incorporate.

5. When your model is finished look for ways of improving it so that it looks even better.

20 Diffusion and surface area

We are learning how to:

- explain the importance of surface area to the rate of diffusion

Diffusion and surface area >>>

The human body relies on diffusion to transport substances into and out of the body. In the lungs oxygen diffuses from the air into the blood, while carbon dioxide diffuses from the blood into the air.

In the digestive system, nutrients diffuse out of the small intestine into the blood. Glucose and oxygen diffuse into cells from the blood. Waste products from different metabolic processes diffuse out of the blood in the kidneys, to be expelled from the body in urine.

How well the body functions depends on the rate at which diffusion can take place. This, in turn, is linked to the surface area across which diffusion is happening. The larger the area of the surface across which diffusion occurs, the more quickly diffusion will take place.

The **lungs** contain about 300 million tiny air sacs through which gases can diffuse. The total surface area of a pair of adult lungs is about the same as that of a tennis court. Each cluster of air sacs is surrounded by a network of tiny blood capillaries. This will give you some idea of the importance of surface area for the diffusion of gases.

The structure of the **small intestine** is also folded to increase the surface area. The intestine wall is lined with finger-like projections called villi, each of which has its own blood capillaries. The villi provide a large area for the absorption of nutrients from digested food.

In Activity B 2.20.1 you will investigate the link between the rate of diffusion and surface area using **agar gel** that has been impregnated with phenolphthalein, allowed to set and then cut into cubes of different sizes. Agar gel is a jelly-like substance obtained from seaweed. It can be dissolved in hot water and will set in a solid form.

Phenolphthalein is an **acid-alkali indicator**. It is colourless in an acid, for example, hydrochloric acid, but turns pink in an alkali, for example, sodium hydroxide solution.

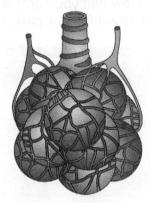

FIG B 2.20.1 Air sacs in the lungs

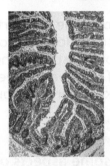

FIG B 2.20.2 Cross section of villi in the wall of the small intestine

FIG B 2.20.3 Agar gel

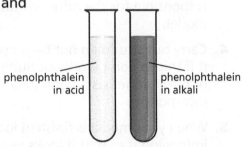

phenolphthalein in acid   phenolphthalein in alkali

FIG B 2.20.4 Phenolphthalein turns pink in alkali

Activity B 2.20.1

Diffusion in agar gel cubes

Here is what you need:

- agar gel cubes impregnated with phenolphthalein indicator: 3 cm cube; 2 cm cube; 1 cm cube
- 0.1 M sodium hydroxide solution 200 cm^3
- beaker 250 cm^3 • spoon
- knife • stopwatch

Here is what you should do:

1. Pour about 20 cm^3 sodium hydroxide solution into a beaker.

2. Use a spoon to put the cubes in the sodium hydroxide solution.

3. Allow the cubes to remain in the sodium hydroxide solution for 10 minutes and during this time use the spoon to turn the cubes over so that all the faces are exposed equally at different times.

4. Remove the cubes with the spoon and put them on a paper towel and blot them to dry.

5. Cut each cube in half and make a sketch of each to show how far the sodium hydroxide solution has diffused. You can tell this by the presence of the pink colour.

6. Into which cube did the sodium hydroxide solution diffuse most? Into which cube did the sodium hydroxide solution diffuse least?

7. Calculate the volume and the surface area of the three different sized cubes you used in this activity and write your answers in a table.

Check your understanding

1. A teaspoon of granulated sugar contains about the same amount of sugar as a sugar cube, but it dissolves much more quickly in tea or coffee than a sugar cube dissolves.

   Explain this observation in terms of surface area.

2. The teeth chop large pieces of food into lots of small pieces before the pieces are swallowed. Explain, in terms of surface area, how this assists the chemicals that digest the food.

Interesting fact

Agar gel is a nutritious jelly. Microbiologists use agar gel plates to grow colonies of bacteria so that they can identify them.

FIG B 2.20.5 Colonies of bacteria on an agar gel plate

Key terms

lungs part of the body where gases are exchanged

small intestine part of the body where nutrients from digested food are absorbed

agar gel nutrient jelly extracted from seaweed

acid–alkali indicator chemical that is differently coloured in acids and in alkalis

FIG B 2.20.6 Different types of sugar

Review of Transport in humans

- The role of a transport system is to move substances around an organism.

- Substances might be transported into, out of or within an organism.

- A unicellular organism consists of a single cell and does not require a transport system because substances can pass in and out simply by diffusion.

- A multicellular organism consists of many cells and requires a transport system so that substances can be delivered to, and pass into and out of the cells inside the organism.

- In the human body blood transports many substances, including the gases oxygen and carbon dioxide, together with nutrients such as glucose and waste products including urea.

- The circulatory system consists of the heart and a network of blood vessels that carry blood to all the cells of the body.

- The heart is a muscular organ that contracts and relaxes throughout a person's life, without ever stopping. It consists of four chambers:

  right atrium, right ventricle, left atrium, left ventricle

- Diastole is the moment when the heart muscle relaxes. During this time:

  o deoxygenated blood from the body enters the right atrium

  o oxygenated blood from the lungs enters the left atrium.

- Systole is the moment when the heart muscle contracts. During this time:

  o the atria contract, forcing blood into the ventricles

  o then, when full, the ventricles contract forcing blood out of the heart.

- Blood is carried away from the heart in arteries and towards the heart in veins.

- Arteries have thick muscular walls and a narrow lumen. They must withstand very high pressures as blood is pumped into them from the heart.

- Veins have thinner walls and a larger lumen. The pressure in veins is lower than in arteries. Long veins have non-return valves to prevent blood flowing in the wrong direction.

- Arteries divide into narrower arterioles and then into capillaries. The wall of a blood capillary is only one cell thick so substances can pass between capillaries and cells. Capillaries combine to form venules. Venules combine to form veins.

- Blood consists of about 90 per cent liquid, which is called plasma, and 10 per cent solids, which is mostly blood cells.

- There are different types of blood cells:

  o Red blood cells that carry oxygen around the body

  o White blood cells called phagocytes that engulf germs

  o White blood cells called lymphocytes that release chemicals that kill germs.

- A pulse is caused by blood being pumped through arteries by the heart.

Review questions on Transport in humans

Knowledge and understanding

1. a) What is meant by the term 'metabolism'?

   b) Why is a transport system necessary for metabolic processes to take place in the human body?

2. Fig B 2.RQ.1 shows how the heart and lungs are connected.

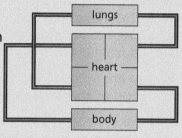

   a) Copy Fig B 2.RQ.1 and draw arrows to show the direction of blood flow between the heart and the lungs, and between the heart and the body.

   b) Why does blood always flow in the same direction in:

      i) an artery?

      ii) a vein?

FIG B 2.RQ.1

3. a) Explain why the blood pumped from the heart to the body is a brighter red than the blood that returns to the heart.

   b) Fig B 2.RQ.2 shows some details of the human heart.

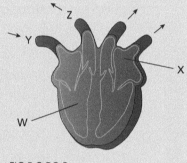

      i) Identify the chambers of the heart marked W and X.

      ii) State where the blood comes from to Y.

      iii) State where the blood goes to from Z.

   c) Some people are born with a hole between the two sides of their heart. Explain why this leaves them feeling weak and lacking in energy.

FIG B 2.RQ.2

Process skills

4 Fig B 2.RQ.3 shows a unicellular organism called paramecium.

Explain why paramecium doesn't need a transport system.

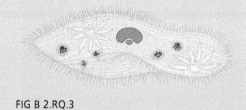

FIG B 2.RQ.3

5. Fig B 2.RQ.4 shows a section through a blood vessel.

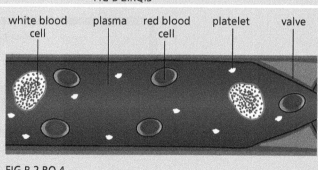

white blood cell   plasma   red blood cell   platelet   valve

   a) Does Fig B 2.RQ.4 represent an artery, a vein or a blood capillary? Explain your answer.

   b) In which direction does the blood flow through this vessel?

FIG B 2.RQ.4

22 Making an artificial heart

Some people with diseased hearts can get a transplant in which they receive a healthy heart from a person who has recently died from other causes, such as a road traffic accident. However, there is a risk that the donor heart may be rejected by the patient's body. Also, there are insufficient donor hearts for every patient who needs one. An alternative to a heart transplant could be to replace a diseased heart with an artificial heart.

The Heart Foundation of Jamaica wishes to raise money for research into building an artificial heart. They have asked you to apply your knowledge of the heart to build a simple model that can be used at fundraising meetings. The model needs to demonstrate how a liquid can be pumped from one container into another, in a circuit, using a small electric motor.

1. You are going to work in small groups to build a simple model that represents the action of the heart. The tasks are:

   • To review the structure of the heart and the movement of blood around the circulatory system.

   • To design a model powered by an electric motor that pumps a liquid from one vessel to another, continuously, in a circuit.

   • To build your model.

   • To test your model.

   • To modify your model on the basis of test results.

   • To demonstrate your model as part of a presentation in which you explain how you went about creating it.

   a) Look back through the unit and make sure that you understand how the heart functions in terms of pumping blood around the body.

   b) In essence, you are being asked to create a model of single circulation. This can be between the right ventricle and left atrium (via the lungs), or the left ventricle and the right atrium (via the body).

   What are you going to use for your containers? They can be open, such as two beakers, or you might decide to use empty plastic bottles.

   What are you going to use to carry the liquid? It might be better to use clear plastic tubing rather than rubber tubing so the liquid can be observed.

   You can make some lifelike 'blood' using water and a few drops of red food colouring.

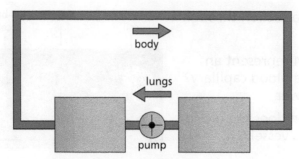

FIG STEAM B 2.22.1 Single circulation

c) The pump is going to provide the kinetic energy needed for your model. How are you going to make a pump out of an electric motor?

One solution might be to attach a circular rotor to the end of the motor. This would have blades twisted at an angle, like a propeller. You could build a waterproof housing around it using an old plastic bottle.

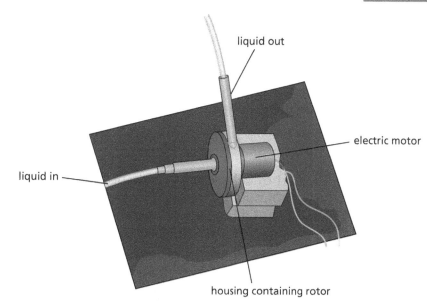

FIG STEAM B 2.22.2 A simple pump

You could build a more lifelike version in which the motor raises and lowers a piston. This would give you pulses similar to how the heart beats, however you would have to devise some valves to ensure that the liquid flows in one direction only.

Take photographs as you build your model. You can use these to illustrate your presentation and make it more interesting.

d) Once you have built your model you need to test it. Run it for a few minutes and make sure the liquid is actually circulating.

To improve performance you might:

- Use silicone sealant to ensure the model is watertight.
- Add a potentiometer (variable resistor) to control the speed of the motor. Your teacher will help you with this.
- Reduce the diameter of the tubing so the liquid circulates more quickly.

e) Your final task is to give an illustrated presentation of how you built your model. This should include a demonstration of how it works.

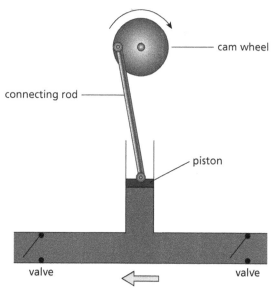

FIG STEAM B 2.22.3 A more realistic pump might include a piston

23 Plant structure

We are learning how to:

- identify the different parts of a flowering plant

Fig B 3.23.1 shows the four main parts of a flowering plant. Each of these parts continually grows as the plant develops. The four parts of a plant have very different functions.

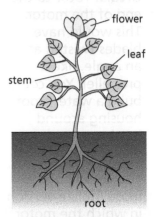

FIG B 3.23.1 Main parts of a flowering plant

Roots

The **roots** are the part of a plant that we do not normally see because they are buried in the soil. Roots are not green because they do not contain the pigment chlorophyll. Roots have the following important functions:

- They anchor the plant in the soil, which prevents it from being blown about in the wind.
- They absorb water containing dissolved minerals from the soil. This is sometimes called soil water. Both the water and the minerals it contains are essential for the plant to flourish.
- They are a place where the plant can store nutrients. This is stored as starch. Examples of plants that store food in their roots are carrots and sweet potatoes.

FIG B 3.23.2 Yellow yam contains lots of starch

Stem

The **stem** is the part of the plant that joins the roots to the leaves and to the flowers. It has the following important functions:

- It supports the parts of the plant that are above the ground. These are the leaves and the flowers.
- It allows water and minerals to move up from the roots to the other parts of the plant, and the movement of nutrients down from the leaves to the roots for storage.
- In climbing plants, like beans, the stem provides attachment by growing in a spiral around another plant or an upright support.
- Green stems can carry out photosynthesis to make sugars, but the leaves are more important for carrying out this process.
- Some plants, for example sugar cane, also store food in their stems.

Interesting fact

Some plants, like begonias, have leaves that are not green or not totally green. These leaves do contain chlorophyll but they also contain other pigments that mask the green colour.

FIG B 3.23.3 This begonia does not have completely green leaves

Leaves ⟫⟫

The **leaves** are the most obvious part of a plant. Each leaf has a network of veins that allows water and nutrients to be transported into and out of the leaf cells.

Leaves are green because they contain a green pigment called chlorophyll, which is able to trap energy from sunlight. This energy is used by the plant to convert carbon dioxide and water to the sugar glucose, and oxygen is also formed.

The leaves have the following important functions:

- They make nutrients by the process of photosynthesis.

- They are involved in gaseous exchange. The leaf has tiny openings, or pores called stomata, through which carbon dioxide is absorbed from the air and oxygen is released.

- They also lose water vapour in a process called transpiration. This water is replaced by absorption through the roots.

- They store some nutrients in the form of starch. Onions, for example, store food in their leaves.

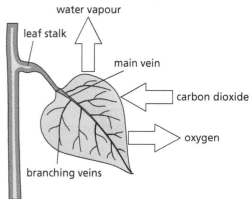

FIG B 3.23.4 Veining in a leaf

Flowers ⟫⟫

Flowers contain the organs for sexual reproduction of a flowering plant.

Activity B 3.23.1

Observing the different parts of a plant

You should work in a group for this activity. You need a plant that is in flower.

1. Carefully examine each of the four parts of the plant mentioned above.

2. Make a drawing of the four parts you have examined.

Check your understanding

1. Fig B 3.23.5 shows a green plant in a jar.

   a) Water passes through the plant from the container. List the parts of the plant through which water passes, in order.

   b) What change took place during the 5 days that the plant was left in the container? Suggest a reason for this change.

Key terms

root part of plant in the ground that absorbs water and nutrients

stem part of plant that joins roots to leaves and flowers

leaf part of plant where food is made, gases are exchanged and water is lost

flower plant organ of sexual reproduction

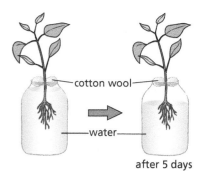

FIG B 3.23.5 A green plant in a jar

24 Substances transported in plants

We are learning how to:

- identify substances transported in plants

Plants obtain the substances they need to flourish in a completely different way to animals.

- Animals eat complex chemicals that are broken down to provide those substances

- Plants absorb and use simple chemicals to create those substances themselves

Consequently substances are transported in different ways.

Transport of gases 〉〉

You learned in the previous unit that:

- all organisms carry out respiration to obtain energy; this process requires oxygen and produces carbon dioxide

- green plants carry out photosynthesis to make food; this process requires carbon dioxide and produces oxygen

Process	Gas needed	Gas produced
respiration	oxygen	carbon dioxide
photosynthesis	carbon dioxide	oxygen

TABLE B 3.24.1

Plants have no organ corresponding to the lungs or gills of an animal. They rely on **diffusion** for transport of gases. Oxygen and carbon dioxide pass into and out of the plant through tiny pores. Many of these pores, or stomata, are located on the underside of leaves.

This is not an active method of transport so gases take much longer to move through a plant than through an animal.

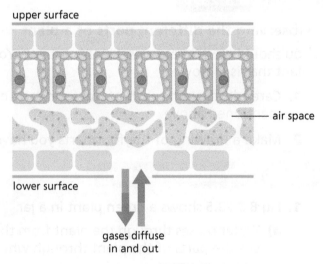

upper surface

air space

lower surface

gases diffuse in and out

FIG B 3.24.1 Section through a leaf

Plants cannot ingest solids in the same way that animals can, so all of the chemicals they need must be absorbed in solution from the soil.

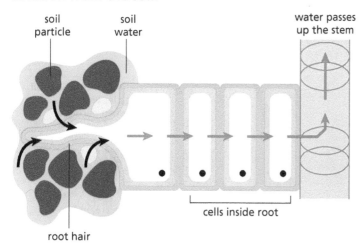

FIG B 3.24.2 Movement of water from soil into plant root and stem

Soil water containing dissolved minerals is absorbed into root hair cells by **osmosis**. The solution passes from cell to cell in the root by the same process until it reaches the stem.

Inside a plant stem there are two types of vessels called the xylem and the phloem. You will learn more about these vessels later in this unit.

- The solution of minerals passes up from the roots to the rest of the plant through the xylem.

- Solutions of substance pass from one part of a plant to another through the phloem.

Plants have no organ corresponding to the heart of an animal. Solutions of substances are not pumped around a plant in the same way as blood circulates in an animal and consequently transport takes much longer.

Check your understanding

1. **a)** How are gases transported in and out of plants?

   b) Why does the movement of gases in plants take much longer than it does in animals?

2. **a)** How are nutrients transported from the soil through the roots of a plant?

   b) Through which vessels are substances transported in a plant?

Key terms

diffusion net movement of particles spreading from an area where they are in high concentration to one where they are in low concentration

osmosis net movement of water from an area of high concentration to one of low concentration through a partially permeable membrane

25 Plant roots

We are learning how to:
- identify different types of plant roots
- describe the functions of a plant root

The roots are the part of the plant that is in the soil. They absorb water containing dissolved minerals from the soil.

FIG B 3.25.1 Fibrous roots (left) and tap roots (right)

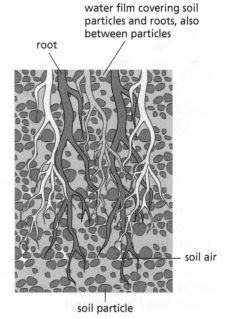

water film covering soil particles and roots, also between particles

root

soil air

soil particle

FIG B 3.25.2 Plant roots divide many times

A plant, such as a pepper plant, might have a **fibrous root** that divides into thinner and thinner roots, or it may be more like a carrot and have a **tap root**, which is a large swollen root with smaller roots growing from it.

Plant roots are ideally suited to absorbing water from the soil. They divide many times so that there is a large surface area available for absorption.

Plant roots consist of plant root cells. Each cell has a **root hair** that grows out into the gaps between soil particles, increasing the surface area of the roots even more. Water containing minerals is absorbed through the root hairs.

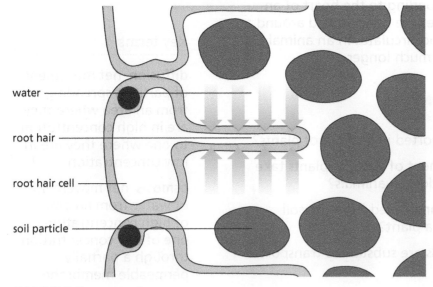

water

root hair

root hair cell

soil particle

FIG B 3.25.3 Plant root cells

Activity B 3.25.1

Examining roots

Here is what you need:

- recently germinated pea or bean plant
- hand lens
- legume plant

Here is what you should do:

1. Carefully remove a plant from a pot so that soil remains around the roots.

2. Look carefully at the roots. Notice how they are spread out to provide the plant with a firm anchor, and also to absorb water and nutrients from different parts of the soil. Notice how the roots divide a number of times to finally produce very thin root hairs.

3. Knock away some of the soil and examine the area immediately around the roots. Can you see any root hairs?

4. Make some drawings of the roots showing their different features.

5. [STEAM] The roots of a group of plants called legumes are associated with fixing or converting atmospheric nitrogen into nitrogenous compounds in the soil. Obtain a legume plant and draw its roots showing how they differ from other plant roots.

Check your understanding

1. Fig B 3.25.4 shows two different types of root system.

tap root system   fibrous root system

FIG B 3.25.4 Different types of root system

a) Which root stores more nutrients?

b) In what ways are the root systems designed to gather water and nutrients efficiently?

Key terms

fibrous root root that divides many times, producing a network of tiny roots

tap root large thick root swollen with food reserves

root hair finger-like projection on a root cell, which increases its surface area for absorption

26 Xylem and phloem

We are learning how to:

- identify the xylem and the phloem in a plant stem

You have already seen how water containing dissolved minerals is absorbed by the roots and passes to other parts of the plant. However, there is also a flow of other substances in the plant.

The leaves use energy from sunlight to make food in the form of glucose. The glucose is then distributed to the other parts of the plant either to provide the plant's cells with energy, or to be stored as starch.

The plant therefore needs two vessels to transport dissolved substances:

- The **xylem** transports water and water-soluble minerals from the soil to different parts of the plant

- The **phloem** transports glucose, proteins and other organic chemicals within the plant

In the root of a plant the xylem and phloem together form a vascular cylinder.

Inside the vascular cylinder the xylem forms the centre, which is surrounded by the phloem.

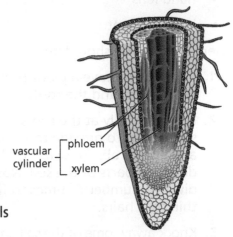

FIG B 3.26.1 Vascular cylinder in the plant root

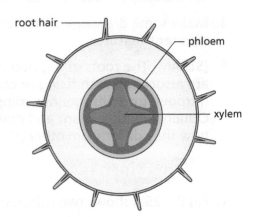

FIG B 3.26.2 Section through vascular cylinder in the plant root

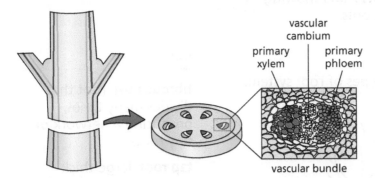

FIG B 3.26.3 Vascular bundle in a plant stem

A cross section of a plant stem shows that the vascular cylinder forms a series of **vascular bundles**. These are arranged symmetrically around the stem but the pattern is different in different plants. Each vascular bundle consists of xylem cells towards the centre of the stem and phloem cells towards the outside. These cells are separated by **vascular cambium** cells.

The flow through the xylem vessels is upwards from the roots towards other parts of the plant. The flow

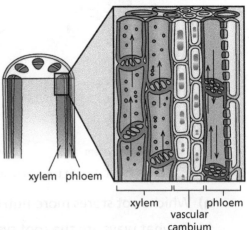

FIG B 3.26.4 Direction of flow in a vascular bundle

through the phloem may be in either direction as substances are carried between the different parts of the plant.

Activity B 3.26.1

Arrangements of vascular bundles

Here is what you need:
- poster-sized sheet of paper
- different coloured card × 2
- scissors
- glue

Here is what you should do:

1. Cut 20 discs of two different colours and sizes from coloured card. 10 will represent the xylem and 10 the phloem.

2. Arrange the discs to show how the xylem and phloem are arranged in the root of a plant and in the stem of a plant.

3. When you are satisfied with your arrangement, glue your discs in place so your poster can form part of a classroom display.

Check your understanding

1. Fig B 3.26.5 shows a section across a plant stem.

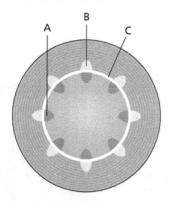

FIG B 3.26.5 A section across a plant stem

a) Name the parts labelled A, B and C.

b) What is carried in:

   i) A   ii) B?

c) In which direction is the flow through:

   i) A   ii) B?

Key terms

xylem vessels carrying solution of minerals from the soil to different parts of the plant

phloem vessels carrying solution of nutrients and other chemicals around the plant

vascular bundle structure containing xylem and phloem vessels

vascular cambium cells between the xylem and phloem in a vascular bundle

27 Movement of substances through the xylem and phloem

We are learning how to:

- describe the movement of substances along the phloem and the xylem of a plant

Both the xylem and the phloem appear to be long thin tubes, like narrow drinking straws, but their structures are very different.

Structure of the phloem

Phloem tissue consists of two main types of cells; sieve elements and companion cells, together with other types of cells that make up the structure.

Sieve elements are long narrow cells that join together to form a **sieve tube**. At the ends of each sieve element there is a sieve plate. Sieve plates are porous and therefore allow substances to flow between cells along the sieve tube.

Sieve elements have no nuclei but they do have thick rigid cell walls made of cellulose. These are needed to withstand the hydrostatic pressures that bring about the flow through the phloem.

Sieve elements would not be able to function without companion cells. The companion cells make the movement of materials through the sieve plates possible.

Substances can move in both directions through the sieve tubes. Movement is the result of hydrostatic pressure from the xylem.

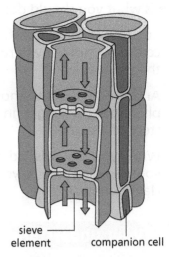

sieve element   companion cell

FIG B 3.27.1 Sieve elements and companion cells in the phloem

Structure of the xylem

The xylem consists of stacks of dead cells, which are joined together to form tubules.

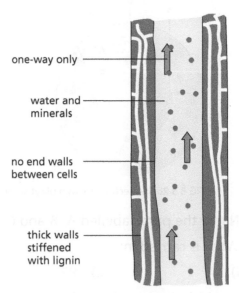

one-way only

water and minerals

no end walls between cells

thick walls stiffened with lignin

xylem vessel

FIG B 3.27.2 A stack of dead cells makes up a xylem vessel

Since the xylem doesn't contain living cells it is not possible for the solution of mineral salts to pass up the plant by osmosis. Instead, the solution of minerals rises up through the xylem by **capillarity**. This occurs when liquids are in tubes that have very small diameters.

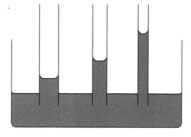

FIG B 3.27.3 The narrower the tube the greater the effect of capillarity

Activity B 3.27.1

Examining the tubes that carry water up a stem

Here is what you need:

- solution of red ink
- stick of celery
- sharp knife

Here is what you should do:

1. Cut off the bottom part of a fresh celery stalk and stand it in the red ink solution at the start of a lesson.

2. Near the end of the lesson take the stalk out of the ink solution and cut across the middle with a sharp knife.

3. Examine the cut part of the celery. Look for the cut xylem tubes which will look like red dots where the ink has been drawn up through the stem.

Check your understanding

1. Decide whether each of the following statements describes the xylem, the phloem, or both the xylem and the phloem.

   a) Carries substances dissolved in solution.

   b) Substances travel in two directions.

   c) Substances can only travel by capillarity.

   d) Contains sieve elements.

   e) Consists of stacks of dead cells.

Interesting fact

Cut flower stems can absorb solutions that will alter the natural colour of the flowers.

FIG B 3.27.4

Florists use this trick to make unusual floral displays.

Key terms

sieve tube a tube composed of sieve elements in the phloem

capillarity movement of a liquid up a narrow tube

28 Transpiration

The absorption of water and minerals from the soil is only one part of a bigger process called **transpiration**.

Transpiration is the movement of water through a plant. Water is absorbed by the roots and passes through the plant. It is eventually lost by evaporation, mainly through the leaves. This is sometimes called a transpiration stream.

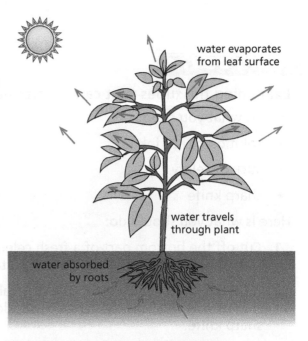

water evaporates from leaf surface

water travels through plant

water absorbed by roots

FIG B 3.28.1 Transpiration through a plant

FIG B 3.28.2 Transpiration causes condensation inside a polythene bag

If the stem and leaves of a plant are sealed in a polythene bag and left for 24 hours, condensation forms inside the bag. The water is not coming from the soil, but from the leaves of the plant.

As a result of transpiration, water is continually being lost from the surface of the leaves and more water is drawn up through the xylem to replace it. In turn, soil water containing minerals is absorbed by the plant roots to replenish the water in the xylem. This is called transpiration pull.

Interesting fact

Although carnivorous plants, like the Venus flytrap, absorb water through their roots just like other plants, they do not rely on soil water for minerals.

FIG B 3.28.3 A Venus flytrap

Carnivorous plants obtain nutrients by trapping and digesting insects.

Activity B 3.28.1

Investigating water loss from both surfaces of a leaf

Here is what you need:

- plant with green leaves
- blue cobalt chloride paper
- plastic paper clip
- scissors

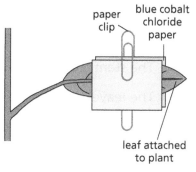

FIG B 3.28.4 Investigating water loss experiment

Here is what you should do:

1. Cut out two pieces of blue cobalt chloride paper roughly the same size as a leaf. (They do not have to be exactly the same size as the leaf.)

2. Using a paper clip, attach the cobalt chloride paper to each side of a leaf that is attached to a plant, as shown in Fig B 3.28.4.

3. Make sure the plant is well watered and leave it for several hours.

4. Observe the colour of the cobalt chloride paper covering the upper surface and the lower surface of the leaf. Blue cobalt chloride paper turns pink in the presence of water.

5. [STEAM] Devise an experiment to measure the pressure created by transpiration as water passes up a leafy shoot.

In addition to allowing the uptake of minerals, transpiration has some more important benefits for a plant.

- Transpiration allows the plant to get rid of excess water.

- Transpiration creates hydrostatic pressure, which allows substances in water to be transported around the plant.

- When water **evaporates** from the surface of a leaf it removes heat energy. A plant can increase the rate at which water is lost from the leaves in order to cool its leaves and prevent them being damaged by heat from the Sun.

Key terms

transpiration movement of water through a plant

evaporate when a liquid changes to a vapour below its boiling point

polythene bag

FIG B 3.28.5 Transpiration experiment

Check your understanding

1. In an experiment carried out to demonstrate transpiration, a polythene bag was placed over the leaves and stem of a plant. The open end of the bag was sealed around the stem, as shown in Fig B 3.28.5.

   a) Predict how the plant and bag will appear after 24 hours.

   b) Explain your prediction.

Review of Transport in plants

- A plant consists of four parts: roots, stem, leaves and flowers.
- The roots anchor the plant in soil and absorb water containing dissolved minerals.
- The stem connects the roots with the leaves and flowers.
- The leaves use energy from sunlight to make glucose.
- The flower is the organ of sexual reproduction.
- Gases pass into and out of plants through tiny pores called stomata.
- Gases move through plants by diffusion.
- Plants take in substances dissolved in water through the roots.
- Dissolved substances are transported from the roots to the rest of the plant.
- Dissolved substances are transported from one part of a plant to another.
- A plant may have fibrous roots or a tap root.
- Tap roots contain stores of food in the form of starch.
- Fibrous roots divide many times to give a network of roots that has a large surface area.
- Root cells have finger-like projections called root hairs that increase the surface area for absorption.
- Substances move around a plant through the xylem and the phloem.
- The xylem transports water and water-soluble minerals from the soil to the different parts of the plant.
- The phloem transports glucose, proteins and other organic chemicals within the plant.
- In the root the xylem and phloem form a vascular cylinder.
- In the stem the xylem and phloem form vascular bundles.
- Substances pass only one way up the xylem.
- Substances may pass either way in the phloem.
- Substances rise up the xylem by capillarity.
- Transpiration is the movement of water through a plant.
- Plants absorb water through the roots and lose it mostly through the leaves.
- Transpiration cools the leaves so they are not damaged by heat from the Sun.

Review questions on Transport in plants

Knowledge and understanding

1. Fig B 3.RQ.1 shows the outline of a plant.

   a) Identify parts A to D.

   b) In which part

      i) is most water lost?

      ii) is water absorbed?

   c) What is the function of part A?

2. Fig B 3.RQ.2 shows two different types of root.

   a) What names are given to these different types of root?

   b) Which root has the larger total surface area?

   c) Which root contains the most stored food?

   d) Why is it an advantage for roots to have a large surface area?

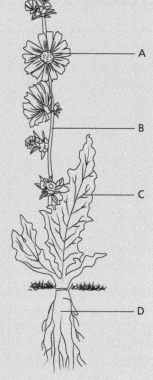

FIG B 3.RQ.1

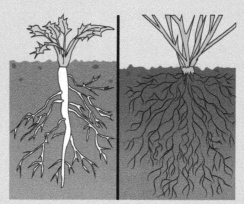

root A   root B

FIG B 3.RQ.2

3. **a)** In a plant, what is the function of

      i) the xylem?

      ii) the phloem?

   b) Draw a labelled diagram to show how the xylem and phloem form vascular bundles in a plant stem.

Process skills

4. The plants shown in Fig B 3.RQ.3 were left in a warm place for 24 hours.

   a) Predict what will happen.

   b) Explain your prediction.

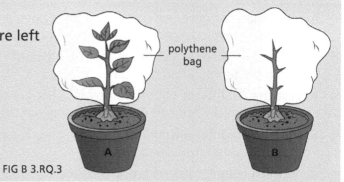

FIG B 3.RQ.3

5. Blue cobalt chloride paper turns pink in the presence of water. Design an experiment using blue cobalt chloride paper to investigate how quickly water is lost from the lower surface of a leaf under the following conditions:

   i) cool still air   **ii)** cool moving air   **iii)** warm still air   **iv)** warm moving air

30 Providing pot plants with adequate water

A company is planning to market a device that will automatically water plants in a pot when there is no one home to water them. The device will be designed to water a 20 cm diameter pot.

FIG STEAM B 3.30.1 Self irrigation

The device consists of a reservoir of water and a mechanism by which a certain amount of water is released into the plant soil each day. The company intends to offer the device in two sizes – a smaller size that will provide water for 1 week, and a larger size that will provide water for 2 weeks.

However, there is a problem. The engineer designing the device does not know how much water a plant loses each day. This information is needed to determine the sizes of the reservoirs. The more water a plant loses the bigger the reservoir will have to be.

As a science specialist you have been hired by the company to investigate and make recommendations. You are going to work in small groups to investigate how much water a typical plant loses each day under different conditions. The tasks are:

- To review how plants absorb and lose water.
- To devise a method of measuring the amount of water lost by a potted plant in a day.
- To investigate whether external conditions have any effect on the rate at which a potted plant loses water.
- To determine an average value for the amount of water lost by a potted plant in one day.
- To test the validity of your value by watering a potted plant with this amount of water each day over a week.
- To make recommendations to the company for reservoir sizes based on your observations.
- To suggest other research work that the company might undertake, which builds on what you have done.
- To compile a report including a PowerPoint presentation in which you should explain how you went about solving the problem and how you arrived at your recommendations. You should illustrate your report by taking photographs at different stages during testing.

a) Look back through the unit and make sure that you understand how plants absorb and lose water.

b) How are you going to determine how much water a potted plant loses in a day?

You may decide to water the plant first thing in the day, let it drain and then weigh it. You could then weigh it first thing the following day to find out how much water has been lost.

c) The weather changes from day to day. What external conditions might affect the loss of water from a potted plant? Perhaps plants lose more water on warmer days than on cooler days. How are you going to find out?

d) Over a period of a week or a fortnight the weather and the amount of water lost by a potted plant each day will vary. Basing the size of the reservoir on the amount of water lost on the hottest day might lead to an overestimate of what is needed. You need to find an 'average' amount of water loss over a week and a fortnight. How will you do this?

e) How are you going to test whether your average amount is sufficient? What will you do if it turns out not to be so?

f) How are you going to use your results to recommend the size of reservoir needed for a device that waters a potted plant for a week, and one that waters a potted plant for a fortnight?

g) Do you think that the development work you have carried out provides the company with sufficient information to go ahead and manufacture their product or do you think there are other factors that might be important? For example, do all types of plants lose the same amount of water each day?

h) Prepare a PowerPoint presentation in which you describe what you did in order to find the average amount of water lost by a potted plant each day. You should illustrate your account with photographs.

Show the data you obtained and explain how you interpreted it in order to make recommendations about reservoir size.

Discuss other issues that you think the company should consider and perhaps research further before finally deciding on the sizes of the reservoirs needed for their device.

FIG STEAM B 3.30.2 Weighing a potted plant

31 Importance of responding to change

We are learning how to:

- appreciate the importance of being able to respond to change

Organisms continually experience changes to their environment. Those changes that result in a reaction by an organism are called **stimuli**.

Organisms react to a whole range of different stimuli. Different organisms don't all react to the same stimuli or react in the same way. Organisms react in a way that is beneficial to them.

Organisms that live in water will move away from stimuli such as harmful chemicals and increasing temperature in order to remain safe.

Microscopic aquatic organisms like algae are attracted towards light because they need light to make food. Animals such as *Daphnia* that feed on the algae are attracted towards the light because they know they will find food.

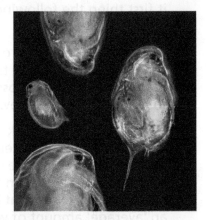

FIG B 4.31.1 *Daphnia*

Plants respond to a limited number of stimuli but much more slowly than animals. Plant roots always grow downwards while the stems always grow upwards.

In this way the plant roots obtain water and nutrients from the soil while the stems receive the light needed for photosynthesis to take place.

FIG B 4.31.2 Plant stems grow towards light

Complex animals, including humans, respond to a whole range of different stimuli.

FIG B 4.31.3 Responding to stimuli enables animals to communicate

Being able to respond to what we see and hear enables us to communicate with others.

FIG B 4.31.4 Responding to stimuli enables animals to find food

Being able to respond to what we see and what we smell helps us to find the food we need.

FIG B 4.31.5 Responding to stimuli enables animals to keep safe

Being able to respond to what we see, hear, feel and smell helps us to remain safe as we go about our daily routines.

Key term

stimuli changes in the environment to which an organism responds

Interesting fact

The leaves on a tree move to change the way they face over the course of a day as the Sun travels across the sky. In this way they capture the maximum amount of sunlight needed for photosynthesis. However, the movement is far too slow for us to see. It can only be captured using time–lapse photography.

Activity B 4.31.1

Why is being able to respond to change important for me?

In your group, discuss why having the ability to respond to change is essential to your everyday life. Use the following to guide your discussions.

- How does responding keep me safe?
- How does responding allow me to communicate?
- How does responding provide me with what I need to live?
- How does responding enrich my life?

Check your understanding

1. Many birds migrate from Northern America to Jamaica in the winter. What changes might cause birds to decide it is time to fly south for the winter?

32 The nervous system

We are learning how to:

* identify the different parts of the nervous system

The nervous system

The nervous system is a network of nerve cells and fibres that carry nerve impulses between different parts of the body. The nervous system allows us to gather information about the environment immediately surrounding us, using our senses, and to act on it. The nervous system is also essential in processes like movement and controlling body temperature.

There are two main parts to the nervous system:

* The **central nervous system (CNS),** which comprises the brain and the spinal cord. This is the main control centre for the body.

* The **peripheral nervous system (PNS),** which consists of a complex network of nerves that extends from the CNS to all parts of the body.

Any damage to the CNS will impair the ability of the body to function and might be fatal. The brain is protected by the skull, while the spinal cord is contained within the vertebrae that make up the backbone.

The PNS contains both sensory cells, called **receptors,** and **effectors**. The receptors are located in the sense organs, such as the eyes and the ears. Their role is to gather information. This is often the result of a change in the environment, called a stimulus.

The information is sent as nerve impulses from the PNS to the CNS along sensory nerves. In the CNS decisions are made about how the body should respond. Messages are then sent as nerve impulses from the CNS along motor nerves to the effectors in the body. Effectors are muscles or glands that bring about the response.

FIG B 4.32.1 The nervous system

brain

cranial nerves

nerves

spinal nerves

spinal cord

■ central nervous system (CNS)

■ peripheral nervous system (PNS)

FIG B 4.32.2 Damage to the spinal cord can prevent the legs from working

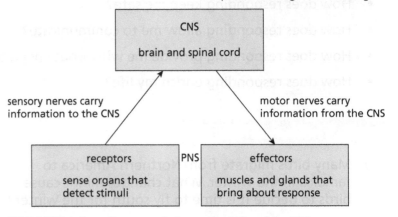

CNS
brain and spinal cord

sensory nerves carry information to the CNS

motor nerves carry information from the CNS

receptors
sense organs that detect stimuli

PNS

effectors
muscles and glands that bring about response

FIG B 4.32.3 Information passes between the PNS and the CNS

Here is how your nervous system might react to the stimulus of a car coming around the bend as you are crossing a road.

1. The receptors in your eyes and your ears send messages to the brain along the sensory nerves, with the information that a car is coming.

2. The brain reasons that if you do not move more quickly you are going to be run over and hurt.

3. The brain sends a message, along the motor nerves, to the muscles in your legs, to make them move more quickly.

In this example the car provides the stimulus while the response is to move more quickly.

FIG B 4.32.4 Crossing a road

Activity B 4.32.1

Labelling a neuron

You will not require any equipment or materials for this activity, but you may need sources of reference material.

Nerve cells are called neurons. They look different from any of the other cells that you have already seen, such as the red and white blood cells.

Fig B 4.32.5 shows a neuron. The labels point to the:

axon, cell membrane, cytoplasm, dendrite, nerve ending, nucleus

1. Copy the diagram into your notebook.

2. Add the labels by choosing from the terms above. You might have to do some research to identify some of the parts.

3. Information can pass along a nerve as quickly as 120 m/s. Convert this value to km/hour, and comment on whether it is faster or slower than a car is allowed to travel along the roads in Jamaica.

> **Interesting fact**
>
> The skull is the body's crash helmet that protects the brain. The average thickness of an adult male skull is 6.5 mm, while the average thickness of an adult female skull is 7.1 mm.

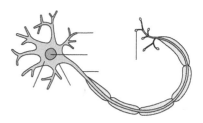

FIG B 4.32.5 A neuron

Check your understanding

1. A student is out for a walk in the woods on a windy day when a tree is blown down just in front of her. Describe how the student's nervous system might react to this situation.

FIG B 4.32.6

Key terms

central nervous system brain and spinal cord

peripheral nervous system network of nerves around the body

receptor sensory cell that receives information

effector muscle or gland that responds to a stimulus

33 The sense organs

We are learning how to:

- identify the sense organs
- explain how the sense organs provide us with information about our surroundings

The sense organs are those parts of the body that respond to stimuli by sending a message to the brain. The sense organs allow us to gather information about our surroundings.

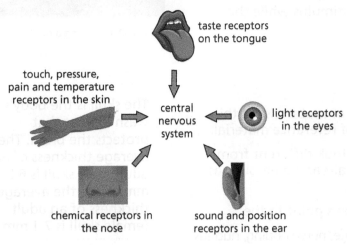

FIG B 4.33.1 The sense organs

Each sense organ responds to a different stimulus or stimuli.

At the back of the eye there is a layer of light-sensitive cells called the retina. These cells detect light and send messages to the brain via the **optic nerve**.

The ear detects sound as vibrations that pass through the air. These vibrations are magnified by the ear and messages are carried to the brain by the **auditory nerve**.

The inside of the nose is lined with cells that can detect different chemicals. We learn to associate different smells with familiar things within our environment. Information is sent from the nose to the brain along the **olfactory nerve**.

The tongue detects chemicals in the foods that we eat and passes information to the brain. Different areas of the tongue detect different tastes.

- The taste buds for 'sweet' are on the tip of the tongue.
- The 'salt' taste buds are on either side of the front of the tongue.
- The 'sour' taste buds are in the middle of the tongue.
- The 'bitter' taste buds are at the back of the tongue.

FIG B 4.33.2 Eyes detect light

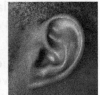

FIG B 4.33.3 Ears detect sound

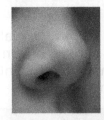

FIG B 4.33.4 The nose detects smell

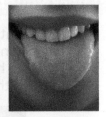

FIG B 4.33.5 The tongue detects tastes

In some ways the skin is the most sophisticated of all the sense organs in that it can detect more than one type of stimulus. The skin contains receptors that detect whether an object is hot or cold, and can sense touch, pressure and pain. All this information is passed on to the brain. Some areas of the skin, like the fingertips, have a much higher concentration of sense cells than other areas, such as the skin on the back. This makes them more sensitive to stimuli.

FIG B 4.33.6 Skin detects a number of stimuli

Activity B 4.33.1

Investigating touch receptors in the skin

You must work with a partner for this activity.

Here is what you need:

- card
- sticky tape
- two long dressmaker's pins

Here is what you should do:

1. Attach the pins to a piece of card so that the points are about 1 cm apart.

2. Your partner should not watch what you do next, so ask them to look away.

3. Choose an area of their skin, such as their forearm.

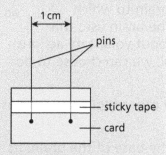

FIG B 4.33.7

4. Touch their skin (but do not stab them!) with either one pin or two pins, but do not tell them which.

5. Ask them whether they felt one pin or two pins and record whether they were correct or not.

6. Do this on the same area of skin four more times and record how many times out of five they were correct.

7. Repeat this by taking sets of five readings from different areas of skin.

8. Write your results in the form of a table.

9. For which area(s) of the skin did your partner score the most correct answers?

10. For which area(s) of the skin did your partner score the fewest correct answers?

11. Which area contained the highest concentration of sensory cells and which area contained the lowest concentration of sensory cells?

Interesting fact

The skin is the largest organ of your body. It is an important sense organ and contains receptors that can be stimulated by touch, hot and cold, pressure and pain.

Key terms

optic nerve carries nerve impulses from the eye to the brain

auditory nerve carries nerve impulses from the ear to the brain

olfactory nerve carries nerve impulses from the nose to the brain

Check your understanding

1. Draw a table showing the five sense organs and what they detect.

34 The brain

We are learning how to:

- identify the main regions of the brain
- explain the functions of the main regions of the brain

The brain is the 'central processor' of the body. It gathers information from all of the sensory organs and then decides how the body should respond.

The brain can be divided into three main parts. Each of these parts has particular functions.

The **cerebrum** is the large part that you might recognise from a photograph of the brain. It is divided into two cerebral hemispheres and the surface is grooved.

The cerebrum is the part of the brain to which information is sent and stored. The brain uses this information to make decisions about voluntary actions. These are actions that we control; we can choose to do them or not.

The cerebrum also controls some other functions, such as speech, learning and memory.

The **cerebellum** is the region at the base of the brain. Its function is to coordinate muscle action so that we can maintain our balance.

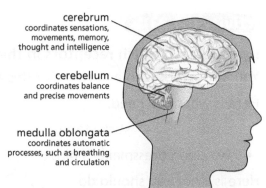

cerebrum
coordinates sensations, movements, memory, thought and intelligence

cerebellum
coordinates balance and precise movements

medulla oblongata
coordinates automatic processes, such as breathing and circulation

FIG B 4.34.1 The three main regions of the brain

FIG B 4.34.2 The cerebrum is where we think

FIG B 4.34.3 Good balance allows us to do things like dancing and sports

The ability to maintain balance allows us to stand and move about without falling or tripping ourselves up. This is described as involuntary action because it happens automatically; we have no control over it.

The **medulla oblongata** is also called the brain stem. It is the part of the brain that joins the spinal cord. This region controls a number of different functions, including breathing, heartbeat, peristalsis (the movement of food along the alimentary canal) and digestion.

The medulla oblongata is also responsible for maintaining a constant body temperature. All of these actions are involuntary because we have no control over them.

FIG B 4.34.4 Temperature control is essential for our wellbeing

---

Activity B 4.34.1

Identifying different parts of the brain

Here is what you need:

- An outline of the brain, like the one in Fig B 4.34.5.

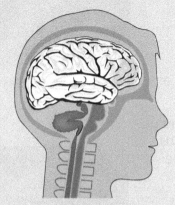

FIG B 4.34.5 The three main regions of the brain

Here is what you should do:

1. Label the skull and the vertebral column.

2. Lightly shade in and label the cerebrum, the cerebellum and the medulla oblongata.

Check your understanding

1. In which parts of the brain does each of the following take place?

a) Balance is coordinated.

b) Information is stored.

c) Breathing is controlled.

d) Decisions are made.

e) Body temperature is maintained.

Key terms

cerebrum largest part of the brain where information is gathered and stored

cerebellum part of the brain that coordinates muscle action

medulla oblongata part of the brain that joins the spinal cord, and which coordinates a number of essential body functions

35 Voluntary, involuntary and reflex actions

We are learning how to:

- describe actions as voluntary, involuntary or reflex

Some parts of the brain are concerned with voluntary actions and others with involuntary actions.

- A **voluntary action** is one over which we have complete control. We can decide whether to do it or not. Standing, walking, sitting and talking are examples of voluntary actions.

- An **involuntary action** is one over which we have no control. The body takes this action without us having to think about it or make decisions. Breathing, swallowing and blinking are involuntary actions.

FIG B 4.35.1 Running is a voluntary action

A **reflex action** is an involuntary response to a stimulus. Like all involuntary responses, it happens without us thinking about it. Reflex actions help to protect the body in dangerous situations.

Accidently touching a hot pan is painful and might burn the skin. Let's think what would happen if we had to rely on voluntary actions in this situation.

- The heat receptors in the hand would send a message to the cerebrum in the brain telling it that they had touched a hot pan.

- The brain would decide to move the hand away to avoid being damaged.

FIG B 4.35.2 Breathing and heartbeat are involuntary actions

- A message would be sent from the brain to the muscles in the arm telling them to move the hand away.

Even in the short time it would take the messages to travel to and from the brain, the skin on your hand would be damaged and it would feel very painful.

Instead of a voluntary action, your nervous system takes over and moves your hand without you having to think about it. This is called a reflex action. It takes place as a result of a **reflex arc**.

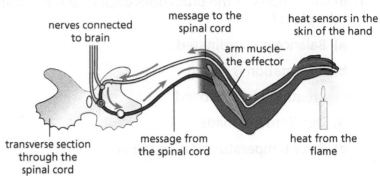

nerves connected to brain

message to the spinal cord

heat sensors in the skin of the hand

arm muscle– the effector

transverse section through the spinal cord

message from the spinal cord

heat from the flame

FIG B 4.35.3 Reflex arc

Here is how a reflex arc would prevent your fingers from being seriously damaged:

- The heat receptors in the hand send a message to the spinal cord.
- The reflex response is sent directly from the spinal cord to the muscles in the arm.

The brain is not involved in any decision making but a message is sent from the spinal cord to the brain so that you are aware of what your body is doing.

Blinking and the knee jerk reflex are other examples of reflexes. Blinking keeps the surface of your eye moist and removes any particles of dust from it.

The knee jerk reflex is the body's response to tapping just under the knee cap to stretch the tendons.

> **Interesting fact**
>
> A doctor can test reflex actions as a simple way of checking whether a patient's nervous system is working properly.

Activity B 4.35.1

Observing reflex actions

You will not require any equipment for this activity, but you must work with a partner. Each partner should observe the reflex actions, in turn.

1. Firstly, investigate the knee jerk response. One student sits with one knee crossed over the other, while the other student taps just under their partner's knee cap with the side of their hand. You don't have to tap hard, but it is necessary to tap in exactly the correct place to produce the response.

2. Secondly, investigate the eye's pupil reflex. The black centre of the eye is called the pupil. It is actually a hole through which light enters the eye.

3. Your partner should turn his or her back away from the window and cover their eyes with their hands for a few minutes. When they remove their hands look quickly at the size of their pupils.

4. Repeat this but with your partner looking towards a bright window. Once again, when they remove their hands look quickly at the size of their pupils.

5. Draw what you observed. Did your partner appear to have any control over this action?

Check your understanding

1. This person is shivering.

   a) Give a stimulus that often causes people to shiver.

   b) Is shivering a reflex action? Explain your answer.

   c) How does shivering help the body?

FIG B 4.35.4 Shivering

Key terms

voluntary action an action that the body controls

involuntary action an action that the body doesn't control

reflex action involuntary response to a stimulus

reflex arc pathway taken by nerve impulses during a reflex action

36 Reaction time

We are learning how to:

- measure reaction time
- reduce reaction time by repetition

The nervous system allows the body to respond to stimuli by taking voluntary actions. The time it takes to respond to a stimulus is called the reaction time.

Reaction time depends on:

- how quickly the brain can process the information provided by the stimulus and decide on a suitable response
- how quickly the muscles can act to bring about that response.

When we are young we are still learning about the world around us and our muscles are still developing. So, it is not surprising that young children have slow reaction times.

As children grow they become more knowledgeable and physically developed, so they are able to respond more quickly to a stimulus.

As we grow we also build up a 'library' of stimulus–response situations that we experience regularly. For example, our cell phones ring and we answer them. We do not need to think about what we are doing or which buttons to press because we may do this several times each day.

People can reduce their reaction time through practice.

Cricketers practise batting in the nets. This allows them to respond more quickly to balls bowled at different speeds, heights and directions. They get used to playing different shots so they do not have to think about what to do.

> ### Interesting fact
>
> A cricket ball bowled by the fastest pace bowlers travels at up to 160 km/h. The batsman has less than half a second to make up their mind about which shot to play.

FIG B 4.36.1 Batsmen and batswomen practise in the nets to improve their reaction times

FIG B 4.36.2 The gymnast Toni-Ann Williams practised these moves for the Rio Olympics many times

Gymnasts such as Toni-Ann Williams will practise their gymnastic routines many times, so that they can go quickly from one move to the next. They do not have to stop and think about them during their displays.

Activity B 4.36.1

Measuring reaction time

You must work with a partner for this activity. Each partner should measure the other's reaction time, in turn.

Here is what you need:

- 30 cm ruler

Here is what you should do:

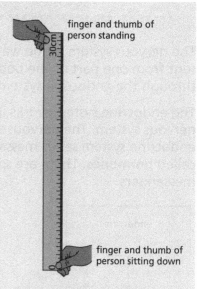

finger and thumb of person standing

finger and thumb of person sitting down

FIG B 4.36.3 Ruler experiment

1. Arrange yourselves so that one partner is standing, and the other is sitting

2. The standing partner then holds the top of the ruler at the very end so that it is hanging in front of the partner who is sitting.

3. The sitting partner places their thumb and finger level with 0 cm on the ruler, but not touching it, and gets ready to catch the ruler as it falls.

4. The standing partner then releases the ruler. As soon as the sitting partner sees the ruler moving he or she should bring their thumb and finger together to stop the ruler.

5. Record to the nearest centimetre the measurement on the ruler at which the sitting partner stopped the ruler from falling further. The measurement on the ruler at which it was stopped by the sitting person should be recorded to the nearest centimetre.

6. Repeat the procedure five times and take an average value.

7. Calculate the average distance travelled by the ruler in the five tests, for each partner.

8. Explain the link between the distance that the ruler travels and reaction time.

9. [STEAM] Devise a similar activity to investigate how much tiredness affects a person's reaction time.

Check your understanding

1. The graph in Fig B 4.36.4 shows how average reaction time varies with age and gender.

   a) Does the diagram suggest that men or women have the quicker reaction times?

   b) Is it true that a man who is 70 years old has a similar reaction time to a child who is five years of age?

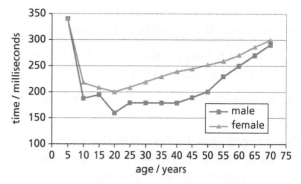

FIG B 4.36.4 Reaction time graph

   c) Suggest how a person might prevent their reaction time from increasing as they grow older.

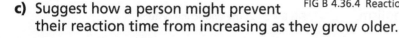

37 The endocrine system

We are learning how to:

- describe how the endocrine system works
- identify some endocrine glands

The nervous system is one way by which messages can be sent from one part of the body to another. A second way is through the endocrine system.

The endocrine system works in a different way to the nervous system. The nervous system uses nerve impulses; the endocrine system sends messages using special chemicals called **hormones**. These are sometimes described as chemical messengers.

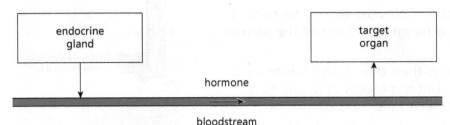

FIG B 4.37.1 Hormones are carried in the blood

Each endocrine gland produces one or more hormones. When a hormone is released into the bloodstream it acts on one particular organ called the **target organ**. Each hormone has a specific role in the body.

The **pituitary gland** is a pea-sized structure found at the base of the brain. It is sometimes called the 'master gland' because it controls the release of hormones by other endocrine glands. The pituitary gland secretes a number of different hormones, including hormones that:

- regulate the growth of the body
- control sperm production in the male and egg production in the female
- control the amount of water in the body.

The **thyroid gland** is found in the throat and its action is controlled by the pituitary gland. It secretes a hormone that:

- controls the rate of metabolism.

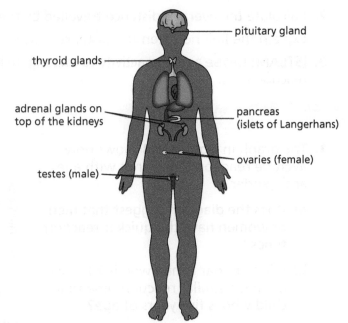

FIG B 4.37.2 The endocrine system

The **pancreas** is connected to the small intestine. It secretes hormones that:

- control the concentration of glucose in the blood.

Blood glucose concentration is sometimes described as blood sugar level.

The **adrenal glands** are located on the tops of the kidneys. They produce hormones that:

- prepare the body for sudden actions or emergencies.

The male **testes** and the female **ovaries** both produce hormones that:

- allow the body to develop secondary sexual characteristics as a person grows to become an adult.

The hormones released by the ovaries also control the menstrual cycle.

There are some glands in the body that release substances into ducts, or tubes, along which the substances are transported. These are called exocrine glands. Endocrine glands do not have ducts and are therefore described as ductless glands. Any substance they produce goes directly into the bloodstream.

> **Interesting fact**
>
> The sweat glands and the salivary glands in your mouth are exocrine glands.

Activity B 4.37.1

Marking the locations of the endocrine glands

Here is what you should do:

1. Mark the position of each endocrine gland on an outline drawing of the human body. You should mark the endocrine glands associated with the reproductive organs according to whether you are a boy or a girl.

2. Label each endocrine gland.

Check your understanding

1. **a)** In which part of the body is the thyroid gland?

   b) Which endocrine gland is sometimes called the master gland?

   c) Which endocrine glands produce different hormones in men and in women?

   d) Which endocrine gland produces hormones that control the concentration of glucose in the blood?

Key terms

hormone chemical messenger released by an endocrine gland

target organ the organ on which a hormone will act

pituitary gland endocrine gland at the base of the brain

thyroid gland endocrine gland in the throat

pancreas endocrine gland attached to the small intestine

adrenal glands endocrine glands on top of the kidneys

testes part of the male reproductive system that releases hormones

ovaries part of the female reproductive system that releases hormones

38 Hormones

Hormones are carried around in the blood. Each hormone has a specific action at a specific target organ, so the body is not confused when several hormones are carried in the bloodstream at the same time. Each endocrine gland is responsible for secreting particular hormones.

The pituitary gland releases a number of different hormones. Some of these control the release of hormones by other endocrine glands. Hormones produced by the pituitary gland include:

- growth hormone, which regulates growth of the body

- **antidiuretic hormone (ADH),** which controls the reabsorption of water by the kidneys during the production of urine

- reproductive hormones that control the production of sperm (in males) and ova (in females).

The thyroid gland releases:

- **thyroxine,** which controls the rate of body metabolism. The release of this hormone is, in turn, controlled by the pituitary gland.

The pancreas releases:

- **insulin** and **glucagon,** which control the level of glucose in the blood.

The adrenal gland releases:

- **adrenalin,** which is sometimes called the 'fight or flight' hormone. It has a number of effects that prepare the body for an emergency. These effects include increasing the heart rate and breathing rate, and increasing the supply of blood to the brain and muscles.

The testes release:

- **testosterone,** which causes the development of male secondary sexual characteristics, such as facial hair and pubic hair, a deepening of the voice and an increase in body size.

The ovaries release:

- **oestrogen,** which causes development of the female secondary sexual characteristics, including pubic hair, enlargement of breasts and broadening of the hips

> **Interesting fact**
>
> A hormone imbalance is a condition where a person's body produces too much or too little of a hormone. Both types of imbalance can have serious implications for the person's health.

FIG B 4.38.1 This man has had a surge of adrenalin

- progesterone, which, together with oestrogen, regulates the menstrual cycle.

The action of a hormone depends on its concentration in the blood. When the weather is hot the body loses water by sweating. The pituitary gland releases lots of ADH into the blood so that the kidneys will retain more water. On a cold day the body loses less water by sweating. Less ADH is released so that less water is retained by the kidneys.

Sometimes two hormones work together to control a process in the body. The concentration of glucose in the blood (blood sugar level) is controlled by the hormones insulin and glucagon.

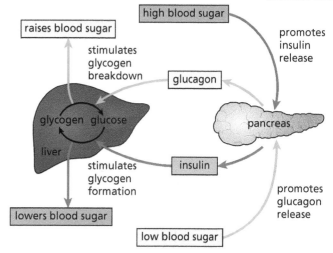

FIG B 4.38.2 Controlling glucose concentration in the blood

- High levels of blood glucose cause the pancreas to secrete insulin, which stimulates the conversion of glucose to a substance called glycogen for storage in the liver.

- Low levels of blood glucose cause the pancreas to secrete glucagon, which stimulates the conversion of glycogen into glucose.

Activity B 4.38.1

Diabetes research

This is a research activity. You should use any reference materials, including the Internet, that you have available.

Diabetes is a condition in which the body needs help controlling the level of glucose in the blood. You might have a relative or friend who has this condition. Find out what you can about diabetes in preparation for a class discussion.

Check your understanding

1. Which endocrine gland releases each of the following hormones?

   a) Testosterone   b) Adrenalin   c) Insulin

2. What is the name of the hormone responsible for:

   a) Controlling the amount of water retained by the kidneys.

   b) Controlling the rate of metabolism of the body.

Key terms

antidiuretic hormone (ADH) hormone that controls water retention

thyroxine hormone that controls the rate of metabolism

insulin hormone involved in the control of blood sugar level

glucagon hormone involved in the control of blood sugar level

adrenalin hormone that prepares the body for emergencies

testosterone hormone responsible for male secondary sexual characteristics

oestrogen hormone responsible for female secondary sexual characteristics

39 Comparing the nervous system and the endocrine system

We are learning how to:

- compare the nervous system and the endocrine system

Although the **nervous system** and the **endocrine system** are both concerned with sending messages from one part of the body to another, there are certain important differences between the two systems.

Nerve messages are electrical impulses that travel along nerve cells, or neurons, rather like an electric current passes along the wires in an electric circuit. The nervous system extends throughout the whole body so the brain can pass a message to different muscles almost instantly.

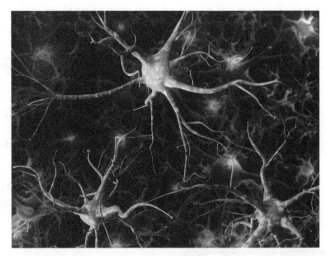

FIG B 4.39.1 Nerve cells, or neurons

Different types of nerve impulse travel at different speeds, but they all travel very quickly. Impulses to the brain from touch sensors travel at around 75 m/s, while from pain sensors the speed is much slower, at around 1 m/s. The speed of impulses travelling in the opposite direction from the brain to muscles may be over 100 m/s.

Nerve impulses are ideal in situations where the body needs an immediate or a short-term response. They are usually the response to a stimulus of one sort or another.

Blood vessels are hollow tubes along which blood flows. The blood moves around your body in a similar way to water in the pipes at home.

Blood moves around the body far more slowly than nerve impulses move along nerve cells. The speed of blood in arteries is around 50 cm/s, while the speed of blood in veins, which do not experience the same pressure from the heart, is only 15 cm/s.

Clearly, hormones are not able to provide an immediate or short-term response to

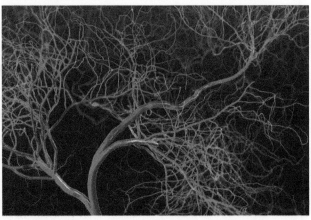

FIG B 4.39.2 Blood vessels

a situation in the same way as nerve impulses. Hormones have a different role in the body. They usually bring about longer-term changes.

Hormones usually cause a gradual change, and are involved with keeping the internal environment of the body stable. Examples are controlling the water content of the body or controlling the level of glucose in the blood. These are very important to our wellbeing, but they do not require an instant change.

Adrenalin is an exception in that it does trigger a quick, short-term response. Its release triggers changes that prepare the body for fighting or other challenging physical activities.

Activity B 4.39.1

Is body temperature controlled by the nervous system or the endocrine system?

You will need to carry out some research for this activity. Use the Internet or any other resources that are available.

Maintaining a constant body temperature is essential to our wellbeing.

1. Is this something that you think involves short-term responses or is it more of a long-term change? What are your first thoughts? Do you think it is controlled by the nervous system or by the endocrine system?

2. Use whatever reference materials are available to find out whether you are correct or not.

Interesting fact

The heart pumps about 7600 dm³ of blood each day, which is about 5 dm³ per minute. This is about the same as the amount of blood in your body. So, if you were able to put a marker into your blood as it left your heart, it would reappear coming back to your heart a minute later.

Check your understanding

1. Copy and complete table B 4.39.1, which compares the nervous system with the endocrine system.

Feature	Nervous system	Endocrine system
nature of the message		
way in which the message is carried		
speed of the message		
speed of response to the message		
reason for the message		

TABLE B 4.39.1

Key terms

nervous system brain, spinal cord and network of neurons along which nerve impulses are sent

endocrine system collection of glands that secrete hormones into the bloodstream

Review of Sensitivity and coordination

- The nervous system is a network of nerve cells, which carry messages around the body.
- There are two main parts to the nervous system: the central nervous system (CNS) and the peripheral nervous system (PNS).
- The CNS comprises the brain and the spinal cord.
- The PNS consists of a network of nerve cells, or neurons.
- Receptors are located in sense organs and respond to stimuli.
- Effectors are muscles or glands that bring about a response.
- There are five sense organs: eyes, ears, tongue, nose and skin.
- Each sense organ responds to a different stimulus.
- The brain is the 'central processor' of the body and consists of three main parts.
- The cerebrum receives and stores information, and uses the information to make voluntary decisions.
- The cerebellum is concerned with balance.
- The medulla oblongata controls a number of body functions, including breathing, heartbeat, peristalsis and digestion.
- A voluntary action is one over which we have complete control.
- An involuntary action is one over which we have no control.
- A reflex action is an involuntary response to a stimulus.
- Reflex actions do not involve the brain.
- Reflex actions may prevent the body from injury.
- Reaction time is the time taken for the body to respond to a stimulus.
- Reaction time decreases as children develop into young adults, and then increases with increasing age.
- Reaction time can be reduced by practice.
- The endocrine system consists of endocrine glands that secrete hormones into the bloodstream.
- Hormones are chemical messengers.
- A hormone secreted by an endocrine gland triggers a response at a target organ.
- Endocrine glands include the pituitary gland, thyroid gland, pancreas, adrenal glands, pineal and thymus, testes and ovaries.
- Each endocrine gland secretes one or more hormones.
- Nerve impulses travel very quickly and bring about a short-term response.
- Hormones travel more slowly in the blood and, with the exception of adrenalin, generally bring about long-term changes.

Review questions on Sensitivity and coordination

Knowledge and understanding

1. State which sense organ makes it possible to:

    a) hear music

    b) detect that an object is cold

    c) see coloured lights

    d) smell food cooking

    e) taste different types of food

2. a) Explain the difference between a voluntary action and an involuntary action.

    b) In which part of the brain do we make decisions about voluntary actions?

    c) Give an example of an involuntary action that is controlled by the medulla oblongata.

3. a) Describe an example of a reflex action.

    b) Why are reflex actions beneficial to the body?

    c) Why are reflex actions triggered by the spinal cord and not the brain?

4. a) Explain why nerve impulses are concerned with short-term responses, while hormones are concerned with longer-term changes.

    b) Give an example of a nervous system response involving the skin.

    c) Give an example of an endocrine system response involving the adrenal glands.

Process skills

5. The bar chart in Fig B 4.RQ.1 shows how a person's reaction time in applying the brakes when driving a car is affected under different circumstances.

    a) Why is it important that a car driver has short reaction times in the event of an emergency?

    b) Which of the circumstances in the chart increases the reaction time the most?

    c) Drinking two alcoholic drinks increases the reaction time by the smallest percentage. Does this mean it is safe to drink alcohol and drive? Explain your answer.

FIG B 4.RQ.1

    d) Predict the effect on reaction time of a person texting on a cell phone after having smoked cannabis.

41 Ensuring documents are legible

An important feature of our ability to detect light is that it allows us to read. Some people are born with defective eyesight. Most people find that their eyesight deteriorates with age.

The Government is concerned that people are not able to read the text on official documents effectively because of poor design. It is your job to provide advice on this.

You are going to work in a small group to investigate the clearest way to provide printed information. The tasks are:

FIG STEAM B 4.41.1 The ability to read deteriorates with age

- To consider the different parameters associated with printed material. These include:
  - » choice of font
  - » font size
  - » font colour
  - » background colour
- To design some printed text that can be used for testing
- To devise methods of testing different texts and a means by which they can be graded in some way
- To make recommendations of certain combinations of features that aid reading and to identify others that should be avoided because they can be harder to read with poor eyesight
- To compile an oral presentation. This should include examples of the texts used, how they were tested and a summary of results.

a) There are many different fonts available on a modern word processor. Some of the fonts in common use are:

Cambria   **Arial**   Verdana   Times New Roman

i) The words above are all in the same-sized font (11 pt). Are they equally clear?

Jamaica   Jamaica   Jamaica   Jamaica   Jamaica

ii) The words above are written in increasing font size. Is there a point beyond which increasing the font size has no effect on the readability of the text?

With modern word processing it is very easy to write text in a coloured font on a contrasting coloured background.

Jamaica   Jamaica   Jamaica   Jamaica   Jamaica

iii) Are different coloured fonts equally easy to read?

Jamaica   Jamaica   Jamaica   Jamaica   Jamaica

iv) Is the background colour important when reading text?

Jamaica   Jamaica   Jamaica   Jamaica   Jamaica

v) What is the effect of different coloured fonts on different coloured backgrounds?

b) You do not have time to test every possible combination of fonts, sizes and colours. Your first job will be to identify a small number of each. You might decide to focus on 4 fonts, 4 font sizes, 4 font colours and 4 background colours.

How are you going to test different combinations of font, size, colour and background effectively? One way might be to prepare short extracts of text presented in different ways.

c) How are you going to carry out your tests? You could aim to obtain both quantitative and qualitative data.
- You could obtain quantitative data by timing how long it takes a person to read an extract.
- You could obtain qualitative data by asking the person how easy or difficult they found the reading. They could score a mark between 0 for the most difficult and 5 for the easiest.

Who are you going to carry out your tests on? If there are some old people living nearby, you might ask them.

d) How are you going to record and present the data you collect? You could do this on a spreadsheet.

e) How are you going to decide how well or how badly each extract performs? If an extract is easy to read then someone should be able to finish reading it relatively quickly. Someone will take longer to finish the same text if the font and colour combinations are not so easy to read.

f) Prepare an oral presentation in which you explain why you chose to explore particular combinations of font, size and colour. You should show some samples of the text you prepared. Describe the tests and detail the results you obtained. You should show photographs and/or a video sequence of carrying out the testing.

Explain how you are using these results to make your recommendations to the Government for use of font, font size, font colour and background colour on official documents.

42 Adolescence and puberty

We are learning how to:
- describe the changes that take place to the body during puberty and adolescence

In general, the rate at which a child grows gradually decreases as he/she gets older. However, the decrease is interrupted shortly before the end of the growth period. At this time there is marked acceleration of growth, called the adolescent growth spurt. In boys this takes place from about 13 to 15 years of age, and in girls from about 12 to 14 years.

Adolescence is a period of life during which we are no longer children but not yet adults. Many changes take place to our bodies, and to the ways in which we think about things. The start of adolescence is marked by **puberty**. This is the time when the male testes start to make sperm cells and the female ovaries start to make egg cells.

All boys and girls are born with a complete set of sex organs, but these only become active when we reach a certain stage in growth and development. When we reach adolescence the **pituitary gland** at the base of the brain starts to make chemical messengers called **hormones**. When these are released into the bloodstream they activate the sex organs which, in turn, start producing sex hormones.

The sex hormones are responsible for changes that take place to the body during adolescence. These changes are sometimes described as secondary sexual characteristics.

The hormone released by the male sex organs is called testosterone. As well as stimulating the production of sperm cells in the testes, this hormone also causes:

- hair to start to grow on the face and body
- the voice to deepen
- the body to become more muscular

The hormone released by the female sex organs is called oestrogen. As well as stimulating the production of egg cells, this hormone also causes:

- hair to grow on parts of the body; mainly the armpits and the pubic area
- breasts to develop
- hips to widen
- the start of menstruation

Adolescence can be a difficult and sometimes emotional time for a person. The release of hormones associated with puberty can bring about mood swings and a chemical imbalance leading to conditions such as acne.

FIG B 5.42.1 Adolescents become very conscious about their appearance

Adolescents must also come to terms with their changing bodies. Adolescence is a time when people start to think in a more adult way about things and experience increased sexual urges. Boys and girls start to appreciate that they are different and that they are attracted to each other.

Adolescence generally finishes around the age of 18 years. The subsequent change to adulthood takes place over several years as adolescents take on their adult forms and their behaviour become more mature. Part of being an adult is taking on responsibilities for yourself and those around you.

> **Interesting fact**
>
> Adolescence tends to start at a slightly younger age in girls than in boys. As a result of this adolescent girls are often regarded as more mature in their behaviour.

Activity B 5.42.1

Testing how well acne treatments work

Some adolescents suffer with acne as a result of changes in their body chemistry. This happens at a time when boys and girls are becoming conscious of their own and each other's sexuality. Acne sufferers might therefore be self-conscious of their appearance.

1. A certain brand of acne treatment claims that it will be effective in reducing acne in just seven days.

   Plan how you could test the claim made about this product. Your plan should include:

   – how you would trial the product

   – what evidence you would gather

   – how you would use your evidence to assess whether the claim made about the treatment is valid or not.

Key terms

adolescence transition period between childhood and adulthood

puberty period during which the body becomes sexually mature

pituitary gland part of the brain that releases hormones into the bloodstream

hormone chemical messenger released in one part of the body, carried in the blood and brings about change in another part of the body

Check your understanding

1. Arrange the following in the order in which they take place.

   adolescence   adulthood   childhood   infancy

2. **a)** What is a hormone?

   b) Name a hormone that is involved in the development of secondary sexual characteristics in:

   i) a girl   **ii)** a boy

43 The male reproductive system

We are learning how to:

- outline the structure of the human male reproductive system and the functions of its parts
- identify the parts of the male reproductive system and their functions

The male reproductive system »»

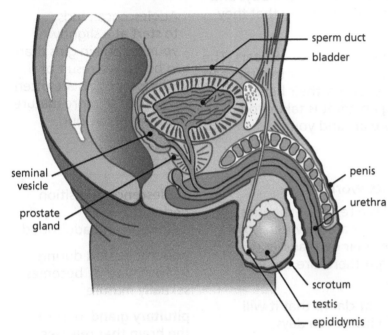

FIG B 5.43.1 Male reproductive system

The male reproductive organs are the two **testes**. These lie outside the body cavity in a sac called the **scrotum**. This allows the testes to remain at a temperature that is slightly below normal body temperature. This favours the production of **sperm**.

Each testis contains many tubes in which sperm cells are formed. These tubes join to connect with the epididymis.

The epididymis leads to the **sperm duct**. The two sperm ducts open into the urethra just after it leaves the bladder. Urine from the bladder and sperm both pass out of the **penis** through the urethra. The body has a mechanism that prevents these events happening at the same time.

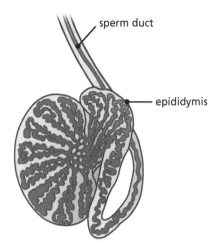

sperm duct

epididymis

FIG B 5.43.2 Structure of a testis

The seminal vesicle branches from each sperm duct just before it enters the prostate gland. The seminal vesicle contains fluid that mixes with the sperm to form semen. The prostate gland secretes a fluid that nourishes the sperm. Millions of sperm are released each time a male ejaculates.

Interesting fact

A vasectomy is a procedure that a man can have if he and his partner agree that they do not want to have any more children. It involves a minor operation during which a short section of each sperm duct is removed and the remaining ends are tied off. This prevents sperm from passing from the testes to the urethra. A vasectomy does not affect a man's ability to have sexual intercourse.

Activity B 5.43.1

Tracing the movement of sperm

Here is what you need:

- model of the male reproductive organs (if this is not available use Fig B 5.43.1)

Here is what you should do:

1. Follow the passage of the sperm from where it is formed to where it leaves the body on the model.

2. Make a list of the parts of the male reproductive system in the order in which sperm passes through them.

Check your understanding

1. In which parts of the male reproductive system are sperm produced?

2. What is the function of the seminal vesicles?

3. What is the name of the duct that joins the epididymis to the urethra?

4. What else apart from sperm leaves the body through the urethra?

Key terms

testes male reproductive organs

scrotum sac outside the body that contains the testes

sperm specialised reproductive cells produced in the testes

sperm duct tube along which sperm pass before they reach the prostate gland

ejaculates releases semen, usually containing sperm, from the body

penis part of male reproductive system through which sperm and urine pass

44 The female reproductive system

We are learning how to:

- outline the structure of the female reproductive system and the functions of the parts
- identify the parts of the female reproductive system and their functions.

The female reproductive system

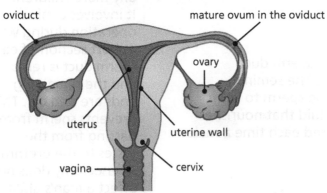

FIG B 5.44.1 All of the parts of the female reproductive system are held within the body cavity

The female reproductive organs are the two **ovaries**. These are found at the back of the abdomen, just below the kidneys. **Ova** develop in the ovaries.

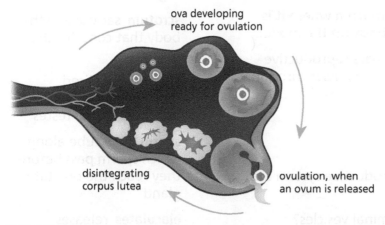

FIG B 5.44.2 Structure of an ovary

When a female is mature, her ovaries will release one ovum each month. This is called **ovulation**.

Interesting fact

Men produce new sperm daily throughout their lives. Women are born with all of their ova. These immature ova develop in the follicles and are stored in the ovaries.

A woman will have between one and two million follicles at birth. Of these, only about 400 will mature during the woman's child-conceiving years, while the rest will die.

When a woman can no longer have children, few or no follicles will remain in her ovaries.

Close to each ovary is the funnel-shaped opening of an oviduct. The oviducts are also called **fallopian tubes**. They are narrow tubes along which the mature ovum passes from the ovaries to the **uterus**. Fertilisation of an ovum by a sperm normally happens in the oviduct.

The uterus is wider than the oviducts. It is the place where a fertilised ovum will develop into an embryo and eventually into a baby.

The uterus, which is usually about 80 mm long, connects with the outside of the body by a muscular tube called the **vagina**. The neck of the uterus is a ring of muscle called the **cervix**.

If an ovum is not fertilised it will pass through the uterus into the vagina and out of the body during menstruation.

Activity B 5.44.1

Tracing the movement of ova

Here is what you need:

- model of the female reproductive organs (if this is not available use Fig B 5.44.1)

Here is what you should do:

1. Follow the passage of the ova from where they are formed to where they leave the body (assuming they are not fertilised) on the model.

2. Make a list of the parts of the female reproductive system in the order that an ovum will pass through them.

Check your understanding

1. In which parts of the female reproductive system are ova produced?

2. What is the name of the duct that joins an ovary to the uterus?

3. What is the cervix and where is it found?

4. How many ova are normally released at one time in human females?

Key terms

ovaries female reproductive organs

ova specialised female reproductive cells

ovulation the release of a mature ovum from the ovary into the oviduct

fallopian tubes narrow tubes along which the ova pass from the ovaries to the uterus

uterus the place where a fertilised ovum will develop into an embryo and eventually into a baby

vagina muscular tube connecting the uterus with the outside of the body

cervix ring of muscle where the uterus joins the vagina

45 The menstrual cycle

We are learning how to:
- describe different stages of the human life cycle
- explain what happens to the female body during the menstrual cycle

When a female has grown to an age when she is able to have children, she will start to have a regular **menstrual cycle**. This typically lasts for 28 days, but varies from female to female.

A female will start having menstrual cycles during puberty at around 12 years old, and will continue to have them until the menopause when she is around 50 years of age. During the menstrual cycle there are changes to the levels of female hormones in the body, and changes in the ovaries and in the uterus.

The cycle starts when the follicle stimulating hormone (FSH) is released from the pituitary gland in the brain. This causes an ovum, or egg, to mature in a **Graafian follicle** inside one or other of the two ovaries.

The Graafian follicle also secretes a hormone called oestrogen. This hormone causes the lining of the uterus to thicken. If fertilisation occurs during the cycle, the fertilised egg will become embedded in the thickened uterus wall and develop into a baby.

As the level of oestrogen begins to decrease, the pituitary gland releases another hormone called luteinising hormone (LH) that triggers ovulation. The mature egg is released by the ovary.

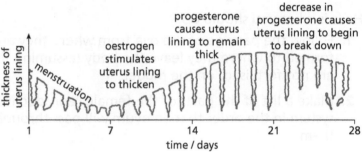

ovum matures inside Graafian follicle

duration day 14

corpus luteum develops

corpus luteum degenerates

events occurring in the ovary

oestrogen secreted by Graafian follicle

oestrogen level

progesterone level

progesterone secreted by corpus luteum

time / days

(a) the menstrual cycle

progesterone causes uterus lining to remain thick

decrease in progesterone causes uterus lining to begin to break down

oestrogen stimulates uterus lining to thicken

thickness of uterus lining

menstruation

time / days

(b) hormones in the menstrual cycle

FIG B 5.45.1 Changes take place in the female body during the menstrual cycle

Start of the cycle → FSH released by the pituitary gland → Egg matures in Graafian follicle

Graafian follicle releases oestrogen, which causes uterus wall to thicken → Pituitary gland releases LH, which triggers the release of a mature egg from the ovary, and corpus luteum forms → Progesterone released by the corpus luteum

If the woman does not become pregnant progesterone production stops and menstruation occurs

If the woman becomes pregnant progesterone and oestrogen continue to be produced

FIG B 5.45.2 The menstrual cycle is controlled by hormones

The remains of the Graffian follicle form another structure called the **corpus luteum**. About a week after the egg is released the corpus luteum starts to produce a hormone called progesterone. If the egg is not fertilised the corpus luteum disintegrates and the level of progesterone falls. The lining of the uterus breaks down and is discharged from the body through the vagina. This process is called **menstruation** or 'having a period'.

The first day of menstruation is taken as the first day of the menstrual cycle because this is the day most easy to identify. Ovulation occurs around the 14th day of the cycle. Sexual intercourse in the days immediately after ovulation is most likely to result in fertilisation and pregnancy.

Although the female body is able to have babies as soon as periods start, which can be as early as 11 or 12 years old, this does not mean that it is sensible for a girl to have a baby when she is young. There is a lot more to bringing up a baby than the biological process of having one.

Interesting fact

Corpus luteum is Latin for body of yellow or yellow body.

Key terms

menstrual cycle regular cycle of ovum maturation and release by a female between the ages of about 12 – 50 years

Graafian follicle structure in the ovary which releases a mature ovum

corpus luteum remains of the Graafian follicle after an ovum is released

menstruation period when blood is lost during the menstrual cycle

Activity B 5.45.1

A diagram to represent the menstrual cycle

Diagrams often make it easier to understand information. Here are two different diagrams that are designed to explain what happens during the menstrual cycle.

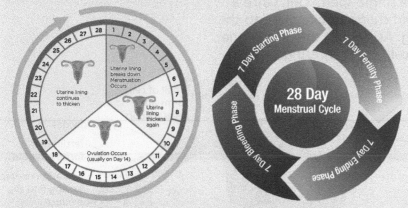

FIG B 5.45.3 Diagrams representing the menstrual cycle

Design and draw a diagram to represent the menstrual cycle which you think will help younger students approaching puberty to understand what it is all about.

Check your understanding

1. **a)** In which structure in the ovary does an egg mature?
   b) Which hormone causes egg maturation to take place?
   c) Which hormone triggers the release of an egg from an ovary?
   d) What happens to the structure in which the egg matured, once the egg is released?
2. **a)** Which hormone causes the uterus wall to thicken?
   b) Why does this happen?
   c) What happens to the thickened uterus wall if the egg is not fertilised?

46 Fertilisation

We are learning how to:
- describe what happens during fertilisation

Fertilisation ▶▶

Fertilisation is when the male and female gametes, the sperm and egg, come together and combine. In human reproduction the sperm is the male sex cell and the egg is the female sex cell. **Fertilisation** takes place in the body of the female, usually in the Fallopian tube, which is also called the oviduct.

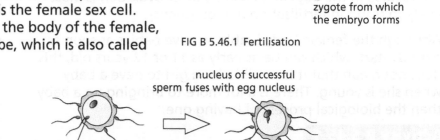

FIG B 5.46.1 Fertilisation

During fertilisation the sperm and the egg combine to form a **zygote**. The zygote develops into the embryo, and then into a baby that is ready to be born.

FIG B 5.46.2 An egg is only fertilised by one sperm

An egg cell is only fertilised by a single sperm cell. Once a sperm has entered the egg, rapid changes take place to the membrane surrounding the egg. As a result the membrane prevents any additional sperm cells from entering.

Fertilisation usually takes place in the woman's oviduct as the egg is passing down from the ovary.

Soon after the zygote forms it starts to divide and this process continues as more and more cells are formed. At around 10 days the zygote becomes an **embryo**.

During the woman's menstrual cycle, her uterus wall has thickened ready to receive an embryo. As the embryo enters the uterus it embeds into the wall, in a process called implantation.

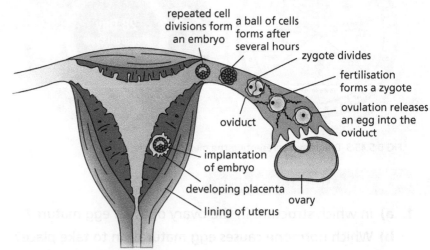

FIG B 5.46.3 Fertilisation usually takes place in the oviduct

Finger-like projections called villi extend from the embryo into the uterus wall. The villi bind to the uterus wall forming a placenta that joins the embryo to its mother. You will learn more about this in the next lesson.

Over the next couple of weeks the attachment develops into the umbilical cord. After eight weeks of pregnancy the major body organs are present in the embryo and it is recognisable as human. At this time the embryo is described as a **foetus**. This term is used for the developing baby until its birth.

Activity B 5.46.1

Identifying the parts of the female reproduction system where different things happen

Carry out this activity on the school field or on any suitable hard court surface. Here is what you need:

- string
- pegs
- sticks or poles to hold labels
- sticky tape
- A4 card for labels

Here is what you should do:

1. Use pegs and string to mark out an outline of the female reproductive system. Use Fig B 5.46.3 as a guide.

2. Walk through your outline and place labels where important things happen, for example:

   a) route taken by sperm

   b) egg is released

   c) fertilisation takes place

   d) zygote starts to divide

   e) embryo implantation

3. Take some photographs of your model, or make a short video in which one student is a sperm and another is an egg. Follow their progress from fertilisation to becoming embedded in the wall of the uterus, and add a suitable sound commentary.

Check your understanding

1. Where does fertilisation normally take place?

2. When does an embryo become a foetus?

3. Why can an egg only be fertilised by one sperm?

4. What happens to the zygote shortly after it is formed?

Interesting fact

Foetus is often also spelt as 'fetus'. You will see both terms used on the Internet and in books. They mean the same thing but the correct spelling to use is 'foetus'.

Key terms

fertilisation coming together of the male and female sex cells

zygote formed by the combination of a male sex cell and a female sex cell

embryo develops from a zygote after about 10 days

foetus the developing baby from about 9 weeks of pregnancy onwards, when recognisable as a human

47 The developing foetus

We are learning how to:

- describe the different stages as the foetus develops

In the first few hours after fertilisation the zygote divides into identical cells. This division takes place several times as the zygote passes from the oviduct into the uterus where it becomes implanted in the uterus wall, and where the embryo, and later the foetus, will develop.

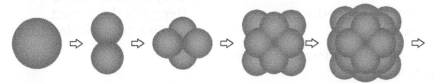

FIG B 5.47.1 Cell division

In humans approximately four days after fertilisation, and after several cycles of identical **cell division**, the complex process of forming different types of cells begins. All of the different types of cells, including skin cells, brain cells, heart cells, muscle cells and many others, must develop through a process known as cell differentiation.

The amount of time taken for the foetus to develop from conception to a baby being born is called the **gestation period**. In humans the gestation period is about nine months.

During the first six weeks of pregnancy the embryo remains small, although cell division is continually taking place. At the end of this time the embryo is around 12 mm long (about the length of your thumb nail) and is embedded in the placenta.

As the embryo becomes bigger it grows out from the placenta but is still attached by the umbilical cord. A membrane called the **amnion** surrounds the embryo, and the cavity inside fills with watery **amniotic fluid**. The developing baby obtains oxygen from the mother via the umbilical cord, so the amniotic fluid does not interfere with the baby getting oxygen.

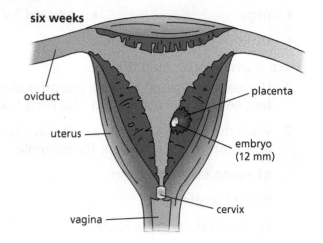

six weeks

oviduct

uterus

placenta

embryo (12 mm)

cervix

vagina

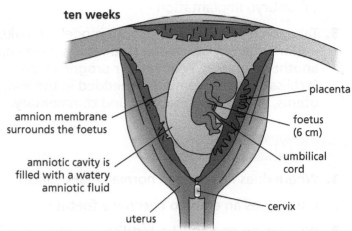

ten weeks

amnion membrane surrounds the foetus

amniotic cavity is filled with a watery amniotic fluid

uterus

placenta

foetus (6 cm)

umbilical cord

cervix

FIG B 5.47.2 Early stages of embryo and foetal development

The fluid-filled sac acts as a shock absorber that protects the embryo or foetus from knocks and bumps should the mother trip over or bang into something. By ten weeks the embryo has grown to about 6 cm and is now called a foetus. This might not sound very big but between six weeks and ten weeks the embryo has grown from 12 mm to 60 mm, or five times its size.

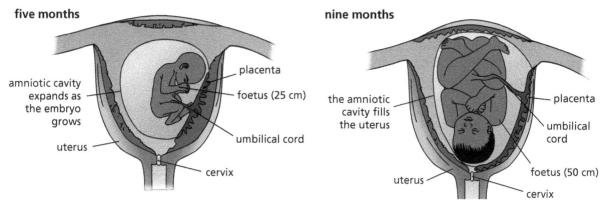

FIG B 5.47.3 Later stages of foetal development

The foetus is nourished throughout pregnancy by the mother via the umbilical cord. As the foetus develops and grows in size the amniotic cavity grows bigger until, when close to birth, it fills the uterus. The cervix supports the foetus as it grows and prevents it falling out of the uterus. When the 'waters break' this means that the amniotic sac has ruptured. It is a sign that the baby is about to be born.

Activity B 5.47.1

Creating a booklet to show the growth stages of the foetus

You will work in a group for this activity, and will need to carry out some research. Use the Internet and/or whatever other resources are available.

Carry out further research about the stages of pregnancy and gather additional information in the form of text, images and data. You might have a friend or relative who is pregnant. Ask them what it feels like. Use the information you have to create an album or booklet about how the embryo and foetus develop.

Check your understanding

1. What is the normal gestation period in humans?
2. What does the 'waters breaking' usually indicate?
3. What is the function of the amniotic fluid?
4. Approximately what length is the developing foetus after five months of the pregnancy?

Key terms

cell division replication to increase the number of cells

gestation period the time between conception and birth

amnion membrane that surrounds the foetus as it develops

amniotic fluid watery fluid contained within the amnion

Interesting fact

The gestation period usually increases with increasing size of the animal species. Mice have a gestation period of 18 days, whereas elephants have a gestation period of 20 months.

48 The role of the placenta

We are learning how to:
- describe the role of the placenta during pregnancy

The **placenta** is a flattened circular organ that develops on the wall of the uterus. The **umbilical cord** develops with the foetus and connects the foetus to the mother at the placenta. It is literally a lifeline for the foetus.

Everything the developing foetus needs throughout the nine months of pregnancy passes from the mother along the umbilical cord. Waste products produced by the developing foetus pass in the opposite direction.

Blood passes from the embryo to the placenta along an artery and blood returns from the placenta to the embryo through a vein.

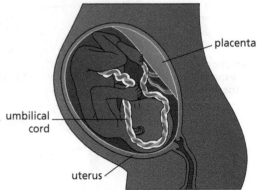

FIG B 5.48.1 The umbilical cord and placenta

placenta

umbilical cord

uterus

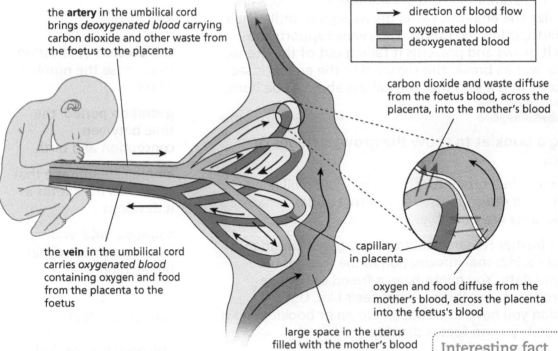

the **artery** in the umbilical cord brings *deoxygenated blood* carrying carbon dioxide and other waste from the foetus to the placenta

direction of blood flow
oxygenated blood
deoxygenated blood

carbon dioxide and waste diffuse from the foetus blood, across the placenta, into the mother's blood

the **vein** in the umbilical cord carries *oxygenated blood* containing oxygen and food from the placenta to the foetus

capillary in placenta

oxygen and food diffuse from the mother's blood, across the placenta into the foetus's blood

large space in the uterus filled with the mother's blood

FIG B 5.48.2 Substances pass along the umbilical cord

Although the nutrients that the foetus requires are provided from the mother's blood supply, the circulatory system of the foetus cannot be directly connected to the mother because the high blood pressure in the mother's arteries would burst the tiny blood vessels in the foetus. Instead, substances pass between the blood of the foetus and that of the mother in the placenta by **diffusion**.

Interesting fact

Some mothers think it is a good thing to eat the placenta after giving birth to their child because it helps to restore their body after pregnancy. This practice is called placentophagy.

Oxygen and food, in the form of glucose and other substances, diffuse from the mother's blood across the placenta into the blood of the embryo. At the same time, waste products such as carbon dioxide and urea pass in the opposite direction.

Harmful substances may also pass between the mother's blood and the baby's blood so the mother must be very careful about what she takes in while she is pregnant.

When a baby is born the midwife cuts the umbilical cord because the baby no longer needs it. Within a short time the piece attached to the baby falls off, but we are all left with a reminder in the form of our navel, or tummy button, that we were once attached to our mothers.

The placenta and the remaining umbilical cord – known as the 'afterbirth' – are expelled from the uterus soon after birth.

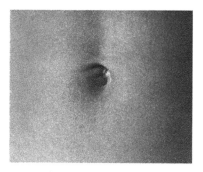

FIG B 5.48.3 Navel, or tummy button

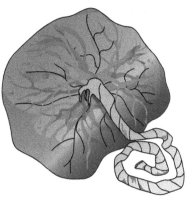

FIG B 5.48.4 Placenta and part of umbilical cord

Activity B 5.48.1

Making a model to show how the placenta works

You will work in a group for this activity.

Here is what you need:

- scissors
- tubing
- glue
- other modelling materials.
- paints
- card for labels

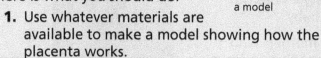

FIG B 5.48.5 One idea for a model

Here is what you should do:

1. Use whatever materials are available to make a model showing how the placenta works.

2. Use different colours to show the blood vessels of the mother and the foetus.

3. Label the parts of your model.

Check your understanding

1. a) Name two substances that pass from the mother's blood to the foetus's blood.

   b) Name two substances that pass from the foetus's blood to the mother's blood.

2. Explain why the blood supply of the foetus cannot be connected directly to that of the mother.

3. What happens to the umbilical cord and the placenta after the baby is born?

Key terms

placenta flattened round organ in the uterus within which substances pass between the blood of the mother and that of the developing foetus

umbilical cord connects the developing baby with the mother's placenta

diffusion net movement of substances from regions of high concentration to regions of low concentration

49 Parental care and maternal behaviour during pregnancy

We are learning how to:

- appreciate the importance of prenatal care and appropriate maternal behaviour during pregnancy

Prenatal care, or antenatal care, is the care provided for the mother and her developing baby before birth.

Expectant mothers regularly attend clinics where they can be monitored to make sure they are in good health and where they can learn about childbirth. Health centres may hold prenatal classes where expectant mothers can share their experiences.

During pregnancy **ultrasound** scans are carried out on the mother. Ultrasound uses very high pitched sound waves to create an image of the foetus in the mother's uterus. Doctors can take measurements of the foetus's brain and spine from the scan to check that the foetus is developing properly.

FIG B 5.49.1 Image of a developing foetus from an ultrasound scan

In addition to the prenatal care provided by health centres and doctors, the expectant mother must also provide her own prenatal care by ensuring that her lifestyle does not jeopardise the development of her unborn baby.

For example, there is scientific evidence that mothers who smoke during pregnancy tend to have smaller babies, because chemicals that enter the mother's blood when she smokes will eventually find their way into the foetus's blood. Excessive consumption of alcohol and taking recreational drugs are also detrimental to foetal development.

FIG B 5.49.2 Smoking during pregnancy reduces birth mass

It is also possible for viruses to pass from the mother to the foetus during pregnancy. Some viruses, such as **rubella,** which is responsible for German measles, can cause the baby to be born with defects including blindness. In some parts of the world, such as Jamaica, girls are vaccinated against rubella when they reach puberty to ensure that they are not affected by this virus in later life during pregnancy.

Another virus that may be passed on to an unborn baby by the mother is **HIV**. It is estimated that around the world more than 1000 babies infected with HIV are born every day. The only way this can be reduced is by safer sexual practice, to reduce the number of people infected with HIV.

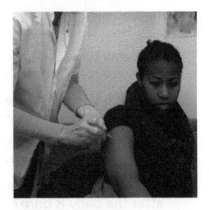

FIG B 5.49.3 Vaccination against rubella

Activity B 5.49.1

Drawing a bar chart to show data about birth mass and cigarette smoking

Here is what you need:

- sheet of graph paper
- ruler 30 cm

Here is what you should do:

Table B 5.49.1 shows the percentage of babies of different masses born to mothers who smoke and to those who do not smoke.

Mass at birth / kg	Percentage born to mothers who smoke	Percentage born to mothers who do not smoke
2.0–2.5	48	52
>2.5–3.0	38	62
>3.0–3.5	33	67
>3.5–4.0	26	74
>4.0–4.5	21	79
>4.5	17	84

TABLE B 5.49.1

Draw a bar chart to show this information. For each range of birth mass values you should draw two bars alongside each other, one bar to represent babies born to mothers who smoke and one bar to represent babies born to mothers who do not smoke.

[STEAM] In addition to reducing birth mass, smoking during pregnancy increases the risk of health problems for developing babies. Carry out research into what these problems are.

Key terms

prenatal care the care a mother receives while she is pregnant and before giving birth

ultrasound very high frequency sound waves

rubella virus that causes German measles and can damage an unborn baby

HIV human immunodeficiency virus, which can be passed from mother to an unborn baby

Check your understanding

1. What does 'prenatal' mean?
2. Which illness is caused by the rubella virus?
3. How is it possible to 'see' the foetus as it develops inside the mother?
4. How can the lifestyle of the mother affect the development of the foetus?

50 Contraception I

We are learning how to:

• understand different methods of contraception

Partners often wish to make love but they do not want this to result in the woman becoming pregnant. To prevent pregnancy different forms of contraception may be used.

Contraception allows people to choose when to have children and to determine the size of their family. This is called **birth control**, or family planning. The decisions are personal and require a mature and responsible attitude. Women do not have to become pregnant by accident.

Methods of contraception can be divided into four groups. In this topic we will look at examples of each group.

Natural methods ▶▶▶

These methods require modifications to our behaviour.

Barrier methods ▶▶▶

These methods prevent sperm from reaching the egg so that fertilisation cannot take place, or they prevent implantation of the embryo.

Method	How it works	Advantages	Disadvantages
Withdrawal of the penis or coitus interruptus	The male withdraws his penis before ejaculation.	No side effects.	Very unreliable. Provides no protection against sexually transmitted infections (STIs).
Rhythm method	Intercourse is avoided at times when the woman is most likely to conceive.	No side effects.	Very unreliable.
Abstinence	Refrain from sexual intercourse.	100% effective.	Requires self-discipline.

TABLE B 5.50.1

The effectiveness of barrier methods of contraception may be increased if they are used in conjunction with spermicidal creams.

Method	How it works	Advantages	Disadvantages
Condom for males penis condom FIG B 5.50.1	The condom is rolled down over the erect penis.	No side effects. Protects against STIs. Cheap to buy and readily available.	Can only be used once. Thought by some to reduce sensitivity.

Intra-uterine device (IUD), or coil	Inserted into the uterus by a doctor and prevents implantation of a fertilised egg.	Reliable and inexpensive. Remains effective for several years.	May interfere with menstrual cycle. Can cause uterine infections.
Condom for females	This is a pouch that is inserted into the vagina before intercourse. It is larger than the male condom.	It is safe, effective, readily available and convenient.	It can cause irritation of the vagina. Thought to reduce sensitivity during intercourse.
Cap / diaphragm cap fitted over the cervix FIG B 5.50.2	The cap is inserted into the vagina and placed at the top of the cervix.	No side effects. Offers some protection against STIs.	May be damaged during intercourse. If not fitted well some sperm may get past and reach the egg.

TABLE B 5.50.2

Activity B 5.50.1

You should work in a group for this activity. In some countries condoms are made available free of charge in places like washrooms and hotel rooms.

- Those in favour of this say that it reduces unwanted pregnancies and reduces the spread of sexually transmitted infections.

- Those against this say that free condoms encourage sexual promiscuity.

Debate in your group whether you think the availability of free condoms is a good practice or not.

Check your understanding

1. Why is 'coitus interruptus' not a reliable method of birth control?

2. Apart from contraception what other advantage is there in using condoms?

3. How does a coil (IUD) prevent pregnancy?

Key terms

birth control controlling if and when you have children and the size of your family

condom latex sheath rolled down over the erect penis before intercourse

cap/diaphragm device inserted into vagina at the top of the cervix

51 Contraception II

We are learning how to:

• understand different methods of contraception

Hormonal methods and spermicidal creams »»

The release of an egg each month in the female is controlled by the body releasing chemicals called hormones. Some methods of contraception use hormones to interrupt this cycle.

Method	How it works	Advantages	Disadvantages
Hormone pill FIG B 5.51.1	One taken each day prevents the ovary from releasing eggs.	Simple and reliable.	Increases the risk of heart disease and high blood pressure. No protection against STIs.
Spermicidal creams spermicide FIG B 5.51.2	Contain chemicals that kill and block sperm from entering the uterus.	Easy to obtain and simple to use.	Not reliable, but useful when used with some other methods of contraception. No protection against STIs.

TABLE B 5.51.1

Surgical methods »»

Surgical methods use simple procedures to modify the reproductive organs so that fertilisation cannot take place.

Method	How it works	Advantages	Disadvantages
Vasectomy sperm duct ends cut and tied sperm duct testis FIG B 5.51.3	The sperm ducts are cut and the ends tied off so sperm cannot travel from the testes to the penis.	100% effective.	Difficult to reverse. No protection against STIs.

Tubal ligation FIG B 5.51.4	The oviducts are cut and the ends tied off so the eggs cannot travel down to the uterus.	100% effective.	Difficult to reverse. No protection against STIs.

TABLE B 5.51.2

The term **sterilisation** is sometimes used to describe surgical procedures that prevent fertilisation taking place. Two examples are given in Table B 5.51.2. These procedures are extremely difficult to reverse and for this reason they tend to be the form of contraception adopted by older couples who have decided that they definitely don't want to have any more children.

Couples who opt for some form of sterilisation may be offered counselling to ensure that they appreciate the implications and have thought them through.

Activity B 5.51.1

Sterilisation

Read the following passage.

In some parts of the world, couples traditionally have lots of children. Two of the reasons for this are:

- *infant mortality was high so many children died young*
- *there was no social system to look after the old, so parents looked to their children for support in their old age*

As health care has improved more children now survive to adulthood. This puts greater financial strain on parents and many families live in great poverty as a result.

In some countries, in order to reduce poverty, couples have been offered money or goods if they will agree to be sterilised.

Discuss in your group whether you agree with this strategy or not. Is it right to persuade people to have fewer children for their own good, or is it wrong to bribe them to give up the ability to have children?

Check your understanding

1. a) What is a vasectomy?

   b) Why might some men think that this affects their virility?

2. A woman comes from a family that has a history of high blood pressure. What form of contraception should she avoid?

Key terms

hormone pill hormones that a woman takes to prevent pregnancy

spermicidal cream a cream that kills sperm

vasectomy cutting the sperm ducts to prevent the passage of sperm

tubal ligation cutting the oviducts to prevent the passage of eggs

sterilisation surgical procedures that prevent fertilisation

Interesting fact

The 'morning after' pill is an emergency contraceptive that is taken within two days of unplanned or unsafe sexual intercourse. It contains a hormone that prevents the implantation of an embryo.

52 Importance of family planning

We are learning how to:

- identify issues that relate to family planning
- discuss the importance of family planning to the individual

The term **'family planning'** might suggest that a couple have complete control over whether they have children or not. This is not the case. There are many factors to be taken into account, such as medical issues, which are beyond the control of the individual. Some couples may try for years to have a child without success, while others have a child soon after they get together.

In this lesson we are going to focus on those issues over which a couple have some control.

Some important issues

When deciding whether to start or extend their family, a couple must give serious considerations to a number of different issues. Some of these are to do with money. Here are examples of things a couple might discuss.

- Can we afford a family or a bigger family? Children are beautiful but they are also expensive! For example, even before a child reaches school age parents must meet the cost of things including medical bills during the pregnancy, baby clothes, diapers and wipes, baby food and childcare.

FIG B 5.52.1 Babies are expensive

- Do we have enough room? Children need their own bedroom and areas where they can play. Space is needed for storing things like baby clothes and toys.

FIG B 5.52.2 Children need their own space

FIG B 5.52.3 Children are demanding on time and resources

- Are we ready to give up our time and resources? Children are demanding on both time and resources. Once a couple start a family their way of life inevitably changes.

- Is the time right? The decision to start a family is sometimes best left for a few years. Young couples, just starting their working lives, might be on low wages and only have a small home. A few years down the line they might earn more and be able to move to somewhere a little larger.

Family planning clinic

Family planning clinics are places where couples can go to get advice from doctors and other professional people.

Couples might need advice on starting a family, or they may be in a situation where they believe their family is large enough and they would like advice on contraception or sterilisation.

FIG B 5.52.4 Jamaica National Family Planning Board logo

Activity B 5.52.1

Family planning discussion

Family planning and the issues around it are things that most students will need to think about in the future. In your group, discuss how you might go about planning a family with a long-term partner.

If possible, visit your local family planning clinic and ask about the work that they do. Invite someone from the clinic to visit your class to talk about the importance of family planning.

Check your understanding

1. Explain why each of the following should be considered before a couple agree to start a family.

   a) How much money they earn each week.

   b) How much space they have in their home.

   c) Whether they are willing to change their lifestyle.

Interesting fact

The Jamaica Family Planning Association (FAMPLAN) was founded in 1957 and pioneered family planning services in Jamaica. It supports the national programme on family planning by providing family planning information and education.

Key term

family planning the practice of controlling the number of children a couple has, and the intervals between them

53 Teenage pregnancy

We are learning how to:

- discuss the problems often associated with teenage pregnancy

Although the female body is capable of having babies as soon as periods start, which can be as early as 9 years old, this does not mean that it is sensible for a girl to have a baby when she is young.

There is a lot more to having and successfully bringing up a child than the biological process. In this lesson we will discuss why it may not be a good idea for a girl in her teens to have a baby.

A woman may not attain her adult size until she is in her late teens. Although the female body can conceive and a girl can become pregnant earlier than this, her body may not be strong enough to carry a baby. The pregnancy might cause her body internal damage, which could affect her ability to have more babies later in life.

FIG B 5.53.1 Teenage pregnancy can be a bad idea

Bringing up a baby is an expensive enterprise. When a baby is born to a mature woman who is in a permanent relationship it is likely that she will have some financial stability and a partner who can continue working to provide for his family. A teenage girl will have no such financial stability and is not likely to have a partner who can provide for her and her baby.

Bringing up a baby requires both knowledge and patience. A mature woman has had time to complete her education and has more time to learn about prenatal and postnatal care. She may also benefit from advice given to her by older relatives and by watching how they raise their own babies. A teenage girl is not likely to have completed her education and may not be old enough to have learnt from others.

FIG B 5.53.2 Babies are expensive

A woman who has a baby when she is an adult is more likely to have had sufficient time to complete her education and worked at a job where she has acquired skills. Once a woman has these skills she will always have the option of returning to work in the future when her children are older. A girl who has a baby when she is young may not

FIG B 5.53.3 Being a good mother takes knowledge and patience

have completed her education or had the opportunity to acquire skills that will allow her to continue with a career later in life.

Teenage girls do not become pregnant 'by magic'. For every teenage mother, there is a father. Although it is the woman who becomes pregnant and has the baby, the man must also share an equal responsibility.

Many of the reasons why a woman should wait until she is an adult before having a baby apply equally well to a man. A mature man who has completed his education and has a job can provide for his partner and their baby, whereas an immature father may not be able to provide for his family reliably.

FIG B 5.53.4 Teenage boys need to be responsible

Activity B 5.53.1

How teenage pregnancy might affect family life

If possible you should work in a mixed group of boys and girls for this activity.

In your mixed group discuss the effects of a teenage pregnancy on the young parents and on their families. Make notes of important points that you can use in a class discussion.

Check your understanding

1. Give as many reasons as you can why it would be far more sensible for a woman to have a baby when she is 25 years old than when she is 15 years old.

Review of Sexual reproduction and birth control

- Adolescence is the period in life between being a child and being an adult.

- Adolescents become sexually mature at puberty.

- Puberty is indicated by certain changes that take place in the body.

- The testes are the male reproductive organs. They are found in the scrotum outside the body cavity.

- Sperm is produced in many tubes inside the testes. These tubes meet and join to connect with the epididymis. During ejaculation sperm passes from the testes through the sperm ducts into the urethra, and leaves the body.

- As sperm passes along the sperm duct it mixes with a fluid from the seminal vesicle to form semen, and is nourished by fluid from the prostate gland.

- The ovaries are the female reproductive organs. They release an ovum once each month. The ovum passes along an oviduct into the uterus.

- If the ovum is not fertilised it will pass down the uterus, through the cervix into the vagina, and eventually leave the body.

- During the years that a woman can have children she has a regular menstrual cycle.

- The menstrual cycle is controlled by the action of the hormones oestrogen and progesterone.

- During fertilisation a sperm combines with an egg to form a zygote.

- Fertilisation normally takes place in the oviduct.

- A fertilised egg undergoes rapid cell division.

- A fertilised egg embeds itself in the uterus wall and a placenta forms.

- The developing baby is initially called an embryo but after 8 weeks it is referred to as a foetus.

- An umbilical cord connects the developing foetus and the placenta on the uterus wall.

- The foetus develops in a sac called the amnion, which is full of watery amniotic fluid.

- The amniotic fluid acts as a shock absorber, protecting the developing foetus from damage.

- Everything that enters and leaves the developing foetus does so through the umbilical cord.

- The mother's blood supply and the foetus's blood supply are not directly joined – substances pass from one to the other by diffusion in the placenta.

- The gestation period is the time taken for a fertilised egg to develop to the point where a baby is born. In humans this takes nine months.

- Expectant mothers attend prenatal clinics where their wellbeing is monitored during pregnancy.

- Ultrasound images show an image of the foetus.

- Harmful substances can pass from the mother's blood into the foetus's blood.

- Doctors advise that expectant mothers should not smoke, drink excessive amounts of alcohol or take recreational drugs during pregnancy.

- Viruses can also pass from the mother to the developing foetus.

- In some countries when girls reach puberty they are vaccinated against the rubella virus that causes German measles.

- Contraception is about preventing a woman becoming pregnant as a result of sexual intercourse.

- Teenage women are physically able to have a baby, but their bodies are not fully developed and there are many other problems with having a baby at a young age.

- Bringing up a baby is very demanding in terms of time, money and dedication.

- A woman is in a much better position to have a baby when she has finished her education, has worked for several years and has acquired skills, and is in a stable relationship with a partner.

Review questions on Sexual reproduction and birth control

Knowledge and understanding

1. Copy and complete the following sentences.

  a) _____ hormones are responsible for changes that take place to the body during adolescence.

  b) The hormone released by the male sex organs is _____ .

  c) During puberty the male voice becomes _____ .

  d) The hormone released by the female sex organs is _____ .

  e) During puberty the female starts to have regular _____ .

2. Explain the following terms.

  a) Adolescence   **b)** Puberty   **c)** Secondary sexual characteristic

3. Name the parts A to E in Fig B 5.RQ.1.

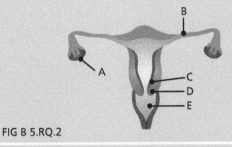

FIG B 5.RQ.1

4. Name the parts A to E in Fig B 5.RQ.2.

FIG B 5.RQ.2

5. a) In which part of the body are the following formed:

  i) sperm?   **ii)** ova?

  b) What travels along:

  i) an oviduct?   **ii)** a sperm duct?

  c) What is the alternative name for a fallopian tube?

  d) How many of the following are normally released by the body at any one time:

  i) sperm?   **ii)** ova?

6. a) Which hormones are involved in controlling the menstrual cycle?

b) State the role of each hormone identified in **a)**.

c) At what age does a girl usually start having periods?

d) What point of the menstrual cycle is usually considered to be day 1?

7. Fig B 5.RQ.3 shows a part of the female reproductive system and some stages leading up to pregnancy.

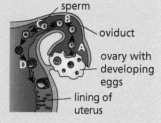

FIG B 5.RQ.3

a) What process is taking place at:

i) A　　　　　　**ii)** B　　　　　　**iii)** C?

b) What happens to the embryo between C and D?

c) What is happening at D?

8. Fig B 5.RQ.4 represents a human foetus in the mother's womb.

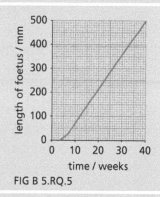

FIG B 5.RQ.4

a) Identify parts A – E on the diagram.

b) This box contains items and substances found in blood.

glucose	carbon dioxide	oxygen
red blood cells	urea	white blood cells

From this list choose two things that pass through part D:

i) from the mother to the foetus　　**ii)** from the foetus to the mother.

c) Describe the function of part A.

d) What normally happens to part B just before childbirth?

Process skills

9. The graph in Fig B 5.RQ.5 shows how a typical foetus increases in length as it grows in the mother's uterus.

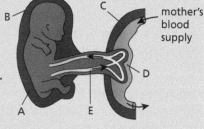

FIG B 5.RQ.5

a) How are doctors able to measure the size of a growing foetus?

b) If the foetus is 250 mm in length, how old is it likely to be?

c) How big will the baby be at birth if this happens at 39 weeks?

10. a) Explain why a doctor might give different advice about a vasectomy to the following patients:

- A 40 year old male with a family of five children
- A 20 year old male with no children.

b) Explain why a doctor should establish that a woman has a healthy circulatory system before recommending contraception using the hormone pill.

c) Explain why some methods of contraception provide protection against sexually transmitted diseases while others do not.

55 Improving communication with teenagers

The following is a quote from a website containing information about teenage pregnancy:

> 'Most experts believe that one of the major causes of teenage pregnancy in Jamaica is ignorance regarding proper sexual behaviour and consequences.' (www.pregnancyexposed.com)

Although much information is available for teenagers it seems that many are not getting the important messages.

A new approach has been suggested that involves providing information about teenage

FIG STEAM B 5.55.1

pregnancy in the form of a comic strip in school magazines and newsletters. It is thought that some teenagers might respond to this more readily than to formal posters and leaflets.

Fig STEAM B 5.55.1 is an example of a comic strip to give you some idea of how one is laid out. Your strip is not meant to make people laugh, but to deliver an important message. However, if it does contain some element of humour this might give it more credibility with the target audience.

1. You are going to work in small groups to produce a comic strip suitable for inclusion in your school magazine or newsletter. The tasks are:

   • To review the parts of the unit which are concerned with contraception and teenage pregnancy and make sure you understand all of the issues discussed.

   • To look at examples of cartoon strips in local newspapers and on the Internet to see how they are laid out and put together.

   • To create the first draft of a comic strip that can be reviewed by people outside your group.

   • To revise your comic strip and produce the final version.

   • To prepare an oral report in which you will explain why you chose a particular focus and to discuss the message you believe is delivered by your comic strip. Your report should also describe any particular techniques that you used in its production.

   a) Look back through the unit, and in particular at those lessons dealing with different forms of contraception and the problems associated with teenage pregnancy.

   b) Look at examples of comic strips in comics and newspapers. How many separate pictures are in the strip? How has the artist avoided covering the characters with the speech bubbles? Do the images look more effective in colour or in black and white?

c) Before you start thinking about drawing you need a story line. What message is your comic strip going to deliver? A simple message delivered well is likely to have a much greater impact than a complicated message that few readers will understand.

d) Once you have decided on your story line you need to assess how many pictures you will need to deliver it. You might be able to deliver it in one picture or you might need a sequence of pictures that follow on. You would be wise to limit this to three or, if really necessary, to four. You are aiming to deliver a message, not create a soap opera.

FIG STEAM B 5.55.2 A picture drawn on a computer

e) How are you going to draw your pictures? Cartoonists often draw pictures to a larger scale than the final version. This allows them to add detail more easily. When a picture is finished it can be reduced by a photocopier or scanned into a computer, reduced and reprinted.

Does your school have any computer-aided drawing packages or other software that would allow you to create your images using a computer? Can you make use of any clip art in your designs? You might be able to drop images of people into a computer-drawn picture.

If you decide to draw freehand don't worry about adding colour at this stage. The outlines and text will provide you with a version that can be reviewed by people outside your group.

f) Who are you going to ask to review your work? You might ask your science teacher about the content and your art teacher about the design, but at the end of the day the message you are planning to deliver is directed towards students around your own age. You need to make sure that what you have done makes sense to them so be sure to include students in your team of reviewers.

g) Once your first version has been reviewed it is time to make whatever changes are necessary. When you are satisfied with the content carry on and produce the final version of your comic strip.

h) Your audience will need to have access to your comic strip when you come to give your oral presentation. You might print copies for circulation in advance or maybe project an image onto a screen.

If your comic strip is successful in delivering its message you should not need to explain what this is to your audience. You should explain why you believe this message is important and how you think it will help to reduce teenage pregnancy.

Your audience might also be interested in how you went about creating your comic strip, so you should be prepared to describe and discuss the different stages. Do not be reluctant to describe things that went wrong – learning through mistakes is an important aspect of scientific development.

1 Development of chemistry I

We are learning how to:

- understand some important contributions to the development of chemistry

Extracting metals ⟫

Most metals do not exist as 'native' metal in the ground but as ores. These are compounds of metals. The ability of chemists to extract metals from their ores has played an important part in the development of science and technology.

Apart from gold and silver, which were used to make jewellery and other fine objects, the first metal to come into common use was bronze.

FIG C 0.1.1 Bronze tools and weapons

Bronze is an alloy of copper and tin. It was relatively easy to extract from its ores simply by heating in a furnace. Bronze implements were a considerable improvement on those made of stone, but bronze is a relatively soft metal.

Iron only became available when early scientists devised furnaces that drew air through them. Such furnaces produced higher temperatures and created the conditions needed to extract iron.

natural draft furnace

early man-made furnace

FIG C 0.1.2 Early iron furnaces

Tribes that had iron implements were at a great advantage. Not only did iron make stronger weapons, it could be used to make tools to shape materials like wood, and implements like spades to farm the land more effectively.

FIG C 0.1.3 Iron weapon

Activity C 0.1.1

Extracting lead from its ore

Here is what you need:

- lead(II, IV) oxide
- carbon block with well
- eye protection
- Bunsen burner
- blowpipe

Here is what you should do:

1. Place a small amount of lead(II,IV) oxide into the well of a carbon block. Take care not to spill any.
2. Heat the top of the block with a Bunsen flame.

3. Using a blowpipe, blow air onto the lead(II,IV) oxide powder. Take care to blow gently so that it is not blown away.

4. When all of the lead(II,IV) oxide has reacted, remove the heat and allow the carbon block to cool.

FIG C 0.1.4 Extracting lead

5. Tip out the contents of the well and see if you have any lead metal.

Although furnaces were now capable of much higher temperatures there are a number of metals, like sodium potassium and aluminium, that cannot be extracted from their ore no matter how hot they are. It was only after the discovery of electricity around 1800 that these metals became available. They were extracted from their ores by a process called electrolysis. This involved passing an electric current through the molten ore.

When aluminium first became available it could only be made in small amounts. Consequently it was more expensive than gold. It was used to make jewellery and Napoleon famously had a dinner set made of the metal.

In 1886 scientists devised a method of making aluminium cheaply on a large scale and the value of aluminium fell by 80% overnight. Today aluminium is a very cheap metal and is widely used.

FIG C 0.1.5 Aluminium is a common metal today

Check your understanding

1. Fig C 0.1.6 shows metals in order of their chemical reactivity. The most reactive is at the top of the list.

   a) Comment on how the reactivity of metals is related to how long ago they were discovered.

   b) Put the following metals in a likely order of discovery, starting with the one that was discovered first.

   potassium   copper   silver   zinc

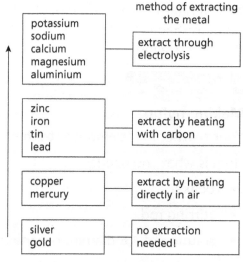

increasing reactivity

	method of extracting the metal
potassium sodium calcium magnesium aluminium	extract through electrolysis
zinc iron tin lead	extract by heating with carbon
copper mercury	extract by heating directly in air
silver gold	no extraction needed!

FIG C 0.1.6

2 Development of chemistry I (continued)

We are learning how to:

- understand some important contributions to the development of chemistry

Polymers 〉〉〉

Polymers are very large molecules made by joining many smaller molecules called monomers. A monomer may be just one chemical or two or more different chemicals.

FIG C 0.2.1 Forming a polymer

There are many examples of naturally occurring polymers, such as cotton and wool. Many of the foods we eat, like proteins, are polymers which are broken down during digestion.

The first synthetic polymer was made in 1907 by Leo Baekeland and was called Bakelite. It is an example of a thermosetting plastic – once it has been formed into a shape it cannot be reshaped. Bakelite was widely used for objects like electric plugs and sockets, radios and telephones.

FIG C 0.2.2 Bakelite telephone

Polythene was discovered in 1933 by accident by two chemists, Eric Fawcett and Reginald Gibson. It took five more years of development before polythene could be made in commercial quantities. The first item made of polythene was a walking stick.

World War II marked a busy time in polymer development. Natural materials like silk and rubber were in short supply and scientists developed synthetic substitutes like nylon and synthetic rubber.

FIG C 0.2.3 Polythene is used to make greenhouses

Many modern plastics are described as thermoplastics. They can be reshaped while hot and harden to take the new shape on cooling.

Activity C 0.2.1

Making nylon

Your teacher may demonstrate this activity.

Here is what you need:

- beaker
- stirring rod
- solution of 1,6-diaminohexane in water

FIG C 0.2.4 Thermoplastic spheres for use in washing machines

- solution of decanedioyl dichloride in cyclohexane

nylon thread wrapped around a stirring rod

solution of decanedioyl dichloride in cyclohexane

nylon forming at the interface

solution of 1,6-diaminohexane in water

FIG C 0.2.5 Making nylon

Here is what you should do:

1. Pour an aqueous solution of 1,6-diaminohexane in a beaker to a depth of about 2 cm.

2. Carefully pour a similar volume of a solution of decanedioyl dichloride in cyclohexane in the same beaker. The solutions will form two layers.

3. Nylon forms at the interface between the layers. If a stirring rod is dipped into the solutions, a thread of nylon can be drawn out.

4. The nylon thread should be slowly rolled onto the glass rod as it continually forms.

FIG C 0.2.6 Many of the products we use in everyday life are made from plastic

Since the middle of the last century, plastics have replaced traditional materials for a host of applications. They have many advantages but have, sadly, created big problems.

The resistance of plastics to rotting was once viewed as a great advantage but it is now seen by many as a curse. The non-biodegradability of plastics means that they can exist in the environment for many years and are a serious source of pollution.

FIG C 0.2.7 Plastic pollution

Check your understanding

1. **a)** What is a polymer?

   b) Give two examples of natural polymers.

   c) Give two examples of synthetic polymers.

2. Many people believe that the use of plastics by society should be greatly reduced. Traditional materials that are more environmentally friendly should replace plastics for some applications. Identify three applications and suggest suitable materials to replace plastics.

3 Development of chemistry II

We are learning how to:

- understand some important contributions to the development of chemistry

Aspirin ▶▶▶

The drugs synthesised by chemists bring relief from pain and discomfort, and extend people's lives. In this section we are going to consider a particular drug called aspirin. It is one of a group of drugs called analgesics. These are drugs that provide relief from pain.

Throughout history there have always been people within a society who had knowledge of medicines and were able to make preparations to treat different ailments.

The apothecary was the medieval pharmacist. There were few doctors so people went to the apothecary when they were not well. Apothecaries did not have the knowledge or apparatus needed to synthesise drugs. Their cures were natural products often extracted from plants.

The bark of willow trees was known to provide relief from pain as long ago as in Ancient Egypt. Ancient Greek writers recorded that people would drink tea made from crushed willow bark to reduce fevers.

FIG C 0.3.1 The local apothecary

FIG C 0.3.2 Willow bark contained an analgesic drug

Activity C 0.3.1

Making a plant oil

One method used by early chemists was to extract natural products using a suitable solvent. In this activity you are going to extract chemicals from plant materials using olive oil. Your teacher will decide which plant is suitable.

Here is what you need:

- plant stems and flowers that have been cut and allowed to dry
- scissors
- mortar and pestle
- small jar with screw top × 2
- olive oil
- fine gauze

Here is what you should do:

1. Cut the plant into small pieces and place them in a mortar.

2. Crush the plant with a pestle.

3. Place the powder into a small jar and just cover it with olive oil.

4. Screw the top on the jar and leave it on a sunny window ledge for several days. The longer you leave it the better the extraction.

5. Pour the mixture through fine gauze into another jar.

6. The plant oil has dissolved in the olive oil. Has the olive oil changed colour or does it have a different smell?

During the 18th century, chemists were able to extract the active ingredient in willow bark and named it salicylic acid. The extract was used to treat fevers, pain and inflammation.

By the 19th century chemists were experimenting with chemicals similar in structure to salicylic acid to see if they could make a more effective drug. In 1853 the derivative acetylsalicylic acid was made, but its use as an analgesic was not evaluated.

One problem with salicylate medicines was that although they relieved pain, they had the unfortunate side effect of causing the patient a certain amount of irritation. In 1897 acetylsalicylic acid was investigated as an alternative and it was marketed by the company Bayer under the name of 'aspirin'.

Aspirin was widely used during the first half of the 20th century but its popularity declined with the development of other analgesic drugs such as paracetamol (known as acetaminophen in the USA), commonly sold as Panadol or Cetamol, and ibuprofen. However, it is still widely used. More recently it has been discovered that aspirin is a powerful anti-clotting agent that reduces the risk of heart attacks and strokes.

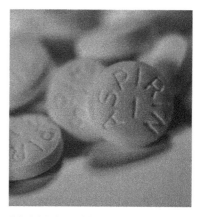

FIG C 0.3.3 Aspirin is still widely used

Check your understanding

1. a) What is an analgesic?
   b) What properties of willow bark were observed?
   c) What is a natural product?
   d) What is an active ingredient?

2. In ancient times many people regarded illness as a punishment from God for their sins. Suggest how this could be reconciled with the use of drugs to treat illness.

4 Development of chemistry II (continued)

We are learning how to:

- understand some important contributions to the development of chemistry

Synthetic dyes

It would be a dull world if everything was either black or white, or some intermediate shade of grey. Since ancient times, people have sought to add colour to their lives and one way of achieving this was to dye their clothing.

Many natural dyes were obtained from different parts of plants, and some from insects. Table C 0.4.1 shows some of the plant parts that can be used to obtain dyes of different colours.

Colour	Plant parts
Yellow	Marigold flowers, sunflowers
Orange	Carrot roots, onion skins
Brown	Walnut husks, fennel
Pink	Rose petals, lavender flowers
Purple	Blueberries, red grapes

TABLE C 0.4.1 Dyes from plants

FIG C 0.4.1 Dyeing fabric with turmeric plant

The dyeing process involved crushing up the plant material and then extracting the substances responsible for the colour by heating in water. The material could then be soaked in the mixture.

Dyes were applied to fabrics and fibres like wool, which were later woven into a fabric. During dyeing the molecules responsible for the colour become fixed to the surface of the fabric. In order to improve fixing, fabrics were sometimes soaked in a chemical called a mordant before being dyed.

Although nature provided a wide range of colours, natural dyes had their limitations. Natural dyes:

- were sometimes easily washed out of the fabric
- sometimes faded rapidly in sunlight.

In 1856 the chemist William Henry Perkin made the first synthetic dye, which was named aniline purple. The name was later changed to mauveine.

FIG C 0.4.2 An image from "The Englishwoman's Domestic Magazine" showing the woman on the right in a dress dyed with mauveine

The synthesis of this dye was something of an accident since at the time Perkins was attempting to find a method of making the antimalarial drug quinine. However, he recognised the importance of what he had discovered and soon set up a factory to make it in large quantities.

Within a few years a chemist called Peter Griess made the first of what was to become a large group dyes which were similar in structure. Bismarck brown was the first diazo dye.

This sparked the interest of other chemists and by the 1880s there was a wide range of synthetic dyes available. Synthetic dyes provide a wider range of colours than natural dyes and they are more colour-fast; that is, they don't fade or wash out as easily as some natural dyes.

FIG C 0.4.3 Synthetic dyes can be used to give new colour to wigs or hair samples

Activity C 0.4.1

Extracting a dye and colouring a fabric

Here is what you need:

- plant material – your teacher will decide what sort
- knife
- beaker 250 cm³
- tripod and gauze
- heat source
- piece of cotton or other fabric
- stirring rod
- tweezers

Here is what you should do:

1. Use a knife to chop up the plant material into small pieces.
2. Place the plant material into a beaker and add water until the beaker is half-full.
3. Heat the plant material mixture and stir it around to help the dye to go into solution.
4. When the water looks to be well-coloured place your piece of fabric into the mix and leave it for 10 minutes.
5. After 10 minutes remove the fabric, wash off the excess dye and leave it to dry.
6. If there is sufficient time you can divide your fabric into four pieces and test whether your dye is easily washed out and/or fades in sunlight.

Check your understanding

1. a) Why is plant material crushed before the dye is extracted?

    b) Why might a mordant be used during dyeing?

    c) What advantages did synthetic dyes offer over natural dyes?

2. The text mentions some advantages of synthetic dyes over natural dyes, but there are also some disadvantages. Suggest two of them.

FIG C 0.4.4 Tie-dyed fabrics

5 What is chemistry?

We are learning how to:

- describe what chemistry is and what it does

Chemistry is the branch of science that is concerned with the different substances from which all matter is composed. Chemists investigate the properties and reactions of substances through experiments.

Traditional branches of chemistry

Chemistry is traditionally divided into three branches, each concerned with a particular aspect of the subject.

- Inorganic chemistry is concerned with the chemistry of metals and non-metals (except carbon).

- Organic chemistry is concerned with the chemistry of carbon compounds except for carbon monoxide and carbon dioxide gases, and metal compounds such as carbonates.

- Physical chemistry is concerned with the physical structure of compounds, the amount of energy they have and how this changes during chemical reactions, and the bonds that hold atoms together.

Applied chemistry

The skills and knowledge of a chemist may be applied in different ways in a modern society. Here are some examples.

Food chemists are interested in the chemical composition of foods and what happens to them when the food is eaten. Dieticians use information about food to make recommendations about what we eat.

Environmental chemists are interested in the chemicals present in soil and in surface water. They have an important role in monitoring for pollution and studying its effects.

Forensic chemists are concerned with detecting substances that may be present at a crime scene. These substances may be in very small amounts and it requires great skill and patience to detect and identify them.

Materials chemists are interested in making and testing new materials that can be used by society in different ways.

FIG C 1.5.1 Food chemistry

FIG C 1.5.2 Environmental chemistry

FIG C 1.5.3 Forensic chemist

FIG C 1.5.4 Materials chemist

Analytical chemist

Discuss in your group:

1. What you think an analytical chemist does.

2. In what areas of chemistry would you expect to find an analytical chemist at work.

Chemistry and other sciences ≫

There are many areas of science that involve using chemistry along with other scientific disciplines. Here are some examples.

Biochemistry is concerned with the biological and chemical processes that occur in living organisms. A biochemist might:

- investigate how substances are made in plants

- develop a drug for use in animals.

Pharmacy is the science of preparing and dispensing medicinal drugs.

This is related to pharmacology, which is concerned with the uses, effects and modes of action of drugs.

Chemical engineers bring engineering expertise to chemical processes in which important products like fuels, fertilisers and drugs are made.

FIG C 1.5.5 Pharmacists dispense drugs

FIG C 1.5.6 Chemical engineers at work

Check your understanding

1. Suggest what each of the following branches of chemistry is concerned with:

   a) polymer chemistry

   b) nuclear chemistry

2. In addition to chemistry, which other areas of science are needed in each of the following?

   a) geochemistry

   b) chemical oceanography

   c) agrochemistry

   d) meteorology

6 Five famous chemists

We are learning how to:

• appreciate the contributions of five people to chemistry

Over the centuries many chemists have made important contributions to our understanding of chemistry. In this spread we will look at the work of five of these people.

John Dalton 〉〉〉

The Ancient Greek Democritus suggested the existence of atoms over two thousand years ago but was unable to offer any evidence for their existence. The concept was largely ignored until John Dalton proposed his atomic theory in 1803. In this theory Dalton suggested that:

1. All matter is made of atoms.
2. Atoms are indivisible and indestructible.
3. All atoms of a given element are identical in mass and properties.
4. Compounds are formed by a combination of two or more different kinds of atoms.
5. A chemical reaction is a rearrangement of atoms.

Dalton's Atomic Theory provided a workable model of atoms and how they behave, which was built on by future generations of chemists.

Humphrey Davy 〉〉〉

Many of the early scientists were able to make valuable contributions to more than one branch of science. Humphrey Davy is well known for his contributions to physics but his work as a chemist is no less important.

At the start of the 19th century, there was no way of obtaining very reactive metals like potassium from their ores. In 1807, Davy had the idea of passing an electric current through a molten compound. We now call this process electrolysis.

He first isolated the element potassium by passing a current through molten potassium hydroxide. In the same year he also isolated sodium using the same method. In the following year, 1808, Davy was the first to isolate barium, calcium, strontium and magnesium, and in the following year boron.

Electrolysis is still used today in the industrial extraction of reactive metals.

FIG C 1.6.1 Five famous chemists

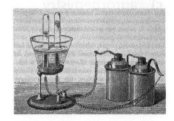

FIG C 1.6.2 An illustration of electrolysis laboratory equipment from 1873

Dmitri Mendeleev >>>

Many new elements were discovered during the 19th century. A number of attempts were made to organise them in a meaningful way but they all suffered from the same problem. The elements placed in some groups had similar chemistry while the elements placed in others did not.

Mendeleev realised the reason for this was that there were elements still to be discovered.

In 1869, working with only 63 known elements, Mendeleev devised what was to be the basis of the modern Periodic Table. He left gaps in his table where he believed there were undiscovered elements, and even made predictions about the properties of some that were later confirmed.

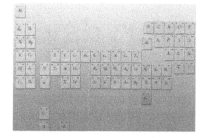

FIG C 1.6.3 Mendeleev's periodic table in 1869

Dorothy Hodgkin >>>

In order to understand the structure of very large molecules like proteins, chemists need to know their shapes and how they fit together with other molecules.

Dorothy Hodgkin developed a technique called X-ray crystallography in order to determine the structure of proteins. The importance of her work was recognised by the award of the Nobel Prize for chemistry in 1964.

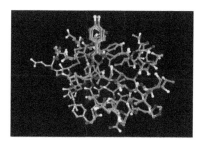

FIG C 1.6.4 A model of insulin, one of the structures determined by Dorothy Hodgkin

Gertrude Elion >>>

The early days of drug development often involved a considerable amount of 'trial and error'.

There were some successes but this procedure often wasted time and resources. Gertrude Elion and her co-workers took a different approach by using differences in the biochemistry of normal human cells and pathogens (agents that cause disease) in order to design drugs that could kill or inhibit the growth of particular pathogens without harming the host cells.

Among the drugs developed by Gertrude Elion were:

- Purinethol – the first treatment for leukemia
- Imuran – used to prevent rejection of organ transplants
- Zyloprim – a treatment for gout
- Daraprim – a treatment for malaria
- Azidothymidine (AZT) – the first treatment for AIDS

The huge contribution she made was recognised by the award of the Noble Prize for physiology or medicine in 1988.

Activity C 1.6.1

Preparing a presentation

1. Choose one of the five chemists whose achievements are briefly described in this spread.

2. Carry out research using whatever resources are available to find out more about the person you have chosen.

3. Prepare a presentation lasting about 3 minutes. Your teacher may ask you to deliver your presentation to the class.

7 Importance of chemistry in everyday life

We are learning how to:

- identify different ways in which chemistry contributes to everyday life

You will have some ideas of how chemistry contributes to your everyday life from reading about the different applications in an earlier section. Let's try to highlight some of these as we go through a day.

FIG C 1.7.1 Personal hygiene products

Chemists make it possible for you to clean your body with products that remove dirt while not damaging your skin. Toothpaste cleans your teeth while helping to protect them from decay.

FIG C 1.7.2 Nutritious foods

Food chemists design foods, such as breakfast cereals, that, while tasting good, provide you with the energy and nutrients you need to stay healthy.

FIG C 1.7.3 Stationery

Material chemists produce paper that you can write on without the ink bleeding into it, and ink that stays liquid in the pen but quickly dries on the paper.

Polymer chemists make plastics that are strong, lightweight, can be given attractive colours and are easily washed. These are ideal for storing food like your lunch.

Petrochemical engineers produce fuels so that vehicles, like the school bus, can travel safely and smoothly on the roads.

Chemists synthesise dyes so that you have attractive coloured clothing to go to the disco. Good dyes don't wash out in the laundry and don't fade in bright sunlight.

Chemists make medicines to give people relief from pain and discomfort. You might be glad for a couple of antacid tablets if you have eaten too much.

FIG C 1.7.4 Plastics

FIG C 1.7.5 Fuels

Activity C 1.7.1

How does chemistry impact my life?

1. Draw a timeline for a typical day from the time you get up to the time you go to bed.

2. Along your time line mark as many places where you think chemistry has contributed in some way to your day. For example, immediately after you get up you might mark 'soap' on your line.

Getting up in the morning

Going to bed at night

soap for washing

FIG C 1.7.8

You can use some of the examples given in this section, but also add some of your own.

FIG C 1.7.6 Dyed fabrics

Check your understanding

1. Briefly discuss how chemistry has contributed to the following:

   a) shampoos

   c) non-stick kitchen utensils

   b) polythene bags

   d) detergents

FIG C 1.7.7 Medicines

8 Selecting apparatus

We are learning how to:

• select appropriate apparatus for an experiment

Chemists have a range of apparatus available for carrying out experiments. In order to carry out an experiment safely and make the necessary observations, it is important that the correct apparatus is used.

• **Ignition tubes** are used to heat solids to very high temperatures. They are made of soft glass and are usually destroyed during heating.

• **Test tubes** are commonly used to carry out experiments using small amounts of substances. They are made of soft glass and will melt if heated too strongly. Substances can be warmed in test tubes but should not be boiled.

• **Boiling tubes** are made of hard glass and can be heated strongly without damage. When substances are to be heated or solutions boiled, a boiling tube should be used. When a solution is to be heated, the boiling tube should not be more than half full. This allows for the expansion of the solution and the bubbling up as it boils.

When tubes are heated, they must be held by suitable tongs or holders.

Beakers and **conical flasks** have a larger capacity than test tubes. They should be used where an experiment involves a large volume of a substance. Beakers and conical flasks come in different sizes. In your laboratory you might find some that hold as little as 50 cm³ and others that can hold up to 1000 cm³.

A liquid in a beaker has a larger surface area than in a conical flask. If it is heated, the liquid will evaporate or boil away more quickly from a beaker. When a beaker or a conical flask is to be used to boil a liquid, it should not be more than half full.

Chemists sometimes need to transfer small amounts of liquids.

When a small amount of a reaction mixture is added to test paper of some kind, such as blue cobalt chloride paper, a single drop can be removed using a glass rod.

When several drops of a reaction mixture or a reagent are required a **dropper pipette** (teat pipette) can be used.

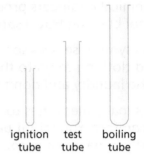

ignition tube   test tube   boiling tube

FIG C 1.8.1 Different types of tube

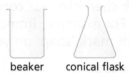

beaker   conical flask

FIG C 1.8.2 Beaker and conical flask

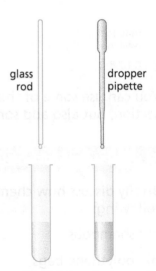

glass rod   dropper pipette

FIG C 1.8.3 Transferring small amounts of liquids

Activity C 1.8.1

Carrying out experiments using different pieces of apparatus

Here is what you need:

- blue cobalt chloride paper
- potassium iodide solution
- lead nitrate solution
- ethanol
- green leaf
- water
- spatula
- eye protection

You will also need some pieces of apparatus. You must choose what you think is appropriate for each experiment, but do not carry out the experiment until your teacher has approved your choice.

Here is what you should do:

Experiment 1

1. Add a single drop of water to a piece of blue cobalt chloride paper.

2. Make a note of any colour change.

Experiment 2

1. Add 10 drops of potassium iodide solution to 10 drops of lead nitrate solution.

2. Make a note of any colour change.

Check your understanding

1. For each of the following state which piece of apparatus would be most appropriate to use.

a) Transferring five drops of hydrochloric acid into a reaction mixture.

b) Heating a small volume of water to dissolve solid sodium chloride and make a solution.

c) Adding 2 cm³ each of two solutions together.

d) Diluting 50 cm³ of sulphuric acid by adding an equal volume of distilled water.

e) Heating hexane (an inflammable liquid).

Interesting fact

Glass is transparent so we can observe changes that take place during a chemical reaction. Early chemists did not have the benefit of glass apparatus. They carried out their experiments in earthenware pots, which made it difficult to make accurate observations.

Key terms

ignition tube small tube for heating solids strongly

test tube used to carry out chemical reactions on a small scale

boiling tube used to heat solids or liquids

beaker used to carry out chemical reactions on a larger scale or as a **water bath**

water bath method of heating inflammable liquids without exposing them to a naked flame

conical flask used to carry out chemical reactions on a larger scale

dropper pipette used to transfer small amounts of a reaction mixture or reagent

9 Using apparatus

We are learning how to:
- use apparatus properly

There are several reasons why it is important for a chemist to use apparatus properly.

- Incorrect use may lead to injury. You should always wear eye protection.

- Some apparatus is very expensive and costly to repair or replace.

- Incorrect use produces incorrect observations or readings.

Here are some pointers that will make you a more proficient chemist.

Balances 》》

Most modern balances have a **tare** button.

If you put a beaker, on the balance and then press the tare button, the scale resets to zero. This means that when you add a substance to the beaker, the reading you get is only the mass of the chemical.

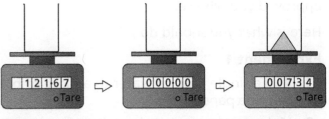

FIG C 1.9.1 Using tare

Thermometers 》》

Thermometers generally have thin glass bulbs and should not be used for stirring. To obtain an accurate temperature it is essential to read a thermometer from the top or bottom of the meniscus.

A column of water and/or alcohol (Fig C 1.9.2 a) forms a meniscus which falls at the centre. The reading is always taken from the bottom of the meniscus. The same is true when measuring aqueous solutions accurately using a pipette or a burette.

A column of mercury (Fig C 1.9.2 b) forms a meniscus which rises at the centre. The reading is always taken from the top of the meniscus.

In order to avoid a **parallax error** in both instances the reading should be taken with the eye level with the meniscus.

30°C — ┄┄ 26°C

20°C —

a) alcohol thermometer

30°C — ┄┄ 27°C

20°C —

b) mercury thermometer

FIG C 1.9.2 Reading a thermometer

Bench mats >>>

Bench mats serve the same purpose in the laboratory as coasters do in the home. They protect the laboratory bench from damage.

FIG C 1.9.3 Bench mat

Activity C 1.9.1

Here is what you need:

- digital balance
- beaker 250 cm³
- tripod and gauze
- bench mat
- heat source
- thermometer

Here is what you should do:

1. Measure about 100 g of water in a beaker using the tare on the balance.
2. Put the beaker on a tripod and gauze sitting on a bench mat.
3. Take the temperature of the water.
4. Heat the water for 5 minutes, taking the temperature every minute.
5. Remove the heat source and allow the water to cool, taking the temperature of the water for a further five minutes.
6. Record the temperatures in a suitable table.
7. Plot a graph to show how the temperature of the water changes over time.
8. Study the gradient of your graph and explain its significance.

Burettes >>>

Burettes are used to measure accurate volumes of liquids. They are supported on a stand and clamp. Rubber-lined jaws should be used to hold the burette securely without the need for overtightening and the risk of cracking it.

To give an accurate reading, the burette must be vertical both from the svides and front-to-back.

Burette taps sometimes seize up. If the tap on the burette won't turn easily don't try to force it. This will simply snap off the section below the scale. Ask your teacher for assistance.

Check your understanding

1. Explain how the tare button allows you to record the mass of a chemical but not the mass of its container.

2. a) Draw a diagram to show the meniscus formed in a mercury thermometer.

   b) Draw an arrow at the place where your eye should be when recording the temperature.

3. Give two reasons why it is sensible to use a bench mat when carrying out experiments.

4. Explain why the level of liquid in a burette can only be read accurately when the burette is held in a vertical position.

FIG C 1.9.4 Using a burette

Key terms

tare button on balance that resets it to zero

parallax error position of object changes with changes to the position of the eye

Review of Introduction to chemistry

- Chemistry is concerned with the different substances from which all matter is composed.

- Chemistry is traditionally divided into inorganic chemistry, organic chemistry and physical chemistry.

- Chemistry is applied in many different contexts in a modern society.

- There are many areas of science that involve using chemistry with other scientific disciplines.

- John Dalton proposed an atomic model which was built on by other scientists.

- Humphrey Davy discovered a number of reactive metals using electrolysis.

- Dmitri Mendeleev created a table of elements that formed the basis of a modern Periodic Table.

- Dorothy Hodgkin determined the structure of proteins using X-ray crystallography.

- Gertrude Elion devised ways of synthesising drugs to treat many illnesses.

- Chemistry is important for many of the things that contribute to our daily lives.

- It is important to select suitable apparatus to carry out experiments.

- It is essential to use apparatus correctly to ensure safety and accuracy.

Review questions on Introduction to chemistry

Knowledge and understanding

1. **a)** What is chemistry?
   b) What is studied by an:
   i) inorganic chemist?   **ii)** organic chemist?

2. **a)** What did Dalton propose in his Atomic Theory?
   b) Why is Dalton's theory regarded as important in our understanding of the composition of matter?

3. **a)** Which metals were first isolated by Humphrey Davy?
   b) How did he isolate them?
   c) Why hadn't scientists isolated these metals a hundred years earlier?

4. **a)** What did Mendeleev's table of elements lead to?
   b) In what way was Mendeleev's table better than other attempts to classify elements around this time?

5. **a)** Why were chemists unable to determine the shape of protein molecules from knowledge of the percentage of different elements in their composition?
   b) What technique did Dorothy Hodgkin use to determine their structure?

6. **a)** What is meant by the 'trial and error' approach to finding drugs to fight diseases?
   b) In what ways is this approach wasteful?
   c) How was the approach to drug design by Gertrude Elion different?

Process skills

7. Briefly describe how chemistry might contribute to the following:
   a) Production of nutritious foods
   b) Development of lubricating oils to protect moving parts of engines
   c) Insecticides to protect food crops from damage
   d) Washing detergents that are environmentally friendly.

8. Suggest what science discipline, other than chemistry, might be used in each of the following areas of study:
   a) astrochemistry   **c)** minerology
   b) plant chemistry   **d)** environmental chemistry

9. Read each of the following thermometers to the nearest half of a degree centigrade.

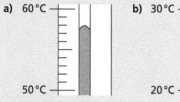 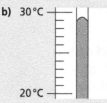 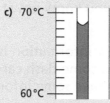

FIG C 1.RQ.1

11 Help cards for use in the laboratory

In some countries, evaluation of the potential hazards involved in carrying out different science experiments have been assessed with a view to making the school chemistry laboratory a safe working environment. This is sometimes called risk analysis.

Such information is useful to:

- The teacher who is planning an experiment to complement the theory taught in class

- The technician who is preparing the apparatus and materials required for the experiment

- The student who is carrying out the experiment and who may not be familiar with some of the apparatus or materials to be used.

CLEAPSS

STUDENT SAFETY SHEETS

FIG STEAM C 1.11.1 Student safety sheets

1. You are going to work in a small group to produce a series of help cards that will help younger students, who are unfamiliar with chemical apparatus, to use different pieces of apparatus correctly in order to be safe and to obtain reliable data. The tasks are:

   - To look back through the lessons on choosing and using different pieces of apparatus.

   - To research which pieces of apparatus are likely to be used by students in lower secondary science lessons.

   - To make a list of the pieces of apparatus you will provide advice about.

   - To design and make your help cards.

   - To trial your help cards in lower school science lessons and receive feedback from students on how useful they were.

   - To revise your help cards and add additional ones on the basis of the feedback that you receive.

   a) Look back through spreads C 1.8 and C 1.9 which describe common pieces of apparatus and give advice on their use. Make sure that you know how to select and use apparatus correctly.

   b) Look at some examples of how information is laid out on help cards. You might have some flash cards that you use for revision or you might have some information cards from a game.

What are the good features of the cards? For example, is colour used to good effect?

What are the bad features of the cards? For example, is there too much text that reduces the impact of the card?

c) What are your cards going to look like? Here are some points for you to consider.

- Students may not bother to read a card if there is lots of small text on it.
- Cards are more likely to interest students if they are attractive in appearance.
- A diagram is often more attractive and more informative than several lines of text.
- You might colour-code your cards in some way, for example, using glassware could be one colour, reading measurements could be another, etc.
- If you decide to use symbols to indicate potential danger, you should use them in a consistent way.

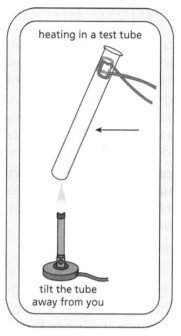

FIG STEAM C 1.11.2 A possible design

Design your cards incorporating those features that you think are important. Once you are satisfied with your designs, make your cards. You might do this directly onto card or you might design them on paper and glue the paper to the card later on.

If there is a laminator available you might consider sealing your cards in plastic to protect them and increase their lifetime.

d) Once your cards are complete, you will need to make arrangements with a member of staff to try them out with students in lower years of the school. How are you going to decide whether the cards are of any help to the students or not?

Here are some ideas:

- You could observe how effective the cards are and how easy students find them to use.
- You could interview the students.
- You could ask students to complete a questionnaire. If you decide to do this you will need to design the questionnaire in advance.

e) Review the feedback that you receive from students and make whatever changes you think necessary to make your cards more effective. You might also consider adding to your cards if students identify particular procedures which they find difficult.

FIG STEAM C 1.11.3 Observing a science class

12 Elements

We are learning how to:

- represent elements by symbols

You know that elements are substances that cannot be made any simpler by chemical methods. There are 94 naturally occurring elements in the world.

Each element is composed of atoms. The atoms of one element are different from the atoms of any other element. Atoms are the building blocks from which all substances are made. Atoms of different elements can combine to form compounds.

Atomic symbols are a shorthand way of representing **elements** or **atoms** of an element. Modern chemists use symbols based on letters of the alphabet but this hasn't always been the case.

> **Interesting fact**
>
> Alchemists are sometimes described as early chemists but they did not apply scientific methods to their work. In their writing, alchemists used symbols to represent certain elements.

Dalton's symbols

At the beginning of the 19th century, the chemist John Dalton proposed a series of symbols (Fig C 2.12.1) for the substances that were thought at that time to be elements.

These symbols worked for the small number of elements known at that time but they were time-consuming to draw and difficult to print.

Modern symbols

Every element has a unique atomic symbol consisting of either one or two letters. The first letter is always written in upper case, and any second letter is written in lower case. For example, the symbol for helium is He, and not HE, hE or he.

The symbols of the first 20 elements of the **Periodic Table** are given in Table C 2.12.1.

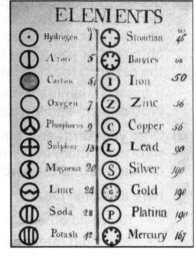

FIG C 2.12.1 Dalton's atomic symbols

Atomic number	Element	Symbol	Atomic number	Element	Symbol
1	Hydrogen	H	11	Sodium	Na
2	Helium	He	12	Magnesium	Mg
3	Lithium	Li	13	Aluminium	Al
4	Beryllium	Be	14	Silicon	Si
5	Boron	B	15	Phosphorus	P
6	Carbon	C	16	Sulphur	S
7	Nitrogen	N	17	Chlorine	Cl
8	Oxygen	O	18	Argon	Ar
9	Fluorine	F	19	Potassium	K
10	Neon	Ne	20	Calcium	Ca

TABLE C 2.12.1 Symbols of the first 20 elements

In general, the symbol of an element is the first letter of its name. Where there are two elements whose names start with the same letter, an additional letter is added. For example, the symbol for carbon is C, while the symbol for calcium is Ca.

There are a small number of elements that do not seem to fit this pattern. The reason for this is that their symbols are derived from their Latin names. Some examples are given in Table C 2.12.2.

English name of element	Latin name of element	Symbol
Copper	Cuprum	Cu
Iron	Ferrum	Fe
Lead	Plumbum	Pb
Silver	Argentum	Ag

TABLE C 2.12.2 Symbols derived from Latin names

In Activity C 2.12.1 you will also find it useful to know the symbols for the elements bromine (Br) and iodine (I).

FIG C 2.12.2 An element card, front and back

Activity C 2.12.1

Learning the symbols of the elements

You will need to work with a partner on this activity. Here is what you need:

- small pieces of card (3 cm × 5 cm) × 26

Here is what you should do:

1. Write the name of an element on one side of a card and its symbol on the other.

2. Do this for each of the first 20 elements and also for copper, iron, silver, lead, bromine and iodine.

3. Mix the cards up so that some show the name face up while others show the symbol face up.

4. Put the pack on the table and look at the first card. If it is a name of an element give its symbol, if it is a symbol give its name.

5. Turn the card over and see if you were correct. Take turns and see who gets the most questions correct.

Key terms

atomic symbol one or two letters used to represent an element

element substance that cannot be made into simpler substances

atom smallest particle of a substance that can take part in a chemical reaction

Periodic Table table of the chemical elements arranged in order of atomic number

Check your understanding

1. Give the symbols of the following elements:

   a) carbon   c) copper

   b) oxygen   d) lithium

2. Which elements are represented by the following symbols?

   a) H   c) B

   b) Mg   d) Ne

13 Atoms, ions and compounds

We are learning how to:

- identify atoms as the building blocks from which all substances are made
- how atoms form ions
- how atoms combine to form compounds

Atoms

An **atom** is the smallest particle of an element that can take part in a chemical reaction. All of the atoms of one element are the same and are different from the atoms of every other element.

Atoms of different elements can be shown as spheres of different colours. The atoms are not really different colours but it helps us to visualise how atoms combine.

You will learn more about the structure of atoms in the next spread.

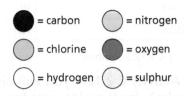

= carbon = nitrogen
= chlorine = oxygen
= hydrogen = sulphur

FIG C 2.13.1 Representing atoms of different elements

Molecules and compounds

Many elements don't exist as individual atoms, but as **molecules** composed of two or more atoms of that element. In a molecule a bond forms between the atoms.

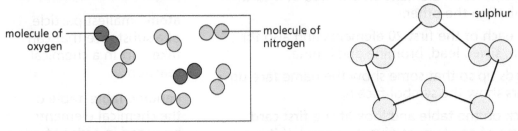

molecule of oxygen — molecule of nitrogen

sulphur

FIG C 2.13.2 Molecules of some elements

Both oxygen and nitrogen exist as molecules containing two atoms. A sulphur molecule consists of eight atoms arranged in the shape of a crown.

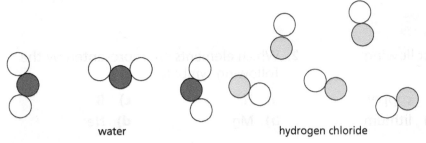

water   hydrogen chloride

FIG C 2.13.3 Molecules of some compounds

When atoms of different elements combine, they form molecules of **compounds**. A molecule of water consists of two atoms of hydrogen and one atom of oxygen chemically bonded together. Hydrogen chloride molecules contain a single atom of hydrogen and a single atom of chlorine bonded together.

Activity C 2.13.1

Making molecules using balls and sticks

Here is what you need:

- items that represent atoms, such as polystyrene balls
- items that represent the bonds between atoms, such as tooth picks
- paints

Here is what you should do:

1. Decide how many atoms you need to make a model of an oxygen molecule.
2. Paint the atoms an appropriate colour.
3. Join the atoms together to make a molecule of oxygen.
4. The length of an oxygen molecule is 2.92×10^{-10} m.

    a) Measure your model of an oxygen molecule and express the value in metres.

    b) Use this information to calculate the scale of your model.

5. Make a molecule of the compound ammonia in a similar way. This compound contains three hydrogen atoms, each bonded to a nitrogen atom.

Key terms

atom smallest particle of a substance that can take part in a chemical reaction

molecule two or more atoms chemically bonded together

compound substance composed of atoms of two or more elements

ion charged particle formed by the loss or gain of one or more electrons from an atom

Ions 》》

Ions are atoms that acquire a charge by the transfer of one or more electrons. Ions may be:

- positively charged due to losing electrons;
- negatively charged due to gaining electrons.

Compounds are also formed by combining oppositely charged ions. You will learn more about such compounds later in this unit.

Check your understanding

1. Copy and complete Table C 2.13.1.

Formula of the compound	Elements present in the compound	Number of atoms of each element
H_2O	Hydrogen, oxygen	2 hydrogen atoms and 1 oxygen atom
HCl		
	Carbon, oxygen	1 carbon atom and 2 oxygen atoms
SO_2		

TABLE C 2.13.1

14 Structure of the atom

We are learning how to:
- recall that atoms contain protons, neutrons and electrons and state their respective charges
- conduct investigations with due regard for safety
- work cooperatively in groups

Atom comes from the Greek word *atomos*, which means indivisible. Atoms are the building blocks from which all things are made.

FIG C 2.14.1 Some common elements: a) aluminium, b) carbon, c) silicon

An **element** is a substance that cannot be made into simpler substances. All of the atoms of one element are similar in structure, but different from the atoms of any other element.

There are 94 naturally occurring elements and many will be familiar to you. These elements can be divided into three groups according to their properties:

- metals, like aluminium and copper
- non-metals, like oxygen and carbon
- semi-metals, like silicon.

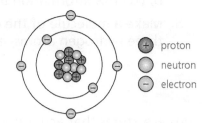

FIG C 2.14.2 Structure of an atom

Sub-atomic particles ▶▶▶

As knowledge increased scientists discovered that atoms are not indivisible. They are, in fact, composed of even smaller particles called **sub-atomic particles**.

An atom consists of a nucleus containing protons and neutrons (Fig C 2.14.2). Surrounding the nucleus are layers of electrons. Table C 2.14.1 summarises the properties of these three particles.

Notice that:

- The mass of an electron is only $\frac{1}{1836}$ the mass of a proton or a neutron, which isn't very much so it is usually written as 0.

Particle	Relative mass	Relative charge	Position in the atom
Proton	1	+1	In the nucleus
Neutron	1	0	In the nucleus
Electron	0	−1	In shells around the nucleus

TABLE C 2.14.1 Three sub-atomic particles

- Although the masses of a proton and an electron are very different, the charges they carry are equal in size but opposite in charge.
- A neutron carries no charge at all.

Activity C 2.14.1

Building a model of an atom of carbon

You should work in a small group for this activity.

Here is what you need:

- small polystyrene balls or similar spheres (12 large and 6 small)
- thin wire
- glue
- paints
- thread

Here is what you should do:

1. Decide on colours to represent protons, neutrons and electrons.

2. Paint six of your balls with each colour. Remember that the electrons are smaller.

3. Glue your protons and neutrons together to form the nucleus of your atom.

4. Make a loop of wire a little larger than your nucleus and thread two of your electrons onto the wire. Keep them in position on your loop with glue. Remember the correct positioning of the electrons.

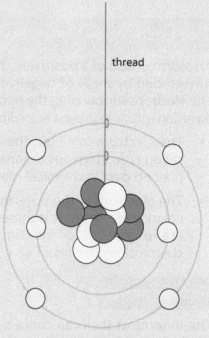

FIG C 2.14.3 Model of a carbon atom

5. Make a second loop a little larger than the first and then thread the remaining four electrons onto it. Hold them in position with glue.

6. Attach a piece of thread with glue, firstly to the nucleus and then loop it round the rings of electrons and hold it in position with glue.

7. Find a suitable place in your classroom to suspend your atom.

Check your understanding

1. Copy and complete the following sentences.

   a) 'Atom' comes from a Greek word that means
      ....

   b) An .... is a substance that cannot be changed into simpler substances.

   c) An .... is the smallest particle of an element that can exist.

   d) .... particles are found inside an atom.

Key terms

atom the smallest particle of a substance that can take part in a chemical reaction

element substance that cannot be made into simpler substances

sub-atomic particles particles found within the atom

171

15 Electronic configuration

We are learning how to:

* write the electronic configuration of atoms in numerical form
* draw the electronic configuration of atoms

Core electrons and valence electrons ≫

An atom consists of a positively charged nucleus surrounded by shells of negatively charged electrons. The electrons surrounding the nucleus of an atom can be classified into two groups according to their positions.

* The electrons in all but the outermost shell are called core electrons or inner electrons. They play no part in chemical reactions.

* The electrons in the outermost shell are called valence electrons. It is these electrons that are responsible for the combining power and chemical properties of an element.

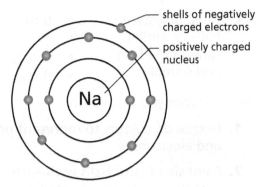

shells of negatively charged electrons

positively charged nucleus

FIG C 2.15.1 Structure of a sodium atom

Electron shells ≫

The innermost shell can contain only two electrons. Helium has just two electrons in a single electron shell. Lithium is the next element in the Periodic Table and it has three electrons. The third electron is in a second electron shell all on its own. See Fig C 2.15.2.

The second electron shell can hold up to eight electrons. Neon, with ten electrons in all, has two in its inner shell and eight in its outer shell. The next element after neon is sodium. Its eleventh electron has to become the first electron in a third electron shell. The third electron shell can also hold up to eight electrons.

The term electronic configuration means the arrangement of the electrons of the atom.

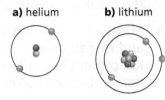
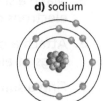

a) helium   **b)** lithium

c) neon   **d)** sodium

FIG C 2.15.2

Activity C 2.15.1

1. Fill in table C 2.15.1.

2. Draw the atomic structure of:

   a) nitrogen   **c)** argon

   b) magnesium   **d)** silicon

Atom	Atomic number	Number of shells
chlorine		
helium		
potassium		
lithium		
calcium		
neon		
magnesium		

Table C 2.15.1

Writing electronic configuration

Written electronic configuration is a shorter way of showing the arrangement of the electrons in any atom.

Atom	Li	Be	B	C	N	O	F	Ne
Electronic configuration	2, 1	2, 2	2, 3	2, 4	2, 5	2, 6	2, 7	2, 8

TABLE C 2.15.2 Written electronic configuration of atoms

Activity C 2.15.2

Drawing and writing the electronic configuration of atoms

Here is what you should do:

1. Using the same method as in Activity C 2.15.1, complete electronic configuration drawings for all the other elements in your chart.

   Remember the rules:

   - The first shell can have no more than two electrons.

   - The second shell can have no more than eight electrons.

   - The third shell can have no more than eight electrons.

2. Now write the numerical configurations for each element. Remember that these are written starting with the number of electrons in the innermost shell.

The atoms of helium, neon and argon have full outer electron shells. This means they are very stable elements and do not react or burn easily. They can be used in lighting tubes as they are unreactive.

Check your understanding

1. What is the numerical electronic configuration of hydrogen?

2. Copy Table C 2.15.1 and add a row for the next eight elements. Complete this row. What do you notice?

3. On your completed chart of electronic configurations, look at the outer shells of the atoms of elements in the right-hand column. What do you notice?

helium

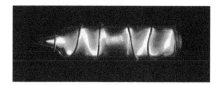

neon

argon

krypton

xenon

FIG C 2.15.3 The noble gases are found in the right-hand column of the Periodic Table. Their electronic configurations mean they are stable elements, so they are used in lighting for many different purposes.

16 Ionic bonding and compounds

We are learning how to:

- form ions from atoms
- write the formulae of different ions
- combine ions to form ionic compounds

Why do atoms form ions? ⟫⟫

Atoms become more stable when they have a full outermost shell. They can achieve this in two ways.

- Elements whose atoms have only one, two or sometimes three electrons in the outermost shell can lose these electrons. Since an electron carries a negative charge, losing electrons forms positively charged particles called **cations**.

- Elements whose atoms only need to gain one, two or sometimes three electrons to fill their outermost shell can gain these electrons. Since an electron carries a negative charge, gaining electrons forms negatively charged particles called **anions**.

Elements that form cations	Cation	Elements that form anions	Anion
Hydrogen	H^+	Chlorine	Cl^-
Lithium	Li^+	Bromine	Br^-
Sodium	Na^+	Iodine	I^-
Potassium	K^+		
Copper	Cu^+		
Magnesium	Mg^{2+}	Oxygen	O^{2-}
Calcium	Ca^{2+}	Sulphur	S^{2-}
Barium	Ba^{2+}		
Copper	Cu^{2+}		
Zinc	Zn^{2+}		
Iron	Fe^{2+}		
Aluminium	Al^{3+}	Nitrogen	N^{3-}
Iron	Fe^{3+}	Phosphorus	P^{3-}

TABLE C 2.16.1 Ions formed by common elements

Elements that form positively charged cations, which are mostly metals, combine with elements that form negatively charged anions, which are non-metals. There has to be enough of each type of **ion** to form a **neutral compound**.

Ionic compounds ⟫⟫

When atoms of combining elements have equal but oppositely charged ions, they combine in the ratio of 1:1.

Na^+ and Cl^- have equal but opposite charges, therefore the formula of sodium chloride is NaCl.

When ions of elements carry different charges they combine in a ratio that forms a neutral compound.

Mg^{2+} and Br$^-$ have opposite charges but the charge on a magnesium ion is twice that on a bromine ion, so they combine in the ratio of

> 1 magnesium ion : 2 bromide ions

Therefore the formula of magnesium bromide is MgBr$_2$.

K$^+$ and S^{2-} have opposite charges but to form a neutral compound they must combine in the ratio of

> 2 potassium ions : 1 sulphide ion

FIG C 2.16.1 Cards representing ions

The formula of potassium sulphide is therefore K$_2$S.

Activity C 2.16.1

Making compounds by combining ions

Here is what you need:

- small pieces of card (4 cm × 4 cm) × 26

Here is what you should do:

1. Make cards to show the ions in Table C2.16.1. Make:
   a) one card for each positive ion
   b) three cards for each negative ion with a charge of –1
   c) one card for each of the other negative ions.
2. Use your cards to form as many compounds as you can, for example, ZnO or CuCl$_2$
3. Write the formula of each compound you make and the ions it contains, for example, MgBr$_2$, Mg^{2+} and 2Br$^-$.
4. Using a dot (·) to represent the outer electrons of a metal atom and a cross (x) to represent the outer electrons of a non-metal atom, draw dot-and-cross diagrams to show how the ionic bonds form in different ionic compounds you make.

Although ammonium is not a metal, it forms the ion NH$_4^+$. Similarly, sulphate ions have the formula SO$_4^{2-}$, and nitrate ions NO$_3^-$. These ions form compounds in exactly the same way as metals and non-metals.

For example, the ammonium ion has a charge of 1+ while the chloride ion has a charge of 1– so the formula of ammonium chloride is NH$_4$Cl.

Similarly, the sodium ion has a charge of 1+ while the sulphate ion has a charge of 2– so the formula of sodium sulphate is Na$_2$SO$_4$.

Key terms

cation positively charged ion

anion negatively charged ion

ion charged atom formed by the loss or gain of electrons

neutral compound a compound in which the particles are electrically neutral

Check your understanding

1. Write the formula of the ions formed by the following elements:
   a) hydrogen   b) iodine   c) barium
   d) oxygen   e) aluminium   f) copper

17 Properties of ionic compounds

We are learning how to:

- describe the properties of a typical ionic compound

Melting point and boiling point

A solid ionic compound consists of a **lattice** in which each ion is in a fixed position and surrounded by oppositely charged ions. See Fig C 2.17.1.

Oppositely charged ions are attracted to each other so it takes a large amount of energy to overcome the forces of attraction. For this reason most ionic compounds have high **melting points** and high **boiling points**.

The melting point of magnesium oxide is 2852 °C, which is higher than that of many metals. See Fig C 2.17.2.

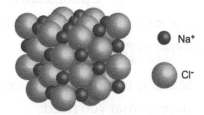

FIG C 2.17.1 Structure of solid sodium chloride

Conducting electricity

Electric charge is transferred along a conductor, like a metal wire, by the flow of negatively charged electrons. Ions can also transfer charge but to do this the ions must be **mobile**.

As we have already seen, in an ionic solid the ions are held in fixed positions and are therefore not mobile. Solid ionic compounds therefore cannot conduct electricity.

When an ionic compound melts or dissolves in water, the ions are free to move (Fig C 2.17.3) and will conduct an electric current.

> ### Interesting fact
>
> Some ionic compounds are described as refractory materials because they are used to make crucibles or line furnaces which contain molten metals.

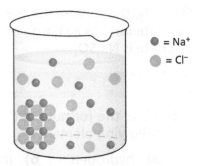

FIG C 2.17.2 A crucible that is used in melting gold

Activity C 2.17.1

Investigating conductivity

Here is what you need:

- a circuit consisting of three cells, a lamp, two probes and connecting wires
- solutions of different substances provided by your teacher

Here is what you should do:

1. Make up the circuit shown in Fig C 2.17.4.

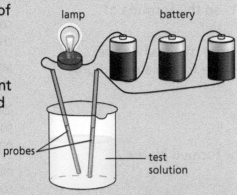

FIG C 2.17.4 Apparatus to investigate conductivity

FIG C 2.17.3 Ions are mobile in solution

2. Dip the probes into the first test solution, making sure that they are not touching each other.

3. If the test solution contains ions, it will conduct an electric current and the lamp will light up. If the solution doesn't contain ions, the lamp will remain off.

4. Repeat this test on all of the solutions you have been given.

5. Give your results in the form of a table with two columns: one for ionic substances and one for non-ionic substances.

Solubility in water

Many ionic substances are **soluble** in water. These include:

- all the salts of sodium and potassium, for example, sodium chloride and potassium hydroxide
- all nitrates, for example, magnesium nitrate;
- all salts of ammonium, for example, ammonium sulphate.

However, there are many ionic compounds that are effectively insoluble. Common examples include calcium carbonate, barium sulphate, copper(II) oxide, silver chloride and lead(II) iodide.

There are also compounds that are soluble in water but are not ionic compounds. Common examples include glucose, sucrose, ethanol, citric acid and ethanoic acid.

It is therefore incorrect to say that solubility in water is a characteristic of all ionic compounds.

Key terms

lattice an ordered arrangement of particles

melting point temperature at which a solid becomes a liquid

boiling point temperature at which a liquid becomes a gas

mobile able to move about

soluble able to dissolve in water or another liquid

Check your understanding

1. Fig C 2.17.5 shows an experiment in which lead(II) bromide is connected in a circuit to a battery and a lamp, and heated until it has melted.

   a) Explain the following observations:

      i) At the start of the experiment the lamp was off.

      ii) As the lead(II) bromide started to melt, the lamp glowed dimly.

      iii) As the lead(II) bromide got hotter, the lamp glowed more brightly.

   b) The melting point of lead(II) bromide is 373 °C. Comment on whether or not this is typical of ionic compounds.

   c) Lead(II) bromide is effectively insoluble in water. Does this indicate it is not an ionic compound? Explain your answer.

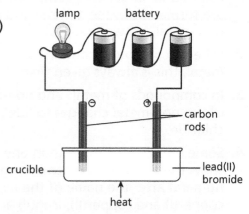

FIG C 2.17.5

18 Chemical formula

We are learning how to:

- combine atoms of different elements to make compounds
- deduce the formulae of compounds from the type and number of atoms that have been combined to make them

Combining power

Atoms of different elements combine to form compounds. The chemical formula of a compound shows the elements present and the relative proportions of each element in the compound.

The simplest compounds are formed from atoms of only two different elements, such as, sodium chloride (NaCl), iron(II) sulphide (FeS) and carbon dioxide (CO_2). These are called **binary compounds**. Other compounds contain atoms of more than two elements, for example, calcium carbonate ($CaCO_3$) and copper sulphate ($CuSO_4$).

In order to determine the formula of a binary compound, we need to know how many bonds the atoms of one element will form with the atoms of another. This is called the **combining power** of the element (see Table C 2.18.1).

When using the information in this table you should bear in mind that:

1. It is not possible to combine any two elements to make a compound. In general, compounds are formed between a metal and a non-metal, or two non-metals.

2. When a compound contains a metal, this is always given first.

3. In compounds of metals and non-metals the ending of the non-metal changes to 'ide', for example, oxide, chloride.

4. Some metals have more than one combining power. To show this we show the combining power as a Roman numeral after the name of the metal, for example, copper(I) and copper(II), iron(II) and iron(III).

Combining power		
1	2	3
Hydrogen (H)	Magnesium (Mg)	Aluminium (Al)
Lithium (Li)	Calcium (Ca)	Iron (Fe(III))
Sodium (Na)	Barium (Ba)	Nitrogen (N)
Potassium (K)	Copper (Cu(II))	Phosphorus (P)
Copper (Cu)	Iron (Fe(II))	
Chlorine (Cl)	Zinc (Zn)	
Bromine (Br)	Oxygen (O)	
Iodine (I)	Sulphur (S)	

TABLE C 2.18.1 Combining of common elements

Chemical formula

A simple way to work out the chemical formula of a binary compound is to write the combining powers beneath each

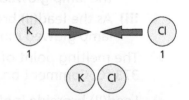

FIG C 2.18.1 The chemical formula of potassium chloride is KCl

element and draw an appropriate number of arrows
(Fig C 2.18.1) from one element to the other element.

The combining power of both potassium and
chlorine is 1. One potassium atom bonds with one
chlorine atom to form potassium chloride.

The combining power of magnesium is 2 and
of bromine is 1 (Fig C 2.18.2) . One magnesium
atom bonds with two bromine atoms to form
magnesium bromide.

Once you are familiar with combining powers, you will
be able to work out the chemical formulae of all binary
compounds.

Activity C 2.18.1

Finding the formulae of binary compounds

Here is what you need:

- small pieces of card (4 cm × 4 cm) × 26

Here is what you should do:

1. Make cards to show the combining power of the
   elements in Table C 2.18.1. Make:

   a) one card for each metal with a combining power
   of 1

   b) three cards for each non-metal with a combining
   power of 1

   c) one card for each element with a combining
   power of 2 or 3.

2. Use your cards to form as many compounds as you
   can. Write the formula of each compound you make,
   for example Fig C 2.18.4 shows why the formula of
   aluminium chloride is $AlCl_3$.

Certain groups of atoms are found together in many
compounds and can pass unchanged through chemical
reactions. These groups are called radicals (see Table
C 2.18.2).

Combining power	
1	2
Hydroxide (OH)	Sulphate (SO_4)
Hydrogencarbonate (HCO_3)	Carbonate (CO_3)
Nitrate (NO_3)	

TABLE C 2.18.2 Combining power of some common radicals

These radicals can combine with metals, for example,
sodium nitrate, $NaNO_3$.

C 2.18

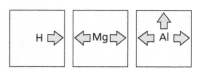

FIG C 2.18.2 The chemical formula of
magnesium bromide is $MgBr_2$

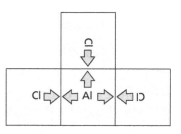

FIG C 2.18.3 Different elements have
different combining powers

FIG C 2.18.4 Aluminium chloride, $AlCl_3$

Key terms

binary compound
formed from the atoms
of only two elements

combining power
number of bonds an
atom can make with
other atoms

Check your understanding

1. Use Table C 2.18.1
   to work out the
   chemical formula of
   each of the following
   binary compounds.

   a) hydrogen bromide

   b) magnesium
   sulphide

   c) aluminium iodide

   d) iron(III) oxide

179

19 Word and symbol equations

A chemical equation describes what happens during a **chemical reaction**. The general form of a chemical equation is:

$$\text{reactant(s)} \rightarrow \text{product(s)}$$

The **reactants** are the chemical or chemicals we start with and the **products** are the chemical or chemicals produced. A simple example is:

$$\text{copper} + \text{oxygen} \rightarrow \text{copper(II) oxide}$$

Copper and oxygen are reactants. Copper(II) oxide is the product.

The simplest way to describe a chemical reaction is by a word equation. This gives the names of the reactants and products. This word equation represents a **synthesis reaction**:

$$\text{iron} + \text{sulphur} \rightarrow \text{iron sulphide}$$
$$\text{(reactants)} \qquad \text{(product)}$$

Word equations are useful but they have their drawbacks.

• They can be long to write.
• They cannot be understood if they are written in another language.
• They don't show the numbers of atoms and molecules involved in a reaction.

In a symbol equation the names of the reactants and products are replaced by symbols:

$$\text{Fe} + \text{S} \rightarrow \text{FeS}$$

• Symbol equations are short to write.
• They can be understood by everybody because the same atomic symbols and formulae are used by scientists of all nationalities.
• They show the numbers of atoms and molecules involved in a reaction.

Although they are less useful, word equations play an important part in learning to write symbol equations.

For example, when charcoal, which is essentially carbon, burns in air it combines with oxygen to form the gas carbon dioxide. This is an example of a **combustion reaction**. It is also an **oxidation reaction** because carbon combines with oxygen. A large amount of heat is also released during this chemical reaction.

The word equation for this reaction is:

carbon + oxygen → carbon dioxide

FIG C 2.19.1 Carbon reacts with oxygen to form carbon dioxide

The symbols for the reactants and product are carbon = C, oxygen = O_2 and carbon dioxide = CO_2. The symbol equation for this reaction is therefore:

$$C + O_2 \rightarrow CO_2$$

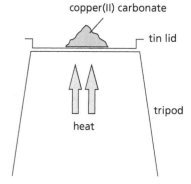

FIG C 2.19.2

Activity C 2.19.1

Writing a chemical equation

Here is what you need:

- copper(II) carbonate
- tin lid
- tripod
- heat source
- eye protection

Here is what you should do:

1. Put a small amount of copper(II) carbonate on a tin lid and stand this on a tripod (Fig C 2.19.2).

2. Gently heat the copper(II) carbonate until no further change takes place. What evidence is there that a chemical reaction has taken place?

3. Carbon dioxide gas has been given off and the solid that remains is copper(II) oxide. Write a word equation for this reaction.

4. The chemical formula of copper(II) carbonate is $CuCO_3$ and the chemical formula for copper(II) oxide is CuO. Write a symbol equation for this reaction.

Check your understanding

1. Write a word equation and then a symbol equation for each of the chemical reactions described below.

   a) Calcium carbonate **decomposes** on heating to form calcium oxide and carbon dioxide gas.

   b) Sulphur reacts with oxygen to form sulphur dioxide gas.

   c) Magnesium reacts with chlorine to form magnesium chloride.

Key terms

chemical reaction process in which atoms of different elements rearrange themselves to form a new substance(s)

reactants starting materials in a chemical reaction

products produced by a chemical reaction

synthesis reaction two or more substances combine to form a single product

combustion reaction substance combines with oxygen and heat is given out

oxidation reaction substance combines with oxygen

decomposition reaction one substance breaks down to form two or more products

20 Law of conservation of mass

Although there are many different possible chemical reactions, they all have one important feature in common:

> During a chemical reaction no mass is lost or gained, therefore the total mass of the products is equal to the total mass of the reactants.

This is the law of conservation of **mass** and is true for all chemical reactions. It might sometimes appear that mass is lost during a chemical reaction but this is due to gaseous products escaping into the air.

For example, here is what happens when 1.00 g of copper(II) carbonate is heated in air.

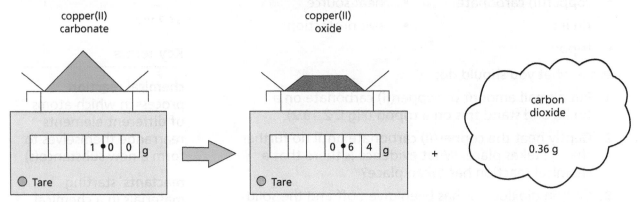

FIG C 2.20.1 Thermal decomposition of copper(II) carbonate

copper(II) carbonate → copper(II) oxide + carbon(II) dioxide

1.00 g   =   0.64 g   +   0.36 g

This is a decomposition reaction in which 1.00 g of copper(II) carbonate decomposes to give 0.64 g of copper(II) oxide and 0.36 g of carbon dioxide gas.

Activity C 2.20.1

Confirming the law of conservation of mass using a precipitation reaction

Here is what you need:
- potassium chloride solution
- lead nitrate solution

- beaker 100 cm³ × 2
- measuring cylinder 10 cm³
- wash bottle containing distilled water
- eye protection

Here is what you should do:

1. Measure about 5 cm³ of potassium chloride solution into a beaker using a measuring cylinder.

2. Thoroughly wash out the measuring cylinder with distilled water.

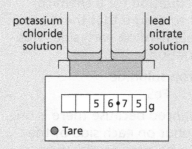

3. Measure about 5 cm³ of lead nitrate solution into the second beaker.

4. Put the beakers on a top-pan balance and record their total mass.

FIG C 2.20.2

5. Pour the contents of one beaker into the other, swirl the mixture and replace the beaker on the balance.

6. What evidence is there that a chemical reaction has taken place?

7. What evidence is there to support the law of conservation of mass?

8. The products of this reaction are lead chloride and potassium nitrate. Write a word equation for the reaction.

Key terms

mass amount of matter

precipitation reaction one in which an insoluble precipitate is formed

Check your understanding

1. Calculate the unknown mass of reactant or product in each of the following chemical reactions:

   a) magnesium + oxygen → magnesium oxide

        1.2 g   0.8 g   ?

   b) calcium carbonate → calcium oxide + carbon dioxide

         1.0 g   0.56 g   ?

   c) copper sulphate + iron → iron sulphate + copper

       15.95 g   ?   15.20 g   6.35 g

   d) potassium iodide + silver nitrate → potassium nitrate + silver iodide

          ?   1.70 g   1.01 g   2.35 g

21 Balancing symbol equations

We are learning how to:

- balance symbol equations which represent chemical reactions

As we have seen from the law of conservation of mass, matter is neither created nor destroyed in a chemical reaction. When writing a symbol equation for a chemical reaction, it is therefore important to ensure that there are equal numbers of atoms of each element on each side. This process is called balancing the equation.

$$\text{iron + sulphur} \rightarrow \text{iron sulphide}$$
$$Fe + S \rightarrow FeS$$

The above equation is already balanced because there is one atom of iron and one atom of sulphur on each side of the equation, but an additional step to balance an equation is often necessary.

Magnesium burns in air with a very bright flame to produce magnesium oxide:

$$\text{magnesium + oxygen} \rightarrow \text{magnesium oxide}$$
$$Mg + O_2 \rightarrow MgO$$

If you count the number of oxygen atoms on both sides of the equation, you will see that an atom of oxygen has been lost. We can correct this by writing a '2' on the right-hand side:

$$Mg + O_2 \rightarrow 2MgO$$

Now the number of oxygen atoms is the same but an atom of magnesium has been added! We must write a '2' on the left-hand side also:

$$2Mg + O_2 \rightarrow 2MgO$$

Now the equation is balanced.

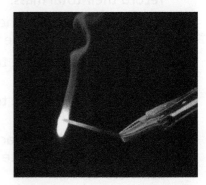

FIG C 2.21.1 Magnesium burns brightly in air

Zinc reacts with dilute hydrochloric acid (Fig C 2.21.2):

$$\text{zinc + hydrochloric acid} \rightarrow \text{zinc chloride + hydrogen}$$
$$Zn + HCl \rightarrow ZnCl_2 + H_2$$

Can you see a problem with this symbol equation? If not then count the atoms on each side of the equation:

Left-hand side	Right-hand side
$1 \times Zn$	$1 \times Zn$
$1 \times H$	$2 \times H$
$1 \times Cl$	$2 \times Cl$

Another 'HCl' must be added to the left-hand side:

$$Zn + 2HCl \rightarrow ZnCl_2 + H_2$$

FIG C 2.21.2 Zinc reacts with dilute acids

The following three steps will help you to write balanced chemical equations.

1. Write a word equation giving the names of the reactant(s) and the product(s).
2. Replace the names with atomic symbols and formulae.
3. If necessary, balance the equation by increasing the proportions of reactants and/or products.

Activity C 2.21.1

Writing a balanced equation for the neutralisation reaction between sodium carbonate (Na_2CO_3) and dilute sulphuric acid (H_2SO_4)

Here is what you need:

- sodium carbonate
- dilute sulphuric acid
- test tube
- wooden splint
- eye protection

Here is what you should do:

1. Put a small amount of sodium carbonate in a test tube.
2. Add enough dilute sulphuric acid to cover the sodium carbonate.
3. What evidence is there that a chemical reaction is taking place? When there is no further reaction, light the end of a wooden splint and hold it into the top of the test tube.
4. The gas produced during this reaction is carbon dioxide. State two properties of this gas based on your observations.
5. The word equation for this reaction is:

   sodium carbonate + dilute sulphuric acid →
   sodium sulphate + carbon dioxide + water

   Write a balanced symbol equation for the reaction.

Check your understanding

1. Write chemical equations for the following reactions using the three-step method described above.

   a) Carbon (C) reacts with oxygen (O_2) to form carbon dioxide (CO_2).

   b) Copper (Cu) reacts with oxygen (O_2) to form copper(II) oxide (CuO).

   c) Magnesium (Mg) reacts with dilute hydrochloric acid (HCl) to form magnesium chloride ($MgCl_2$) and hydrogen (H_2).

Key term

neutralisation chemical reaction in which an acid reacts with an alkali to produce a solution which is neither acidic nor neutral

22 Precipitation reactions and ionic equations

We are learning how to:
- recognise precipitation reactions
- write ionic equations

The **solubility** of a substance compound is determined by how much will dissolve in a given volume of water (or some other solvent). A general summary of the solubility of metal and ammonium compounds in water is given in Table C 2.22.1.

All compounds of ammonia, potassium and sodium are soluble in water. All nitrates are also soluble.

Family of compounds	Soluble	Insoluble
Chlorides, bromides, iodides	All others	Lead and silver
Sulphates	All others	Barium, calcium, lead
Carbonates	Ammonium, potassium, sodium	All others
Nitrates	All	

TABLE C 2.22.1 Solubilities of different families of compounds in water

Precipitation reactions are carried out in solution. A **precipitate** is a solid that separates out from solution during a chemical reaction. In a typical precipitation reaction two soluble reactants form one soluble product and one insoluble product.

Precipitation reactions are useful because the products can be easily separated by filtration. When the reaction mixture is poured into a filter paper, the soluble product passes through as the **filtrate** while the insoluble product forms the **residue**.

Silver iodide is an insoluble compound. It can be made by the reaction of a soluble silver compound with a soluble iodide:

$$AgNO_3 \quad + \quad KI \quad \rightarrow \quad AgI \quad + \quad KNO_3$$

soluble   soluble   insoluble   soluble

Here is another equation describing the same reaction but now the individual ions present in each solution are shown:

$$Ag^+ + NO_3^- + K^+ + I^- \rightarrow AgI + K^+ + NO_3^-$$

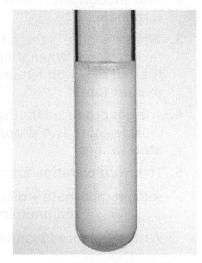

FIG C 2.22.1 Silver iodide precipitate

If you look carefully at this equation, you will see that the nitrate ions, NO_3^-, and potassium ions, K^+, play no part in the reaction. Ions that take no part in a reaction are called spectator ions.

$$Ag^+ + \cancel{NO_3^-} + \cancel{K^+} + I^- \rightarrow AgI + \cancel{K^+} + \cancel{NO_3^-}$$

If the spectator ions are deleted from the equation, what is left is called an ionic equation:

$$Ag^+ + I^- \rightarrow AgI$$

Ionic equations make it easier to see exactly which species are involved in a chemical reaction.

- Spectator ions are those that do not change in a reaction between ionic compounds.

- Ionic equations include only ions that change in a chemical reaction.

Activity C 2.22.1

Making lead iodide by a precipitation reaction

Here is what you need:
- lead nitrate solution
- potassium iodide solution
- test tubes × 2
- boiling tube
- filter funnel
- filter paper
- stand and clamp
- eye protection

Here is what you should do:

1. Support a boiling tube using a stand and clamp. Fold a filter paper and fix it in a filter funnel. Stand the filter funnel in the boiling tube.

2. Pour lead nitrate solution into a test tube until it is about one-third full. Pour a similar amount of potassium iodide solution into a second test tube.

3. Pour the lead nitrate solution into the test tube containing the potassium iodide solution. What is the colour of the precipitate formed?

4. Pour the reaction mixture into the filter paper and leave it to separate.

5. What colour is the filtrate? What colour is the residue?

6. Write a balanced symbol equation for this reaction.

7. Write an ionic equation for this reaction.

8. [STEAM] Using the information on solubility in Table C.22.1, write down the names of 3 other insoluble compounds and write ionic equations for their formation.

Check your understanding

Each of the following equations represents a precipitation reaction. The precipitate formed is written in **bold**.

1. For each equation, rewrite it showing the ions present in the reactants and the products.

   a) $Ca(NO_3)_2 + Na_2CO_3 \rightarrow$ **$CaCO_3$** $+ 2NaNO_3$

   b) $Pb(NO_3)_2 + Na_2SO_4 \rightarrow$ **$PbSO_4$** $+ 2NaNO_3$

   c) $AgNO_3 + KCl \rightarrow$ **$AgCl$** $+ KNO_3$

2. Delete the spectator ions and write an ionic equation for the reaction.

Key terms

solubility amount of solid that will dissolve in a given amount of a solvent

precipitate insoluble solid formed during a chemical reaction

filtrate passes through a filter paper during filtration

residue retained by a filter paper during filtration

23 Displacement reactions

We are learning how to:

- recognise displacement reactions
- write ionic equations to represent displacement reactions

In a **displacement reaction** one substance displaces another. A more reactive metal will displace the ions of a less reactive metal from a solution of its salts. For example, Fig C 2.23.1 shows what happens when pieces of magnesium are added to copper sulphate(II) solution.

Magnesium is a more reactive metal than copper so magnesium atoms displace copper(II) ions from solution. We observe during the reaction that:

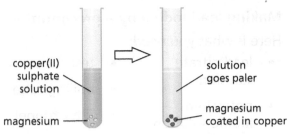

FIG C 2.23.1 Displacement reaction between magnesium and copper(II) sulphate solution

- The copper(II) sulphate solution becomes paler. As the Cu^{2+} ions are displaced, their concentration decreases, hence the loss of colour.

- The pieces of magnesium turn brown. The copper(II) ions become copper atoms and these are deposited on the surface of the pieces of magnesium. They eventually cause the reaction to stop.

The ionic equation for this reaction is:

$$Mg + Cu^{2+} \rightarrow Mg^{2+} + Cu$$

Notice that the reverse reaction does not take place. If pieces of copper are placed in magnesium sulphate solution, no reaction will occur. This is because copper is less reactive than magnesium.

We can also carry out displacement reactions with chlorine, bromine and iodine.

As was the case with the metals, a more reactive element will displace a less reactive element. In this case:

- Chlorine is the most reactive of these elements so it will displace bromine from bromides and iodine from iodides.

- Bromine will displace iodine from iodides.

- Iodine is the least reactive element so it will not displace either of the other elements.

When chlorine water is shaken with potassium bromide solution, bromide ions are displaced and bromine is formed. Bromine is more soluble in a solvent called **hexane** than it is in water so if a small amount of hexane is added

Interesting fact

In countries that have cold winters, people may use hand warmers to warm themselves. One type consists of a metal powder and a different metal salt solution held in separate containers. When the pack is activated a displacement reaction occurs that gives out heat.

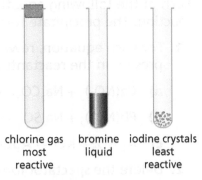

chlorine gas most reactive   bromine liquid   iodine crystals least reactive

FIG C 2.23.2 Chlorine, bromine and iodine

the bromine will dissolve in it forming an orange-brown layer and it makes the displacement more obvious.

The ionic equation for this reaction is:

$$Cl_2 + 2Br^- \rightarrow 2Cl^- + Br_2$$

Similarly, chlorine will displace iodide ions from solution forming iodine. This dissolves in the hexane layer giving a purple solution.

The ionic equation for this reaction is:

$$Cl_2 + 2I^- \rightarrow 2Cl^- + I_2$$

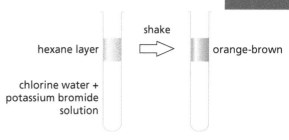

FIG C 2.23.3 Chlorine displaces bromide ions from solution

Activity C 2.23.1

Displacing iodide ions from solution with bromine

Here is what you need:

- dilute bromine water
- potassium iodide solution
- hexane
- test tube
- eye protection

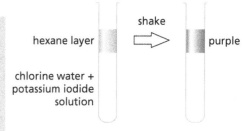

FIG C 2.23.4 Chlorine displaces iodide ions from solution

Here is what you should do:

1. Pour bromine water into the test tube to a depth of about 1 cm.

2. Add a similar volume of potassium iodide solution to the test tube.

3. Pour hexane into the test tube to form a layer about 0.5 cm deep above the aqueous layer. Fix a stopper in the test tube and gently shake the mixture for 10 seconds.

4. Allow the layers of water and hexane to settle out. What colour is the hexane layer?

5. Write an ionic equation for the displacement reaction that took place.

Check your understanding

1. Zinc is more reactive than copper. Predict what will happen in these cases and write an ionic equation if appropriate.

   a) Zinc powder is added to an aqueous solution of copper(II) sulphate.

   b) Copper powder is added to an aqueous solution of zinc sulphate.

Key terms

displacement reaction a reaction in which one species displaces another

hexane an organic solvent

24 Oxidation and combustion reactions

We are learning how to:

- classify oxidation reactions in terms of combining with oxygen
- describe combustion as an oxidation reaction

Oxidation ⟫⟫

Oxidation describes a chemical reaction in which something reacts with oxygen. Oxidation reactions may be fast or slow.

Fireworks contain a mixture of metal salts together with an **oxidising agent** which provides oxygen. When the firework is ignited, the metal salts are oxidised providing a colourful display. The oxidation reaction is over in a few seconds.

When iron is left exposed to moisture and oxygen in the air, it is oxidised to brown iron(II) oxide, which we call rust. This reaction is very slow and we would not observe any change from day to day.

Air is composed of about one fifth oxygen and four fifths nitrogen so is in a sense 'dilute' oxygen. Substances are oxidised much more vigorously in pure oxygen than in air.

When elements react with oxygen, they form oxides. Magnesium burns in oxygen to form magnesium oxide:

$$2Mg + O_2 \rightarrow 2MgO$$

FIG C 2.24.1 Oxidation reactions

Activity C 2.24.1

Making magnesium oxide

Here is what you need:

- strip of magnesium ribbon
- heat source
- tongs
- eye protection

Here is what you should do:

1. Carefully examine the magnesium ribbon.
2. Hold one end of the magnesium ribbon with tongs and hold the other end in the heat source until it ignites.
3. Hold the ribbon above the bench while it burns and avoid looking at it.
4. When the ribbon has finished burning, examine what remains.
5. What evidence is there from your observations that a chemical reaction has taken place?

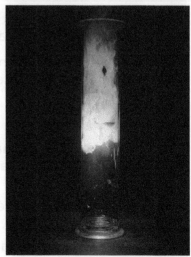

FIG C 2.24.2 Oxidising magnesium

6. Predict whether the mass of the magnesium oxide formed will be greater than, equal to or less than the mass of magnesium used.

7. Using a dot (·) to represent the outer electrons of an atom of magnesium and a cross (X) to represent the outer electrons of an atom of oxygen, draw dot-and-cross diagrams to show how the ionic bonds form in magnesium oxide.

8. [STEAM] Describe how you could use this experiment to demonstrate that mass is neither gained nor lost during a chemical reaction.

FIG C 2.24.3 Charcoal is an impure form of carbon

Combustion reactions

Combustion is another term for burning. When fuels burn they undergo oxidation. Charcoal is an impure form of carbon. When it burns in a good supply of air, the main product is carbon dioxide:

$$C + O_2 \rightarrow CO_2$$

Methane and fuels like petrol and diesel are **hydrocarbons**. They are composed of carbon and hydrogen only and burn in a good supply of air to produce carbon dioxide and water:

$$CH_4 + 2O_2 \rightarrow CO_2 + 2H_2O$$

When carbon-containing fuels are burned in a poor supply of air, only partial combustion takes place. Both carbon soot and carbon monoxide gas may be produced:

$$2C + O_2 \rightarrow 2CO$$

Not only does partial combustion produce less heat energy but carbon monoxide is a very poisonous gas. If the concentration of this gas in the air increases in an enclosed space, like a poorly ventilated room, people will lose consciousness and may die.

Check your understanding

1. A stove produces heat by burning propane gas.
   a) The formula of propane is C_3H_8. Explain why propane is a hydrocarbon.
   b) Which gas from the air combines with propane when it burns?
   c) Give the names and formulae of the gases produced when propane burns in a good supply of air.
   d) A label on the stove warns the user not to obstruct the panel where air is drawn into the stove. Explain why it might be dangerous to do this.

Interesting fact

Carbon dioxide is an important **greenhouse gas** believed by many scientists to be responsible for **global warming**. In the future these traditional fuels might be replaced by hydrogen gas, which burns to produce only water.

$$2H_2 + O_2 \rightarrow 2H_2O$$

Key terms

oxidising agent chemical which releases oxygen

combustion another term for burning

hydrocarbon compound composed of atoms of hydrogen and carbon only

greenhouse gas a gas that contributes to the greenhouse effect

global warming small but significant increase in the average surface temperature of the Earth

25 Synthesis reactions

We are learning how to:
- describe the features of a synthesis reaction

A **synthesis** reaction is a chemical reaction in which two or more simple substances combine to form a more complex product. The reactants might be elements or compounds but the product is always a compound.

Some of the reactions you have already studied in this unit, like the formation of magnesium oxide from magnesium and oxygen, are synthesis reactions.

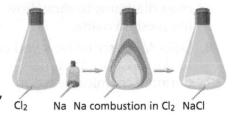

Cl_2 Na Na combustion in Cl_2 NaCl

$$2Na + Cl_2 \longrightarrow 2NaCl$$

FIG C 2.25.1 Synthesis of sodium chloride

Metals and non-metals ⟩⟩

Synthesis reactions often take place between reactive metals and non-metals. For example, sodium burns in chlorine gas to produce sodium chloride. The reaction is very vigorous and a large amount of heat is given out.

$$2Na + Cl_2 \rightarrow 2NaCl$$

A synthesis reaction may not be the best way to prepare a compound. There are easier and safer ways to make sodium chloride involving less vigorous reactions, such as the neutralisation reaction between dilute hydrochloric acid and sodium hydroxide solution. You will learn more about neutralisation in Unit C 3.

Interesting fact

Synthesis reactions are also known as direct combination reactions.

Activity C 2.25.1

The synthesis of copper(II) oxide

Here is what you need:
- copper powder
- tin lid
- tripod and gauze
- heat source
- balance
- eye protection

Here is what you should do:
1. Weigh out about 2 g of copper powder. The exact amount is not important, but you must record the actual mass used.
2. Put the copper powder on a tin lid and place this on a tripod and gauze.
3. Heat the copper powder for several minutes and then allow it to cool.
4. Reweigh the powder on the tin lid.
5. What visible evidence is there that a chemical reaction has taken place?
6. Comment on any change of mass that you observe and explain your observation.

Non-metals

Synthesis reactions also take place between non-metals. In lesson C 2.24 we saw how the non-metallic elements carbon and hydrogen combine with oxygen during combustion.

Other non-metals, like phosphorus and sulphur, readily combine with elements like oxygen and chlorine to form oxides and chlorides respectively.

Industrial processes

Synthesis reactions are the basis of some important industrial processes.

In the Haber process, nitrogen and hydrogen combine to form ammonia:

$$N_2 + 3H_2 \rightarrow 2NH_3$$

This reaction is extremely important because it is the first step in producing ammonium nitrate fertiliser. Nitric acid, HNO_3, is made by the oxidation of ammonia. Ammonia and nitric acid then combine to form ammonium nitrate:

$$NH_3 + HNO_3 \rightarrow NH_4NO_3$$

Every year farmers around the world use millions of tonnes of ammonium nitrate to improve the yield of food crops.

In the Contact process, used to make sulphuric acid, the first stage is a synthesis reaction between sulphur and oxygen to form the gas sulphur dioxide. Sulphur dioxide is further oxidised to sulphur trioxide and then converted to sulphuric acid. In each step a more complex chemical is made:

sulphur → sulphur dioxide → sulphur trioxide → sulphuric acid

Apart from its use in car batteries, sulphuric acid is an important chemical used to make a range of products.

FIG C 2.25.2 Phosphorus burns in air to produce phosphorus pentoxide

FIG C 2.25.3 Ammonium nitrate fertiliser

Key term

synthesis combining components to form something new

Check your understanding

1. Calcium is a reactive metal. When heated strongly in air, it burns to form a cloud of calcium oxide, CaO.
   a) What type of reaction takes place?
   b) Write a balanced symbol equation for this reaction.
   c) Calcium oxide reacts with water to form calcium hydroxide. Write a balanced symbol equation for this reaction.
   d) A second method for making calcium hydroxide is to react calcium with water. Why might a chemist choose to make calcium hydroxide by the second method rather than the first one described?
2. [STEAM] Farmers sometimes spread lime on their fields in the form of calcium hydroxide to increase the pH of the soil. Research why this should be done at a different time of the year to spreading ammonium nitrate fertiliser.

26 Decomposition reactions

We are learning how to:

- describe the features of a decomposition reaction

In a decomposition reaction a complex compound breaks down, or decomposes, into simpler products. Decomposition is often brought about by heating a substance and is therefore described as **thermal decomposition**.

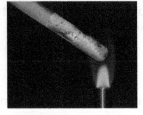

FIG C 2.26.1 Thermal decomposition of lead(II) nitrate

Decomposition of nitrates

Metal nitrates contain the nitrate ion, NO_3^-. With the exception of sodium nitrate and potassium nitrate, all metal nitrates decompose on heating to give nitrogen dioxide and oxygen.

The equation for the decomposition of lead(II) nitrate is:

$$2Pb(NO_3)_2 \rightarrow 2PbO + 4NO_2 + O_2$$

lead(II) oxide   nitrogen dioxide   oxygen

Nitrogen dioxide is recognisable by its brown colour and its unpleasant pungent odour. This reaction should be carried out in a fume cupboard or near an open window.

The presence of oxygen can be shown by relighting a glowing wooden splint (Fig C 2.26.2).

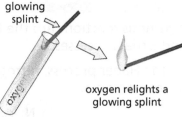

FIG C 2.26.2 Test for oxygen

Decomposition of carbonates

Metal carbonates contain the carbonate ion, CO_3^{2-}. With the exception of sodium carbonate and potassium carbonate, all metal carbonates decompose on heating.

The equation for the decomposition of copper(II) carbonate is:

$$CuCO_3 \rightarrow CuO + CO_2$$

copper(II) oxide   carbon dioxide

The reaction produces carbon dioxide. The presence of this gas can be shown by turning limewater milky (Fig C 2.26.4).

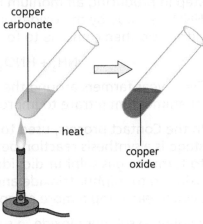

FIG C 2.26.3 Thermal decomposition of copper(II) carbonate

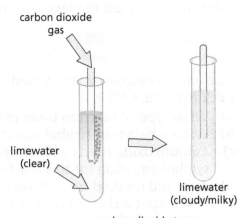

FIG C 2.26.4 Test for carbon dioxide

Here is what you need:

- copper(II) carbonate
- sodium carbonate
- sodium nitrate
- limewater
- wooden splint
- heat source
- test tubes × 4
- eye protection

Here is what you should do:

1. Pour limewater into a test tube to a depth of about 1 cm.

2. Put some copper(II) carbonate powder in a test tube to a depth of about 1 cm. Heat the copper(II) carbonate and observe any changes that take place.

3. Carefully pour the gases above the copper(II) carbonate into the tube containing limewater.

4. Shake the limewater and see if it goes cloudy.

5. Summarise the evidence that copper(II) carbonate decomposes on heating.

6. Repeat the same test using sodium carbonate.

7. Does sodium carbonate decompose on heating? Explain your answer.

8. Pour a small amount of sodium nitrate powder in a test tube. Heat the sodium nitrate and observe any changes that take place.

9. Introduce a glowing wooden splint into the top of the test tube.

10. Does sodium nitrate produce nitrogen dioxide and/or oxygen when it is heated? Explain your answer.

Interesting fact

Nitrogen triiodide (NI_3) is an example of a contact explosive. A mechanical shock will cause it to decompose into nitrogen and iodine.

FIG C 2.26.5 Decomposing nitrogen triiodide

Nitrogen triiodide is so sensitive that even stroking it with a feather (attached to a wooden rod) is sufficient to cause decomposition.

Check your understanding

1. The following equation represents the thermal decomposition of potassium nitrate to form potassium nitrite:

$$2KNO_3 \rightarrow 2KNO_2 + O_2$$

potassium   potassium
nitrate   nitrite

   a) How is the decomposition of potassium nitrate different from that of many other metal nitrates?

   b) Describe a test you could carry out to demonstrate that oxygen is produced.

Key term

thermal decomposition breaking down as a result of heating

27 Exothermic and endothermic reactions

We are learning how to:

- describe exothermic processes as those that give out heat
- describe endothermic processes as those that take in heat

Exothermic and endothermic

During a chemical reaction chemical bonds are broken and new bonds are formed.

- Breaking bonds requires energy, so energy is taken in.

- Making bonds releases energy, so energy is given out.

FIG C 2.27.1 Combustion reactions are highly exothermic

In an **exothermic reaction** the energy needed to break bonds is less than the energy given out when new bonds are formed. The result is that energy is given out in the form of heat, and sometimes of light.

The combustion of fuels is highly exothermic. We use the heat given out to keep warm and to cook our food.

In an **endothermic reaction** the energy needed to break bonds is more than the energy given out when new bonds are formed. The result is that energy is taken in.

Photosynthesis, by which plants make food (Fig C 2.27.2), is an endothermic process. Energy is absorbed from sunlight.

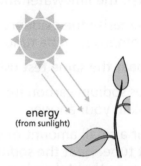

energy
(from sunlight)

FIG C 2.27.2 Photosynthesis is an endothermic reaction

Temperature change

Many of the reactions we carry out in the laboratory are exothermic but they don't burst into flame so we cannot see that energy is given out. We can, however, feel that a reaction mixture is getting warmer.

We can also measure any temperature change using a thermometer. If a reaction is exothermic, heat is given out and the temperature of the reaction mixture rises.

Endothermic reactions in the laboratory are less common, but other processes may be endothermic. When some chemicals dissolve in water to form solutions there is a fall in temperature as heat is removed from the solution.

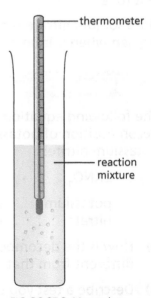

thermometer

reaction mixture

FIG C 2.27.3 Measuring temperature change

Activity C 2.27.1

Exothermic and endothermic changes

Here is what you need:

- a thermometer
- a test tube containing a 1 cm depth of dilute hydrochloric acid and a second test tube containing a similar volume of dilute sodium hydroxide solution
- a test tube containing a 1 cm depth of copper(II) sulphate solution and 1 g of iron filings
- a test tube containing a 1 cm depth of distilled water and 1 g of ammonium chloride
- a test tube containing a 1 cm depth of dilute sulphuric acid and 1 g of zinc powder
- a test tube containing a 1 cm depth of ethanoic acid and 1 g of sodium carbonate powder
- eye protection

Here is what you should do:

1. For each of the above, put the thermometer into the first test tube and note the temperature.

2. Add the contents of the second test tube or the solid and gently mix the substances together.

3. After a couple of minutes note the temperature of the reaction mixture.

4. State whether each change is exothermic or endothermic. Give your results in the form of a table.

> **Interesting fact**
>
> Although combustion reactions are highly exothermic, a small amount of energy has to be provided in order to start a reaction. This is why you need a match to light a fire. Once the fire is burning you get a lot more energy out than you put in.

Key terms

exothermic reaction
a reaction in which energy is given out

endothermic reaction
a reaction in which energy is taken in

Check your understanding

1. In cold countries, people sometimes use hand warmers (FIG C 2.27.4) to warm themselves on a cold day.

   The pack contains iron powder and salt solution in a porous medium. When the pack is opened oxygen from the air reacts with the iron.

   a) Is the reaction between iron and oxygen exothermic or endothermic? Explain how you know.

   b) What is the name of the substance formed during the reaction?

   c) The finer the iron particles are the more quickly the reaction takes place. Suggest why the pack contains coarse particles of iron.

FIG C 2.27.4

Review of Chemical bonding, formulae and equations

- Atomic symbols are a shorthand way of representing elements or atoms of elements.

- Modern atomic symbols consist of one or two letters. When there are two letters the first is written in upper case and the second in lower case.

- A molecule consists of two or more atoms chemically bonded together.

- Some elements exist as molecules.

- A compound contains atoms of different elements.

- An atom is the smallest particle of an element that can take part in a chemical reaction.

- An atom contains the sub-atomic particles: protons, neutrons and electrons.

- Protons and neutrons have a relative mass of 1; electrons have a relative mass of 0.

- Protons and electrons have equal but opposite charges.

- Electronic configuration is the arrangement of electrons in an atom and can be represented diagrammatically or numerically.

- Ions are formed by the loss or gain of electrons by atoms.

- Positively charged ions are called cations.

- Negatively charged ions are called anions.

- Ions combine to form compounds that are neutral.

- Ionic compounds generally have high melting points and high boiling points.

- Ionic compounds conduct electricity when molten or in aqueous solution but not when solid.

- Many ionic compounds are soluble in water but a significant number are effectively insoluble.

- Binary compounds contain atoms of only two different elements.

- Compounds form between a metal and a non-metal, or two non-metals.

- Combining power is the number of bonds an atom of an element can make with other atoms.

- A chemical equation describes what happens during a chemical reaction.

- A word equation identifies substances by name, and a symbol equation identifies them by their symbols and formulae.

- During a chemical reaction mass is neither created nor destroyed.

- In a balanced equation the same number of atoms of each element is present on the right-hand and left-hand sides of the equation.

- Equations cannot be balanced by altering the formulae of compounds.

- A precipitation reaction is one in which an insoluble solid product is formed.

- An ionic equation includes only the ions involved in a chemical reaction.

- Spectator ions are ions that are present during a chemical reaction but take no part in it.

- In a displacement reaction atoms of one element displace ions of another.

- A more reactive element will displace the ions of a less reactive element from a solution.

- An oxidation reaction occurs when a substance combines with oxygen.

- Combustion of fuels is a common example of an oxidation reaction.

- A synthesis reaction is a chemical reaction in which two or more simple substances combine to form a more complex product.

- A decomposition reaction is a chemical reaction in which a complex substances breaks down into simpler products.

- In an exothermic reaction heat is given out and the temperature of the reaction mixture rises.

- In an endothermic reaction heat is taken in and the temperature of the reaction mixture decreases.

Review questions on Chemical bonding, formulae and equations

Knowledge and understanding

1. a) Give the atomic symbols for each of the following elements:

i) sulphur **ii)** iron   **iii)** barium   **iv)** bromine

b) Which elements are represented by the following atomic symbols?

i) Ca   **ii)** N   **iii)** Ar   **iv)** Na

2. Write the formula of the ions formed by the following elements:

a) bromine   **b)** magnesium   **c)** sulphur   **d)** lithium   **e)** iron

3. Give the electronic configuration of each of the following ions:

a) Cl^- **b)** Na^+ **c)** O^{2-} **d)** N^{3-} **e)** Ca^{2+}

4. a) Explain why solid sodium chloride doesn't conduct electricity, but molten sodium chloride does.

b) In what other form does sodium chloride conduct electricity?

5. When a mixture of iron and sulphur is heated, iron sulphide (FeS) is produced.

a) What type of reaction takes place?

b) Write a balanced symbol equation for this reaction.

c) Suggest one difference in the properties of iron and iron sulphide.

Process skills

6. Using the colour key given in Fig C 2.13.1, draw each of the following molecules from the description given. State whether each is a molecule of an element or a compound.

a) A molecule of hydrogen consists of two atoms joined together.

b) A molecule of ammonia consists of three atoms of hydrogen joined to one atom of nitrogen.

c) A molecule of chlorine consists of two atoms joined together.

7. Draw a diagram of an atom that contains two protons, two neutrons and two electrons. Choose appropriate symbols for these particles and include a key alongside your drawing.

8. Draw the electronic configuration of atoms of the following elements and alongside each drawing show the electronic configuration in numerical form.

a) magnesium   **b)** fluorine

c) lithium   **d)** argon

9. Predict the formula of each of the following compounds.

a) potassium iodide   **b)** water   **c)** iron(III) oxide

10. Write a word equation and then a symbol equation for each of these reactions.

   a) Copper(II) carbonate is heated to form copper(II) oxide and carbon dioxide gas.

   b) Hydrogen reacts with chlorine to form hydrogen chloride gas.

   c) Barium reacts with iodine to form barium iodide.

   d) When iron(II) oxide is heated with aluminium, iron and aluminium oxide are formed.

11. Rewrite the following chemical equations so that they are balanced.

   a) $CuO + HCl \rightarrow CuCl_2 + H_2O$

   b) $MgBr_2 + AgNO_3 \rightarrow AgBr + Mg(NO_3)_2$

   c) $Al + O_2 \rightarrow Al_2O_3$

   d) $CH_4 + O_2 \rightarrow CO_2 + H_2O$

12. Describe the chemical reactions represented by each the following equations in words.

   a) $2Cu + O_2 \rightarrow 2CuO$

   b) $Fe + 2HCl \rightarrow FeCl_2 + H_2$

   c) $ZnO + H_2SO_4 \rightarrow ZnSO_4 + H_2O$

   d) $K_2CO_3 + 2HCl \rightarrow 2KCl + CO_2 + H_2O$

13. Each of the following equations represents a precipitation reaction. The precipitate is written in **bold**. For each equation, rewrite it showing the ions present in the reactants and the products. Delete the spectator ions and write an ionic equation for the reaction.

   a) $Mg(NO_3)_2 + K_2CO_3 \rightarrow$ **$MgCO_3$** $+ 2KNO_3$

   b) $CaCl_2 + Na_2SO_4 \rightarrow$ **$CaSO_4$** $+ 2NaCl$

14. a) Explain why zinc powder will displace iron from a solution of iron(II) sulphate but copper powder will not.

   b) Write an ionic equation for the displacement reaction between zinc and iron(II) sulphate.

   c) When carrying out this reaction a student noticed that the test tube containing the reaction mixture felt warm. Explain this observation.

15. Ethanol is sometimes used as a fuel. It has the formula C_2H_6O.

   a) Explain whether ethanol is a hydrocarbon or not.

   b) What type of reaction is combustion?

   c) Name the gases produced when ethanol is burned in a good supply of air.

   d) Explain why burning ethanol in a poor supply of air might produce carbon monoxide gas.

16. The following word equation shows what happened when a sample of magnesium carbonate was strongly heated:

   magnesium carbonate $\rightarrow$ magnesium oxide + carbon dioxide

   a) What type of reaction took place?

   b) Write a balanced symbol equation for this reaction.

   c) Give details of a test you could carry out to demonstrate that carbon dioxide gas is evolved.

29 An aid for learning about bonding

Ionic compounds contain positively charged ions, or cations, and negatively charged ions, or anions. Cations and anions combine in small whole numbers to form compounds.

The salt that we sometimes sprinkle on the food we eat is an example of an ionic compound. Its chemical name is sodium chloride and it has the formula NaCl.

Sodium ions have the formula Na^+ and chloride ions have the formula Cl^- so they combine in the ratio of 1 : 1. Other cations, however, may have charges of 2^+ and 3^+ while other anions may have charges of 2^- and 3^-.

In order to make compounds (which are always neutral) it is sometimes necessary to combine cations and anions in ratios other than 1 : 1. This can be a bit confusing for students.

FIG STEAM C 2.29.1 Salt is an example of an ionic compound

1. You are going to work in a small group to produce a teaching aid that a teacher can use in the classroom to help students understand about bonding in ionic compounds. The tasks are:

   - To look back at the unit content to make sure you understand about ions.
   - To research how reference sources like books and the Internet explain the formation of ionic compounds.
   - To plan your teaching aid and then make it.
   - To try out your teaching aid on a group of students from another class and assess whether they find it helpful.
   - To compile a presentation during which you will demonstrate how your teaching aid should be used.

   a) Look back through the unit and particularly Section C2.18, which describes combining power, and Section C2.13, which describes ions. Make sure that you understand how cations and anions combine to form compounds.

   b) Look at how the formation of ionic compounds is illustrated in some textbooks. You have already carried out an activity in which different ions were represented by cards and compounds were made by combining cards. Look at how the formation of ionic compounds is shown on the Internet. You might find that video sequences, models or cartoons are used.

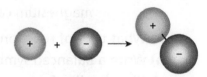

FIG STEAM C 2.29.2 An example from a textbook showing how coloured balls may be used to represent ions

What are the good features of what you have seen that you would like to incorporate in your aid? For example, was colour used to good effect?

What are the bad features of what you have seen that you would like to avoid in your aid? For example, did things become too complicated too quickly?

c) How are you going to demonstrate how ions combine in a simple and entertaining way? Here is one example that might give you some ideas.

Some important features of the above you might consider:

- Cations and anions are represented by different colours.
- Cations have hooks and anions have eyes.
- The charge on the ion is represented by that number of hooks/eyes.

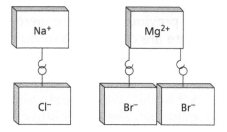

FIG STEAM C 2.29.3 Representing ionic compounds using blocks

What features do you think are important in a good teaching aid? Here are some suggestions:

- Robust
- Easy to use
- Large enough to see clearly
- Material can be obtained easily or cheaply
- Materials are easy to work with.

Design your aid incorporating those features that you think are important. Once you are happy with your design, make a list of the materials and tools that you will need. Once you have collected what you need, make your aid.

d) Once your aid is built you need to try it out with some students from another class. How are you going to decide whether it helped them understand ionic compounds or not?

Here are some ideas:

- You could interview the students.
- You could ask students to complete a questionnaire. You will have to design this in advance of the trial.
- You could ask them to answer the same questions about ionic compounds both before and after the trial. If your teaching aid has worked, you might expect individual marks on the test to improve. You will need to write the questions in advance of the trial.

e) Prepare a presentation in which you describe your teaching aid and demonstrate how it should be used. You should discuss how you trialled your aid and how you assessed whether it was successful or not. You should also describe how, as a result of the trial, your aid might be modified to make it even more effective.

30 Acids and alkalis

We are learning how to:

- classify substances as acids or alkalis

Chemical compounds can be classified into groups according to their composition and their chemistry. For example, in the previous unit there were several examples of **oxides**. These are compounds in which a metallic or a non-metallic element combines with oxygen. Copper(II) oxide and carbon dioxide are both examples of oxides.

In this unit you will learn about some other groups of chemicals called **acids** and **alkalis**. You will also find out how acids and alkalis combine to form **salts**.

The terms acid and alkali may be unfamiliar to you. However, these substances are found in a variety of products that you use, and maybe eat, every day.

FIG C 3.30.1 a) Fruit contains acids b) Baking soda is an alkali

As you will find out, some acids and alkalis are harmless while others are hazardous and must be handled with great care.

FIG C 3.30.2 These household chemicals may contain acids or alkalis

You might observe that some of the reagent bottles in the laboratory carry warning labels like the one in Fig C 3.30.3.

Signs like this warn people of potential hazards. Both acids and alkalis may be corrosive. This means they will attack skin and also materials like clothing.

FIG C 3.30.3 Corrosive warning sign

Activity C 3.30.1

Identifying acids and alkalis in everyday substances

The packaging of products often contains information about what they contain.

1. Examine the packaging of some foods and household chemicals like cleaning agents, indigestion tablets and toothpaste.

2. Look out for the key word: 'acid'.

3. Look out for the key words: 'alkali', 'hydroxide' and 'carbonate'. If any of these are present, the substance contains an alkali.

4. Present your results in the form of a table with separate columns for acids and alkalis.

Check your understanding

1. State and explain whether each of the following statements is true or not.

   a) Alkalis are a group of chemicals with similar properties.

   b) All acids are harmful and should not be eaten.

   c) Some household chemicals contain alkalis.

   d) Many fruits contain alkalis.

   e) The acids and alkalis used in the laboratory are potentially hazardous.

Interesting fact

Some of the vitamins we need in order to remain healthy are actually acids. For example, the chemical name of vitamin C, which we obtain from fresh fruits and vegetables, is ascorbic acid.

Key terms

oxides a group of chemicals formed when elements combine with oxygen

acids a group of chemicals which have similar properties

alkalis a group of chemicals which have similar properties

salts a group of chemicals formed from acids and alkalis

31 Identifying acids

We are learning how to:

- distinguish between substances that are acids and alkalis
- explain the use of an acid–alkali indicator
- give the colour change of an indicator when it is in contact with an acid

Identifying acids

Activity C 3.31.1

Exploring how indicators change colour with different acids

Here is what you need:

- hydrochloric acid
- sulphuric acid
- nitric acid
- red and blue litmus paper
- phenolphthalein

- methyl orange
- test tubes
- tweezers
- droppers
- eye protection

SAFETY

Observe the safety icon on the acid bottles. All indicator papers should be held with tweezers. Avoid spillage.

Here is what you should do:

1. Copy this table.

Acid	Indicator	Colour change
hydrochloric (HCl) sulphuric (H_2SO_4) nitric (HNO_3)	red litmus paper	
hydrochloric sulphuric nitric	blue litmus paper	
hydrochloric sulphuric nitric	phenolphthalein	
hydrochloric sulphuric nitric	methyl orange	

2. Pull up a dropper full of hydrochloric acid from one of the test tubes.

3. Squeeze one drop of hydrochloric acid onto a piece of each of the coloured indicator papers and record the colour you observe.

4. Squeeze a small amount of hydrochloric acid into each of two test tubes.

5. Add one drop of the liquid indicators into each of the two test tubes of hydrochloric acid. Record the colour change you observe.

6. Wash out all the test tubes and droppers thoroughly.

7. Repeat steps 2 to 6 for sulphuric acid and then for nitric acid.

8. Compare the results you found for the various acids. Did all the acids give the same results for each indicator?

The word **acid** is from the Latin *acidus*, meaning sour. An acid is a chemical substance. Solutions formed from these chemical substances usually have a sour taste. In order to identify acids **indicators** are used. Indicators are made from special dyes and the results of your experiments should show the colour changes.

> **Interesting fact**
>
> Most fruits contain acids, such as citric acid, but these are weak acids and we can eat them without coming to any harm. They also provide the tangy flavours of fruits.

Activity C 3.31.2

Check your breath

In this activity you will explore the gas that is exhaled from your body.

Here is what you need:

- test tubes × 2
- universal indicator
- dropper
- drinking straws

Here is what you should do:

1. Add a little water to two clean test tubes.

2. Put one drop of universal indicator into one of the test tubes and observe its colour.

3. Put a straw into each test tube.

4. Ask a volunteer to gently breathe out a few breaths through the straw into each test tube.

5. Is there a colour change in the indicator?

FIG C 3.31.1 Carrying out the experiment

Carbon dioxide is a naturally occurring gas that is important for photosynthesis. It is produced during respiration, decay, fermentation, combustion and volcanic eruptions. Carbon dioxide dissolves in water to form carbonic acid.

Check your understanding

1. What colour changes are observed when the following are added to an acid?

   a) blue litmus paper

   b) phenolphthalein

   c) methyl orange

2. Name three common acids.

Key terms

acid a member of a group of substances that turn blue litmus paper red

indicators substances that change colour depending on whether an acid or alkali is present

32 Identifying alkalis

We are learning how to:

- distinguish between substances that are acids and those that are alkalis
- give the colour change of an indicator when it is in contact with an alkali

Identifying alkalis ⟫⟫

Activity C 3.32.1

Exploring alkalis

Here is what you need:

- sodium hydroxide
- ammonium hydroxide
- calcium hydroxide
- blue litmus paper
- red litmus paper
- phenolphthalein

- methyl orange
- test tubes
- tweezers
- droppers
- eye protection

 SAFETY

Observe the safety icon on the alkali bottles. All indicator papers should be held with tweezers. Avoid spillage.

Here is what you should do:

1. Copy the table.

Alkali	Indicator	Colour change
sodium hydroxide (NaOH) ammonium hydroxide (NH_4OH) calcium hydroxide ($Ca(OH)_2$)	blue litmus paper	
sodium hydroxide ammonium hydroxide calcium hydroxide	red litmus paper	
sodium hydroxide ammonium hydroxide calcium hydroxide	phenolphthalein	
sodium hydroxide ammonium hydroxide calcium hydroxide	methyl orange	

2. Pull up a dropper full of sodium hydroxide solution from one of the test tubes.

3. Squeeze one drop of sodium hydroxide onto a piece of each of the coloured indicator papers and record the colour you observe.

4. Squeeze a small amount of sodium hydroxide solution into each of two test tubes.

5. Pour one drop of each of the liquid indicators into each of the two test tubes of sodium hydroxide solution. Record the colour change you observe.

6. Wash out all the test tubes and droppers thoroughly.

7. Repeat steps 2 to 6 for ammonium hydroxide and then for calcium hydroxide.

8. Compare the results you found for the various alkalis. Did all the alkalis give the same results for each indicator?

The word **alkali** is of Arabic origin, meaning dry. Alkalis belong to the set of bases but they are soluble in water, hence the name **hydroxide**. Dilute solutions of alkalis feel soapy and have a bitter taste. All alkalis conduct electricity. Alkalis can be identified by their colour changes with indicators.

Ammonia is an alkali commonly used as a household cleaner. Other household cleaners such as oven cleaner and scouring creams are also alkaline. Common baking powder is an alkali used in cooking.

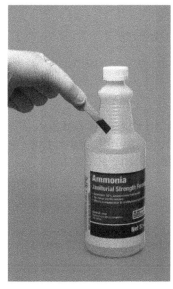

FIG C 3.32.1 Household ammonia solution is strongly alkaline

Interesting fact

Saliva is mildly alkaline. This helps to counteract the acids present in many foods.

Key terms

alkali a member of a group of substances that turn red litmus paper blue

hydroxide a compound of a metal with hydrogen and oxygen, which is often basic; if it is soluble it will form an alkaline solution

Check your understanding

1. Name three common alkalis.

2. What is the effect of an alkali on red litmus paper?

33 Acids and the pH scale

We are learning how to:

- distinguish between substances that are acids and alkalis
- test the strength of an acid

Strength of an acid ⟫

Activity C 3.33.1

Exploring the strength of acids

Here is what you need:

- vinegar
- milk
- lemon or lime
- universal indicator solution
- small pieces of universal indicator paper
- ketchup
- spatulas
- scalpels
- experimental tray
- hydrochloric acid
- sulphuric acid
- nitric acid
- droppers
- eye protection

 SAFETY

Observe the safety icon on the acid bottles. All indicator papers should be held with the tweezers. Take care when using scalpels. Avoid spillage.

Here is what you should do:

1. Copy the table. List the names of the substances you are going to test in the Specimen column, as shown below.

Specimen	Universal indicator (colour change)	
	Paper	**Solution**
vinegar		
milk		
lemon or lime		
ketchup		
hydrochloric acid		
sulphuric acid		
nitric acid		

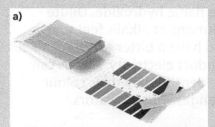
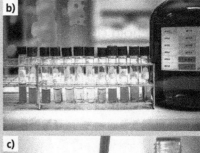

FIG C 3.33.1 **a)** Universal indicator paper **b)** Universal indicator solution **c)** Experimental tray

2. Using a scalpel, spatula or dropper, put a tiny sample of each specimen in the cavities of the experimental tray.

3. Wash your hands and all the apparatus you used thoroughly then dry your hands.

4. Add a small piece of indicator paper to each specimen. Observe and record any colour change.

5. Add one drop of indicator to each specimen. Observe and record any colour change.

6. Were all the colours the same?

7. Do you think that the difference in colours has any significance for acid strength?

Universal indicator is very special. As well as indicating acidity, it also gives the strength of an acid.

FIG C 3.33.2 As acidity weakens, the colour of universal indicator moves from red to yellow

The colours of universal indicator match those on a range called the pH scale. Acids have a **pH** with a number between 0 and 6. The stronger the acid, the more corrosive it is. The stomach produces hydrochloric acid, which is a strong acid.

Check your understanding

1. How can you determine the strength of an acid?

2. Research what scientists use to make indicators.

3. Research what can be used to make homemade indicators.

Key term

pH measure of strength of an acid or an alkali

34 Alkalis and the pH scale

We are learning how to:

- distinguish between substances that are acids and those that are alkalis
- identify the strength of an alkali

Strength of an alkali »

Activity C 3.34.1

Exploring the strength of alkalis

Here is what you need:

- universal indicator solution
- small pieces of universal indicator paper
- tweezers
- spatulas
- scalpels
- experimental trays
- test tubes
- droppers
- bleach
- dishwashing liquid
- baking soda
- sodium
- ammonium
- calcium hydroxide
- eye protection

 SAFETY

Observe the safety icon on the alkali bottles. All indicator papers should be held with the tweezers. Avoid spillage. Take care when using scalpels.

Here is what you should do:

1. Copy the table. List the names of the substances you are testing, as shown below.

Specimen	Universal indicator (colour change)	
	Paper	Solution
bleach		
dishwashing liquid		
baking soda		

2. Using a scalpel, spatula or dropper, add a tiny sample of each specimen to the cavities of an experimental tray.

3. Wash your hands and all the apparatus you used thoroughly.

4. Place a small piece of indicator paper in each specimen. Observe and record any colour change.

5. Add one drop of indicator to each specimen. Observe and record any colour change.

6. Were all the colours the same?

7. Do you think that the difference in colours has any significance for an alkali's strength?

Universal indicator also shows the strength of alkalis. Universal indicator displays colours for alkalis with a pH between 8 and 14.

PH SCALE

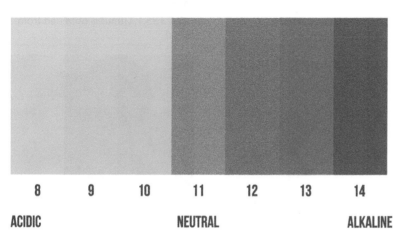

| 8 | 9 | 10 | 11 | 12 | 13 | 14 |

ACIDIC   NEUTRAL   ALKALINE

FIG C 3.34.1 The colour moves from blue to dark purple as the alkali gets stronger

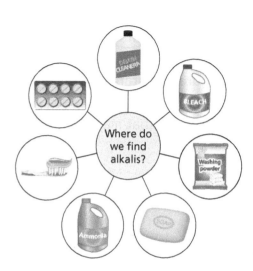

FIG C 3.34.2 Alkalis around us

Alkalis can be found all around us, especially in the home.

So far you have identified acidic and alkaline substances. Indicators tell us that they are at opposite ends of the pH scale.

Check your understanding

1. What would the pH of a strong alkali be?

2. What numbers indicate the pH range of alkalis?

3. How does universal indicator show the strength of an acid?

4. Which number would indicate the strongest alkali?

Interesting fact

An ant injects some acid under your skin when it bites. By placing an ice cube on the bite, it is possible to soothe the sting and prevent swelling.

35 Making an acid–alkali indicator

We are learning how to:

- make an acid–alkali indicator from organic material
- investigate the colour changes of an indicator

Litmus is extracted from lichen. This is a rather unusual organism in which algae and fungi coexist for mutual benefit.

There are many organic materials that contain coloured chemicals which might provide **acid–alkali indicators**. For a chemical to be of any use as an indicator, it must be different colours in acids and in alkalis.

The petals of flowers like the hibiscus contain coloured substances that may be useful indicators.

The leaves of vegetables like the red cabbage contain coloured substances that may be useful indicators.

The roots of vegetables like the beetroot contain coloured substances that may be useful indicators.

FIG C 3.35.1 Litmus is obtained from lichen

FIG C 3.35.2 Plant petals

FIG C 3.35.3 Vegetable leaves

FIG C 3.35.4 Vegetable roots

Whatever the source, the coloured substance must be extracted by physically crushing the organic material to break down the cells and then extracting it using a suitable solvent. Many of the chemicals responsible for colour are soluble in water but are more soluble in a solvent like ethanol. When extracting, it is important not to use too much solvent or the extract will be very dilute and colours will be difficult to see.

> **Interesting fact**
>
> It is thought that litmus was first used around 1300 by the Spanish alchemist Arnaldus de Villa Nova, but it is unlikely that he used it as an acid–alkali indicator. Many coloured organic extracts like this were used in those days to dye cloth.

Activity C 3.35.1

Making an acid–alkali indicator

Here is what you need:

- chopped up coloured plant material
- mortar and pestle
- beaker
- ethanol
- stirring rod
- test tubes × 3
- test tube rack
- dropper pipette
- dilute hydrochloric acid
- dilute sodium hydroxide solution
- eye protection

 SAFETY
Observe the safety icon on the alkali bottles. Avoid spillage.

Here is what you should do:

1. Put a small amount of chopped up coloured plant material in a mortar and pestle and grind it into a mushy paste.

2. Scrape it into a beaker.

3. Repeat this three or four times with small amounts of material each time.

4. Pour a small amount of ethanol into the mortar and wash the mortar and pestle to dissolve any coloured juice.

5. Pour the ethanol into the beaker with the crushed material and stir the mixture for a few minutes so that any coloured juice has a chance to dissolve in the ethanol.

6. Allow the contents of the beaker to settle for a few minutes.

7. Decant off the liquid from the beaker into a test tube, taking care not to pour it over any of the plant material.

8. Pour dilute hydrochloric acid into a test tube to a depth of about 1 cm.

9. Add a few drops of your indicator solution using a pipette. Record the colour of the indicator in a table.

10. Repeat steps 8 and 9 using dilute sodium hydroxide solution instead of the acid.

Check your understanding

1. Why is it necessary to crush organic material before extracting any coloured material?

2. Why is ethanol preferred to water for extracting the coloured chemical from crushed organic material?

3. Why is it essential that an indicator has different colours in acids and alkalis?

Key terms

litmus common acid–alkali indicator

acid–alkali indicator chemical that has different colours in acids and in alkalis

36 Reactions of acids with bases and alkalis

We are learning how to:
- describe chemical reactions involving acids
- define neutralisation

Acid–alkali reactions ⟫⟫

Activity C 3.36.1

Exploring neutralisation

For this experiment you need to work in two groups – one with an acid and the other without.

Here is what you need:
- a dilute acid
- a dilute alkali
- liquid indicator (phenolphthalein)
- measuring cylinder
- droppers
- test tube
- drinking straws
- eye protection

 SAFETY
Observe the safety icon on the reagent bottles. Remember to observe safety rules when working with hazardous materials. Avoid spillage.

Here is what you should do:

1. Measure 1 cm³ of alkali and pour it into the test tube.

2. Use a dropper to add one drop of indicator into the alkali.

3. Observe and record the colour.

For the groups with the acid:

4. Using a second dropper, slowly add some acid to the alkali in the test tube and shake it gently after each drop.

5. Keep adding until a colour difference is seen.

6. Use a third dropper to add drops of alkali and observe any colour changes.

7. Add acid and alkali alternately until you think you have found a midpoint between acid and alkali.

8. Explain what you experienced as you changed from adding acid to alkali and back.

For the group with no acid:

9. Get one student to gently blow exhaled air through the straw into the alkali with the indicator.

10. They should keep exhaling until the colour changes.

11. Use the second dropper to add drops of alkali to observe colour changes.

12. Then the student should exhale into this combination.

13. Repeat until you think you have found a midpoint between exhaled air and alkali.

Alkalis are bases that are soluble in water. Acids and alkalis have opposite chemical properties. When an alkali and an acid combine, there is a point where they cancel out the effect of each other – this is called **neutralisation**. A neutral substance has a pH of 7, the midpoint of the pH scale.

Since acids and alkalis chemically react with each other, a new product is formed.

FIG C 3.36.1 Carbon dioxide, which is slightly acidic, neutralises limewater, calcium hydroxide, which is an alkali

> **Interesting fact**
>
> Indigestion is caused by a build-up of stomach acid. Indigestion tablets are alkaline and so they neutralise the acid.

Check your understanding

1. Describe how to explore the neutralisation of an acid by an alkali. Say what equipment you would need, and what chemicals you would use. Describe what observations you would make.

> **Key term**
>
> **neutralisation** the effect of an acid and an alkali cancelling each other out

37 Neutralisation reactions

We are learning how to:

- name the products of the neutralisation reaction between sodium hydroxide and hydrochloric acid
- name salts prepared from hydrochloric acid, nitric acid and sulphuric acid
- explain how a salt is named

Neutralisation

The reactants in a chemical change are in fixed proportions. To know the exact amount of each chemical to be used for neutralisation, you can use an indicator.

Activity C 3.37.1

Exploring neutralisation

This is a demonstration activity. You are to observe and record.

Here is what you need:

- dilute sodium hydroxide
- dilute hydrochloric acid
- conical flask
- methyl orange indicator
- titration apparatus
- evaporating dish
- heat
- tripod
- gauze

 SAFETY
Take care with chemicals and heat sources.

Here is what you should do:

1. Add one drop of indicator to 10 cm³ of sodium hydroxide in a conical flask.
2. Use the **titration** apparatus shown in Fig C 3.37.1 to find the amount of hydrochloric acid used for neutralising alkalis.
3. Use these amounts of acid and alkali to make a solution containing no indicator.
4. Pour some of this solution into an evaporating dish and heat it using a Bunsen flame.
5. As the liquid evaporates, reduce the heat to a gentle flame.

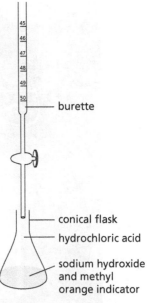

burette

conical flask

hydrochloric acid

sodium hydroxide and methyl orange indicator

FIG C 3.37.1 Titration apparatus set up to find neutralisation point

Interesting fact

In ancient times, Roman soldiers were sometimes paid in salt (Latin: *sal*) – this is the origin of the word 'salary'.

6. If it's a sunny day, some of the solution can be left outside in a crystallisation dish.

7. When evaporation is complete, examine the residue.

8. Write a laboratory report on this activity.

Key terms

titration a technique to make a neutral solution which contains equivalent amounts of acid and alkali

salt the product of neutralisation

residue the material remaining after distillation, evaporation, or filtration

The products of the neutralisation of sodium hydroxide and hydrochloric acid in this **titration** is a **salt** and water. The evaporation occurring was that of the water. The **residue** is the salt (sodium chloride). The chemical reaction that occurred is:

sodium hydroxide + hydrochloric acid → sodium chloride + water

Products of neutralisation ⟩⟩⟩

The products of the neutralisation of an alkali and an acid are a salt and water.

The names of salts have two parts. The first part is the name of the metal involved in the reaction. (Ammonia is not a metal but when it reacts with an acid, the first part of the name of the salt is ammonium.)

The second part comes from the acid used.

If the acid is

- hydro**chlor**ic acid then the salt is a **chlor**ide
- **nitr**ic acid then the salt is a **nitr**ate
- **sulph**uric acid then the salt is a **sulph**ate.

nickel sulphate

copper sulphate

Check your understanding

Complete these word equations for some neutralisations:

1. magnesium hydroxide + hydrochloric acid →
2. aqueous ammonia + hydrochloric acid →
3. aluminium hydroxide + nitric acid →
4. sodium hydroxide + sulphuric acid →
5. copper hydroxide + nitric acid →
6. magnesium hydroxide + sulphuric acid →
7. zinc hydroxide + hydrochloric acid →
8. lead hydroxide + hydrochloric acid →
9. aqueous ammonia + hydrochloric acid →

sodium chloride

cobalt nitrate

FIG C 3.37.2 There are many different metal salts and some of them are brightly coloured

38 Applications of neutralisation in daily life

We are learning how to:

- identify neutralisation reactions that take place in our everyday lives

Chemical reactions are not limited to test tubes in the laboratory. There are many examples of chemical reactions taking place in our everyday lives, including neutralisation reactions. Some have already been mentioned in this unit.

Baking powder >>>

Bread and cakes often have a light texture so they are easy to bite into and chew. Bakers achieve this by adding **baking powder** to the dough before baking. This causes the dough to rise.

Baking powder contains an acid and a carbonate or a hydrogencarbonate. These chemicals react to produce **carbon dioxide** gas. Here is a typical example of the chemical reaction that takes place:

tartaric acid + sodium hydrogencarbonate
→ sodium tartrate + carbon dioxide

The bubbles of carbon dioxide are contained within the dough and expand when the dough is heated in the oven. The result is lots of 'holes' in the bread or cake giving it a light texture.

FIG C 3.38.1 Baking powder contains an acid and a carbonate/hydrogencarbonate

FIG C 3.38.2 Bread with a light texture

Antacids >>>

The lining of the stomach releases hydrochloric acid to assist in the process of digestion. The more we eat the more acid is produced.

When the stomach produces lots of acid we get stomach pain which we call indigestion. In order to reduce the pain we might take an **antacid** which neutralises the excess acid.

FIG C 3.38.3 Antacids neutralise excess stomach acid

Interesting fact

You might be wondering 'why doesn't baking powder react and produce carbon dioxide in its container'? The answer is that many chemical reactions only take place in solution. Provided baking powder is kept dry it will remain active for a long time.

There are lots of different brands of antacids available. They contain carbonates, hydrogencarbonates or weak hydroxides like magnesium hydroxide. All of these compounds will neutralise stomach acid.

Activity C 3.38.1

Home-made fizzy sherbet

You should carry out this activity in the kitchen at home. Your teacher might set this for homework, so then test the fizzy sherbet you make.

Here is what you need:

- 1 measure of sodium hydrogencarbonate (this is often called sodium bicarbonate or baking soda)

- 1 measure of citric acid (this is the acid from citrus fruits like lemons)

The size of the measure will depend on how much you plan to make. You should make small amounts until you hit on a mixture that tastes really good. You can also add icing sugar to make it sweeter and jelly crystals to give some colour.

Here is what you should do:

1. Mix the ingredients as powders in a bowl. Don't add any water or your mixture will react and lose its fizz.

2. Keep your fizzy sherbet dry in a suitable container like a small food box.

3. Test it out on your family and friends.

Key terms

baking powder mixture of chemicals used to make dough rise before baking

carbon dioxide gas produced by the reaction of an acid with a carbonate or hydrogencarbonate

antacid medicine that relieves stomach ache by neutralising excess stomach acid

Check your understanding

1. Milk of magnesia contains magnesium hydroxide. How is it able to relieve stomach ache?

2. Fig C 3.38.4 shows details of an old-fashioned fire extinguisher.

   a) What neutralisation reaction takes place when the extinguisher is activated?

   b) Explain how the fire extinguisher works.

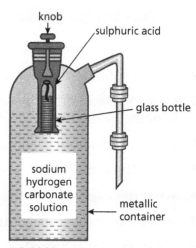

FIG C 3.38.4

39 Acid–carbonate reactions

We are learning how to:

- describe what happens when acids react with carbonates
- test for carbon dioxide gas

Carbonates are a group of compounds that contain the carbonate ion, CO_3^{2-}. They are almost all metal carbonates but ammonium carbonate also exists.

Some metals also form **hydrogencarbonates** which contain the hydrogencarbonate ion, HCO_3^-.

Carbonates and hydrogencarbonates have a characteristic reaction with acids that can be used to identify them.

Activity C 3.39.1

What gas is given off during an acid–carbonate reaction?

This is a demonstration lesson. Volunteers will be needed. Observe carefully.

Here is what you need:

- dilute hydrochloric acid
- samples of metal carbonates
- test tubes
- splint

- Bunsen burner
- limewater solution
- drinking straws
- eye protection

FIG C 3.39.1 Reaction between an acid and sodium carbonate

 SAFETY

Observe care with acids.

Here is what you should do:

1. Put a little carbonate in a test tube.
2. Have a lighted splint available.
3. Pour some acid onto the carbonate and hold the splint in the evolving gas. What happens to the flame?
4. Pour some colourless limewater solution ($Ca(OH)_2$) into a test tube.
5. Allow the evolving gas to flow into the test tube of limewater and shake it.
6. What has happened to the limewater? Can you identify the gas?
7. Using the straw, exhale into a test tube of limewater. What do you observe?
8. What gas was exhaled?
9. Can you now identify the gas that was evolved from the acid–carbonate reaction?

All carbonates and hydrogencarbonates react with acids to release **carbon dioxide** gas. Here are the ionic equations for the reactions:

$$2H^+ + CO_3^{2-} \rightarrow CO_2 + H_2O$$

$$H^+ + HCO_3^- \rightarrow CO_2 + H_2O$$

Notice that only the carbonate ion or hydrogencarbonate ion is involved. The reactions are the same no matter which metal ion is present.

The other product formed during the reaction depends on the metal in the metal carbonate, and the acid used. For example, a reaction between copper carbonate and dilute hydrochloric acid would produce copper chloride.

Carbon dioxide is a colourless and odourless gas so it cannot be observed. However when it is shaken with a small volume of **limewater**, the limewater turns milky.

Limewater is a solution of calcium hydroxide. When carbon dioxide is shaken with limewater the following reaction takes place:

$$Ca^{2+} + 2OH^- + CO_2 \rightarrow CaCO_3 + H_2O$$
$$\text{insoluble}$$

Calcium carbonate is insoluble in water. It is precipitated as tiny particles that make the limewater appear milky.

Check your understanding

1. Copper carbonate is green and sodium carbonate is white. Which ion is responsible for the green colour of copper carbonate? Explain your answer.

2. What are the products of the reaction between sodium carbonate and dilute sulphuric acid?

3. What is the test for carbon dioxide gas?

> **Interesting fact**
>
> Carbon dioxide is denser than air and does not support combustion. This makes it particularly useful as a fire extinguisher. The carbon dioxide forms a layer beneath the air and prevents oxygen from reaching the flames.

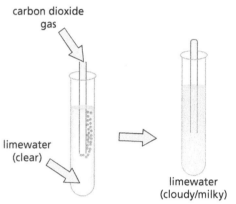

carbon dioxide gas

limewater (clear)

limewater (cloudy/milky)

carbon dioxide turns limewater milky

FIG C 3.39.2 Carbon dioxide turns limewater milky

Key terms

carbonate compound that contains the ion CO_3^{2-}

hydrogencarbonate compound that contains the ion HCO_3^-

carbon dioxide colourless, odourless gas that is denser than air and turns limewater milky

limewater solution of calcium hydroxide

40 Acid–metal reactions

We are learning how to:

- describe what happens when acids react with metals
- test for hydrogen gas

All acids form solutions that contain hydrogen ions, H^+.
The ions present in laboratory acids are:

$$HCl \rightarrow H^+ + Cl^-$$

$$H_2SO_4 \rightarrow 2H^+ + SO_4^{2-}$$

$$HNO_3 \rightarrow H^+ + NO_3^-$$

Acids react with most, but not all, metals.

Activity C 3.40.1

What happens when acids react with metals?

Here is what you need:

- rack of labelled test tubes, each containing a metal: aluminium, magnesium, copper, zinc, lead
- an acid
- eye protection

FIG C 3.40.1 Reaction between zinc and an acid

 SAFETY

Observe the name and the safety icon on the acid bottle.

Here is what you should do:

1. Take out each metal, examine it and then replace it in the test tube.

2. Pour some acid onto each metal, shake gently and feel the outside of the test tube. Look for signs of any reaction and record any observations you make.

3. You can report your findings as a group. Did each metal react the same way with the different acids?

4. With which ones was there effervescence? What does effervescence indicate?

5. [STEAM] Plan how you could use the reaction with dilute hydrochloric acid to compare the reactivity of five metals. How could you use your results to arrange the metals in order of their reactivity?

When a metal reacts with an acid, **hydrogen** gas is released.
Here are some examples of the ionic equations for such reactions:

$$Ca + 2H^+ \rightarrow Ca^{2+} + H_2$$

$$Zn + 2H^+ \rightarrow Zn^{2+} + H_2$$

Notice that only the metal and the hydrogen ions are involved.
The reaction is the same no matter which acid is used.

The other product formed during the reaction depends on the metal and the acid used. For example, a reaction between zinc and dilute sulphuric acid would also produce zinc sulphate.

Hydrogen is a colourless and odourless gas so it cannot be observed. It is much less dense than air so it must be collected in an inverted tube. A mixture of hydrogen and air is explosive. This can be used to test for the gas.

If the open end of an inverted tube containing hydrogen and air is held in a flame there is a loud 'pop' as the gaseous mixture explodes. The product of the explosion is water:

$$2H_2 + O_2 \rightarrow 2H_2O$$

Notice that when hydrogen burns in air, it doesn't produce carbon dioxide like many other fuels. Scientists believe that hydrogen will be an important fuel in the future for this reason.

The metals that do not react with dilute acids are those that have low reactivity and include copper, silver and gold.

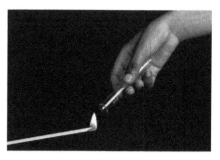

FIG C 3.40.2 A mixture of hydrogen and air explodes when ignited

Check your understanding

1. Fig C 3.40.3 shows what happened a few minutes after pieces of three metals were put into some dilute hydrochloric acid.

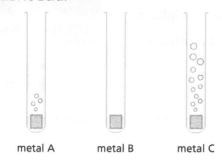

metal A   metal B   metal C

FIG C 3.40.3

   a) Which is the most reactive metal?

   b) Which metal could be silver?

2. What are the products of the reaction between zinc and dilute hydrochloric acid?

3. What is the test for hydrogen gas?

Interesting fact

Hydrogen is the least dense gas. In the past, air balloons were filled with hydrogen. However, because of the risk of explosions the use of hydrogen was discontinued and helium is now used to fill the balloons.

Key term

hydrogen a colourless, odourless gas that is much less dense than air. A mixture of hydrogen and air explodes with a loud 'pop' when ignited

225

41 Ammonium compounds

We are learning how to:

- describe different ammonium compounds
- make and test for ammonia gas

Ammonia is a gas with the chemical formula NH_3. You have already learned about ammonium hydroxide as a solution of ammonia gas dissolved in water.

Ammonia molecules form **ammonium ions** by combining with a hydrogen ion present in water:

$$NH_3 + H^+ \rightarrow NH_4^+$$

The ammonium ion is similar to any metal ion so it is not surprising that it forms salts in the same way as metals.

If the stoppers from bottles of concentrated hydrochloric acid and concentrated ammonia solution are removed and the necks brought close together, a white 'smoke' consisting of tiny particles of ammonium chloride is formed. The acid releases hydrogen chloride gas while the ammonia solution releases ammonia gas.

A more general way of making salts of ammonia is by reacting ammonia solution with dilute acids.

$NH_4OH + HCl \rightarrow NH_4Cl + H_2O$ ammonium chloride

$2NH_4OH + H_2SO_4 \rightarrow (NH_4)_2SO_4 + 2H_2O$ ammonium sulphate

$NH_4OH + HNO_3 \rightarrow NH_4NO_3 + H_2O$ ammonium nitrate

All of these salts are white powders that are very soluble in water.

If an alkali is added to any ammonium compound, ammonia gas is evolved. This reaction is often carried out by heating a mixture of solid ammonium chloride and calcium hydroxide. Ammonia cannot be collected over water because it is too soluble. It is less dense than air so it is collected in an inverted test tube.

Ammonia gas turns damp red litmus paper blue. This is the laboratory test for this gas.

FIG C 3.41.1 Formation of ammonium chloride

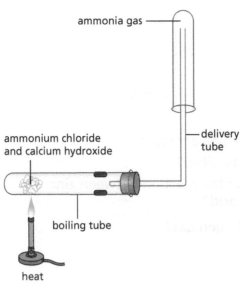

FIG C 3.41.2 Making ammonia gas

ammonia gas

delivery tube

ammonium chloride and calcium hydroxide

boiling tube

heat

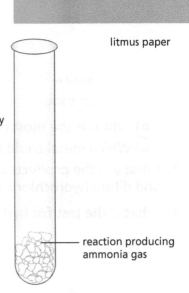

litmus paper

reaction producing ammonia gas

FIG C 3.41.3 Ammonia gas turns damp red litmus paper blue

Making and testing for ammonia gas

Here is what you need:

- ammonium chloride
- calcium hydroxide
- test tube
- test tube holder
- heat source
- red litmus paper
- spatula
- eye protection

Here is what you should do:

1. Put one spatula full of ammonium chloride in a test tube.

2. Put a similar amount of calcium hydroxide into the same test tube.

3. Shake the test tube to mix the solids and then gently heat them.

4. When you start to smell ammonia gas, remove the heat source and hold a piece of damp red litmus paper at the top of the test tube.

5. What evidence is there that ammonia gas is given off?

Check your understanding

1. The following is the formula of an ammonium compound: $(NH_4)_2CO_3$.

   a) Name this compound.

   b) i) Predict what gas would be given off if dilute sulphuric acid were added to this compound.

   ii) Describe a test for this gas.

   iii) Name the compound formed in this reaction.

   c) i) Predict what gas would be given off if calcium hydroxide were added to this compound and the mixture heated.

   ii) Describe a test for this gas.

Interesting fact

'Stink bombs' consist of small glass ampules containing a solution of ammonium sulphide, $(NH_4)_2S$. When the ampule is broken, the ammonium sulphide decomposes to ammonia gas and hydrogen sulphide gas which has the smell of rotten eggs.

FIG C 3.41.4 Stink bombs contain ammonium sulphide

Stink bombs should not be used in an enclosed space because, as well as having an unpleasant smell, hydrogen sulphide gas is very poisonous.

Key terms

ammonia a gas with the chemical formula NH_3

ammonium ions ions with the formula NH_4^+

42 Classifying salts

We are learning how to:

- classify salts in different ways
- make insoluble salts by precipitation

Methods of making salts >>>

So far in this unit you have learned about three different routes for making salts:

- acid + alkali (neutralisation)
- acid + carbonate
- acid + metal

Notice that not all salts can be prepared using each of the above reactions. For example, **unreactive** metals like copper and silver do not react with dilute acids. When planning to make a salt, some thought has to be given to the reaction used and how a pure product will be separated from any remaining reactants.

Classifying salts according to the acid used >>>

Salts can be classified according to the acid used in their preparation:

- Hydrochloric acid is used to make **chlorides**.
- Sulphuric acid is used to make **sulphates**.
- Nitric acid is used to make **nitrates**.

It doesn't matter which of the above routes is used, a particular acid will always produce the same salt. For example, if dilute hydrochloric acid is reacted with zinc oxide, zinc carbonate or zinc metal, the product will always be zinc chloride.

Weak acids also produce salts. For example, citric acid forms citrates and ethanoic acid forms ethanoates.

FIG C 3.42.1

The salts of different metals can have different colours.

iron chloride

magnesium chloride

zinc nitrate

sodium chloride

copper chloride

copper sulphate

aluminium sulphate

potassium nitrate

FIG C 3.42.2 Salts of some different metals

- The salts of sodium, potassium, magnesium, calcium and zinc are colourless and appear as white powders. Ammonium salts are also colourless.

- The salts of other metals, like iron, nickel and copper, are coloured.

Notice that it is the metal ion that is responsible for the colour. So if the chloride of a metal is coloured, then the sulphate and the nitrate of the same metal will also be coloured.

nickel(II) chloride

nickel(II) sulphate

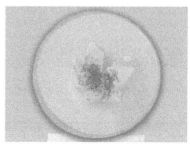
nickel(II) nitrate

FIG C 3.42.3 Salts of nickel

Classifying salts according to solubility and making insoluble salts >>>

You learned in the previous unit that some salts are soluble in water while others are insoluble. Table C2.22.1 contains information about the solubility of different families of compounds.

Interesting fact

No ionic compound is totally insoluble in water. However, the solubility of some is so low that they are effectively insoluble. For example at 20 °C the solubility of barium sulphate is only 0.000 244 8 g/100 g of water.

43 Classifying salts (continued)

We are learning how to:
- classify salts in different ways
- make insoluble salts by precipitation

Insoluble salts can be prepared by precipitation reactions. The general method for these is:

soluble reactant + soluble reactant → insoluble product + soluble product

You have already seen how this method of preparing salts can be used to make silver iodide and lead(II) iodide.

In planning to make an insoluble salt, care must be taken to choose suitable reactants. For example, to make barium sulphate:

- One reactant must be a soluble barium compound, for example, barium nitrate.

- One reactant must be a soluble sulphate, for example, sodium sulphate.

- The second product must be a soluble salt, for example, sodium nitrate.

| barium nitrate | + | sodium sulphate | → | barium sulphate | + | sodium nitrate |
| soluble | | soluble | | insoluble | | soluble |

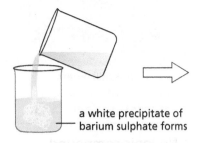

solutions of barium nitrate and sodium sulphate are mixed

a white precipitate of barium sulphate forms

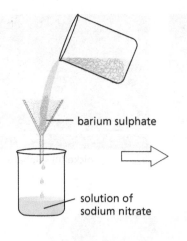

barium sulphate

solution of sodium nitrate

barium sulphate washed with distilled water, scraped off the filter paper and left to dry

FIG C 3.43.1 Separating an insoluble salt

Using this method, the insoluble product is separated by filtration. Barium sulphate forms the residue while the soluble product, sodium nitrate, passes through the filter in solution as the filtrate.

Testing solubility

Here is what you need:

- salts × 10 (your teacher will decide which salts to give you; some will be **soluble** and some **insoluble**)
- test tube
- heat source
- distilled water
- spatula

Here is what you should do:

1. Put a spatula full of the first salt in a test tube and add distilled water to a depth of about 2 cm.

2. Gently shake the test tube for a couple of minutes to dissolve the salt.

3. If the salt doesn't appear to be dissolving, heat the contents of the test tube and then repeat the shaking.

4. Make a note of whether the salt dissolves in cold water, only dissolves in hot water or doesn't dissolve in either.

5. Repeat this procedure for all of the salts you have been given.

6. Present your observations in the form of a table with columns.

7. Solubility is often expressed in g / cm³. Using the solubility of sodium chloride (92.1 g / 100 cm³) as an example, explain how solubility can be converted into g / dm³.

Check your understanding

1. Here is some information about six salts.

Salt	Colour	Soluble/insoluble in water
barium sulphate	colourless/white	insoluble
copper(II) nitrate	blue	soluble
lead(II) iodide	yellow	insoluble
sodium chloride	colourless/white	soluble
silver chloride	colourless/white	insoluble
iron(II) sulphate	green	soluble

Table C 3.43.1

Classify these salts into two groups in two different ways according to different criteria.

Key terms

unreactive doesn't react

chlorides salts made from hydrochloric acid

sulphates salts made from sulphuric acid

nitrates salts made from nitric acid

soluble dissolves in water (or anther liquid)

insoluble doesn't dissolve in water (or another liquid)

44 Safety booklet

We are learning how to:

• keep safe in the laboratory

A typical kitchen contains sharp knives, hot pans and fruit juices that sting the eyes.

We are aware of these dangers from an early age and we learn how to keep ourselves safe. The school laboratory is no more dangerous than your kitchen but some of the hazards are different.

There are always hazards when dealing with chemicals so it is important to take precautions and behave correctly.

Whenever you carry out experiments involving chemicals like acids and alkalis, you must wear eye protection. Splashes of acids and alkalis can irritate the eyes and cause permanent damage.

FIG C 3.44.1 A kitchen is a potentially dangerous place

FIG C 3.44.2 Foolish behaviour leads to accidents

FIG C 3.44.3 Eye wash station

Your laboratory should be equipped with an eye wash bottle or an eye wash station/sink just in case somebody does get chemicals in their eyes.

Even dilute acids and alkalis are **corrosive** and will damage skin. Any spillages should be washed off the skin immediately with cold water.

These chemicals will also damage the fabrics from which your clothing is made. If you splash an acid or alkali onto your clothing, wash the area with lots of cold water immediately. The area in which you work should be kept clean and tidy at all times.

FIG C 3.44.4 Protect your eyes

Activity C 3.44.1

Producing a safety booklet

Your task is to produce a booklet about safety when using acids and alkalis in the laboratory. This will be four pages long and you will make it by folding an A4 sheet of paper in two along the short side.

It is up to you to decide on the format. It might:

- have a mixture of text and diagrams
- use photographs you have taken to illustrate your text
- make use of tables and/or bullet points
- use colour to emphasise important points.

Check your understanding

State why each of the following actions is potentially dangerous in a chemistry laboratory.

1. Leaving your school bag on the floor between the benches.

2. Eating a snack while you are handling chemicals.

3. Looking down into a boiling tube when you are heating it.

4. Putting hot glassware directly on the table top.

Key term
....

corrosive destroys by chemical action

Review of Acids and alkalis

- Acids are chemical substances that have a sour taste.
- Alkalis are chemical substances that conduct electricity and have a soapy feel when diluted.
- Carbon dioxide is a gas that dissolves in water to form a weak acid.
- Bases form a set of chemicals that include oxides, hydroxides and carbonates.
- Both acids and alkalis are identified using indicators.
- There are a variety of indicators used for identifying acidity and alkalinity.
- Both acids and alkalis can be weak or strong.
- Universal indicator gives the degree of acidity or alkalinity using a range of colours to identify pH values from 0 to 14.
- The midpoint on the universal indicator is green and indicates neutrality (pH 7).
- Acid–alkali indicators can be made from coloured organic material.
- Acids and bases can neutralise each other to form new products.
- Acids react with metals to form neutral products called salts.
- Carbon dioxide changes calcium hydroxide (limewater) to a white precipitate.
- Hydrogen explodes, producing a squeaky pop.
- A salt is named after the reactants from which it was formed.
- Hydrochloric acid forms chlorides.
- Nitric acid forms nitrates.
- Sulphuric acid forms sulphates.
- Ammonia forms the ammonium ion, NH_4^+.
- The ammonium ion forms salts just like metal ions.
- Ammonium salts react with alkalis to release ammonia gas.
- Ammonia gas turns damp red litmus blue.
- Salts can be classified in a number of ways.
- The salts of some metals are coloured while the salts of others are colourless and form white powders.
- Some salts are soluble in water while others are not.
- Insoluble salts can be made by precipitation reactions.
- It is essential to create a safe environment when carrying out experiments.
- Eye protection must be worn when working with potentially harmful materials.
- Even dilute acids and alkalis are corrosive.

Review questions on Acids and alkalis

Knowledge and understanding

1. a) What advantage does universal indicator have over litmus as an acid–alkali indicator?

   b) How could you use universal indicator to determine whether an acid is strong or weak?

2. Briefly describe how you would make an acid–alkali indicator using coloured flower petals.

3. a) When an acid neutralises an alkali, what is the pH of the resulting solution?

   b) Write a balanced symbol equation for the neutralisation reaction between sodium hydroxide and sulphuric acid.

   c) i) Explain why any spillage of an acid onto the bench should be mopped up immediately with a damp cloth.

   ii) Some acid has been spilt on the floor. Name a substance that could be sprinkled as a solid onto the floor to neutralise the acid.

   iii) The student next to you has splashed some acid into her eye. What action should be taken?

4. Complete these sentences by filling in the blanks below.

   Salts made from

   a) hydrochloric acid are called _____.

   b) nitric acid are called _____.

   c) sulphuric acid are called _____.

Process skills

5. During a reaction there is vigorous effervescence. Describe what you would do to find out if the gas evolved was carbon dioxide or hydrogen.

6. Give the word equations of four different reactions that would produce zinc nitrate.

7. Copy and complete the following chemical equations:

   a) zinc hydroxide + sulphuric acid →

   b) magnesium carbonate + nitric acid →

   c) aluminium hydroxide + sulphuric acid →

   d) copper oxide + nitric acid →

   e) lead + sulphuric acid →

   f) sodium + hydrochloric acid →

8. Lead(II) sulphate is an insoluble salt.

   a) Suggest suitable starting materials for preparing some lead(II) sulphate.

   b) Write an ionic equation for the reaction that takes place.

   c) Describe how a dry sample of lead(II) sulphate could be obtained from the reaction mixture.

9. You have been given an unknown substance. Explain and give the results of three sets of tests you would carry out to discover whether the substance is acidic or alkaline.

46 Measuring soil acidity to improve yield

Mrs Whittaker's house has a small backyard garden in which she grows vegetables.

Mrs Whittaker grows vegetables with mixed success. She noticed that some vegetables grew well, while others did not – but she doesn't know why. When she discussed this with another gardener in her community, Mrs Whittaker was told that the pH of her soil was an important issue when deciding which vegetables to grow, but she doesn't understand what this means.

You are Mrs Whittaker's nephews and nieces and she has turned to you for help.

FIG STEAM C 3.46.1 Mrs Whittaker has a vegetable garden

1. You are going to work in a small group to investigate soil pH. The tasks are:

   • To carry out research about soil pH testing kits.
   • To devise a method of measuring the pH of soil samples.
   • To measure the pH of the soil in a garden.
   • To research the best pH range for growing different vegetables and to recommend the best vegetables to plant in the garden.
   • To research the use of lime to reduce the pH of soil and calculate the amount of lime needed to treat the garden soil by a given amount.

   a) Take a look at soil pH testing kits for sale in your local garden centre or on the Internet.

Each kit contains
• **Instruction booklet**
• **pH colour chart**
• **Plastic mixing plate**
• **Plastic mixing rod**
• **pH dye indicator liquid bottle**
• **Barium sulphate powder bottle**

FIG STEAM C 3.46.2 Soil pH test kit

Read the information on the boxes to see what they contain and how they work.

Use your knowledge of acid–alkali indicators and pH, and the information you obtain from soil testing kits to devise a way of measuring the pH of some soil.

Test the accuracy of your method by checking your results against those obtained using a pH meter.

b) You might investigate the soil in the garden of one group member or your teacher might divide up a plot of land and assign one part to each group.

Plan how you will measure the pH of the soil in the garden or given area of ground. You should consider such factors as:

- How many samples will you take?
- From which parts of the garden will you take your samples?
- How will you present your results?
- How will you use your results to provide an overall pH value for the soil in the garden?

c) The availability of different nutrients essential for plant growth depends on the pH of the soil.

For example, if the pH of soil falls below pH 6, plants find it very difficult to obtain phosphorus from the soil. Plants that need a lot of phosphorus will do badly in soil with a pH lower than 6.

Research which vegetables grow well in soils that have different pH values. Make a list of vegetables that grow best in acid soils. Make another list of vegetables which grow best in alkaline soils. Is there a range of pH values of soils in which all vegetables grow well?

Recommend which vegetables would be best suited to the soil in the garden.

d) Lime is a common name for several chemicals, including calcium carbonate.

Investigate the effect of calcium carbonate on acids and explain the effect that adding calcium carbonate to soil has on its pH value.

e) Research how lime is used to reduce the pH of soil. Calculate how much lime per square metre would need to be added to the garden soil to reduce its pH value by 1 unit.

f) Give a PowerPoint presentation to the class on what you have found out about soil pH and the advice you will be able to pass on to Mrs Whittaker. Your presentation should include a demonstration of how you measure the pH of a sample of soil.

g) Plant some of the vegetables you have recommended and cultivate them to see if they grow well. This will help you to determine whether your advice was accurate or not.

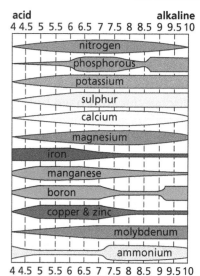

FIG STEAM C 3.46.3 The wider the band the easier it is for the nutrient to be absorbed

FIG STEAM C 3.46.4 Raking lime into the soil

1 Development of physics I

We are learning how to:

• understand some important contributions to the development of physics

There have been many important developments and discoveries that have helped scientists to increase their knowledge of physics. Over the next four spreads we are going to look at four examples.

Structure of the atom ≫

John Dalton, who you read about in the chemistry section, imagined an atom to be a solid hard ball that could neither be divided nor destroyed. The scientists who came after him started to think about this model of the atom. Was it really a hard ball – or was the atom itself made up of even smaller particles?

J. J. Thompson and the discovery of the electron ≫

In 1897 J. J. Thompson discovered the electron while investigating the properties of cathode rays.

He used a discharge tube from which most of the air had been pumped out so the pressure inside it was very low. At one end of the tube there was a positive electrode (anode), and a negative electrode (cathode). When a high potential difference (1500 volts) was applied across the electrodes a beam of rays was emitted from the cathode. These were called cathode rays. At the opposite end of the tube there was a screen that was coated with zinc sulphide. Any cathode rays striking the screen caused the zinc sulphide to glow.

From his observations Thompson came to the conclusion that cathode rays consisted of a stream of negatively charged electrons, and that these particles are present in all matter.

FIG D 0.1.1 Cathode ray tube used by Thompson in his experiments

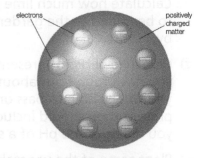

FIG D 0.1.2 Thompson's 'plum pudding' model of the atom

Thompson proposed a different model of the atom than that given by Dalton. He suggested that the negatively charged electrons are spread through the atom, much like plums in a plum pudding, and because the atom is neutral overall, the remainder of the atom must be positively charged.

Rutherford and the discovery of the proton

The understanding of atomic structure took a giant step forward as a result of experiments on scattering alpha particles carried out by the New Zealander Ernest Rutherford and his students Geiger and Marsden in 1910. The essential parts of the apparatus are shown in Fig D 0.1.3.

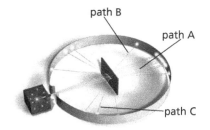

FIG D 0.1.3 Rutherford's apparatus

Alpha radiation is the name given to a stream of positively charged helium particles. In this experiment he directed a stream of alpha particles towards a thin piece of gold foil and observed the directions in which the particles were deflected.

Most of the alpha particles went straight through the gold foil as if it wasn't there without any deflection (path A), a few were deflected through small angles (path B) and, most surprisingly, a very small number of particles, only 1 in 20 000, were deflected backwards (path C).

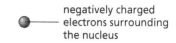

These results didn't fit Thompson's 'plum pudding' model of the atom. As a result of his experiment, Rutherford came to the following conclusions:

1. Much of the atom must be empty space, because so many of the alpha particles were able to pass through the gold foil without being deflected.

FIG D 0.1.4 The Rutherford model of the atom

2. The alpha particles that were deflected must have come close to, or collided with, a large mass at the centre of each atom.

Rutherford proposed a new model of the atom in which almost all of the mass of the atom is in a small, central, positively charged nucleus surrounded by electrons some way from it.

Rutherford also predicted the existence of the neutron, a particle similar in mass to the proton but carrying no charge. The existence of the neutron was confirmed by Chadwick in 1932 and the model of the atom was then modified to consist of a nucleus containing protons and neutrons, surrounded by electrons.

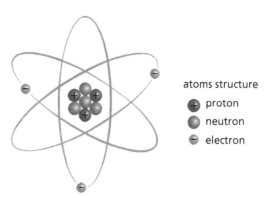

FIG D 0.1.5 Model of the atom after the discovery of the neutron

2 Development of physics I (continued)

Activity D 0.2.1

The story of how physicists developed the model of the atom we use today doesn't stop with Rutherford.

Carry out research using whatever resources are available to you to find out how the Danish physicist Niels Bohr modified the model of the atom proposed by Rutherford.

Check your understanding

1. Why was the model of the atom proposed by Thompson known as the 'plum pudding' model?

2. How did the model of the atom proposed by Rutherford differ to that proposed by Thompson?

Nuclear energy 》》

In 1896 the physicist Antoine-Henri Becquerel found that a sample of uranium gave out invisible radiation that caused photographic film to cloud over. What he discovered was an example of natural radioactivity.

Nuclear energy is the result of changes to the nuclei of atoms. This is a very different process to that of burning fuels. Atoms of some elements undergo spontaneous nuclear decay. The nuclei of these atoms divide to form two or more smaller nuclei of different elements. These are described as radioactive and the process of dividing is called nuclear fission.

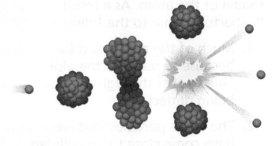

FIG D 0.2.1 Nuclear fission of uranium

Uranium is a radioactive element. It decays spontaneously but it can also be made to happen by firing neutrons at uranium atoms. If we add the masses of the particles formed we find that this is slightly less than the mass of one uranium atom plus one neutron. A tiny amount of mass has been converted into energy – nuclear energy.

Notice that as well as producing energy, this process produces three more neutrons. Fig D 0.2.2 shows what happens if those three neutrons strike more uranium atoms.

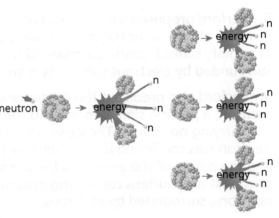

FIG D 0.2.2 A chain reaction

You can imagine what happens if the nine electrons strike nine more uranium atoms and so on. This is called a chain reaction and produces a huge amount of energy very quickly. In order to create a nuclear power station, physicists had to find a way of controlling the chain reaction.

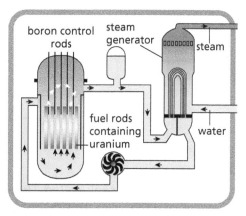

FIG D 0.2.3 Pressurised water reactor

The first nuclear power station began operating in Obninsk, Russia in 1954. They were soon operating in countries around the world.

At the heart of a nuclear power station is a nuclear reactor. This has an array of fuel rods, each containing the uranium fuel. In order to control the reaction, rods of the element boron can be raised or lowered between the fuel rods.

Boron absorbs neutrons. If the nuclear reaction becomes too vigorous, the control rods can be lowered a little into the reactor. These absorb neutrons so there are fewer neutrons available to collide with uranium atoms. If the nuclear reactor slows down, the control rods can be raised a little to allow more neutrons to collide with uranium atoms.

The energy produced during the nuclear reaction boils water to steam, which is then used to drive turbo-generators to make electricity in the same way as in a fossil-fuelled power station.

There are around 450 nuclear power stations in operation around the world. Jamaica currently operates the only nuclear reactor in the Caribbean as part of a research project at the University of the West Indies, but nuclear power is being considered as an alternative source of energy for the future.

Interesting fact

The same nuclear reactions take place in nuclear weapons as in nuclear power stations.

FIG D 0.2.4 Nuclear explosion

This is what happens when a nuclear chain reaction is not controlled.

Activity D 0.2.2

There is considerable controversy regarding the use of nuclear power stations. Some people see it as a safe form of alternative energy that doesn't pollute the atmosphere, while others believe the risk of radioactive substances leaking into the environment make them undesirable.

Carry out research using whatever resources are available to you to find out more about the possibility of nuclear energy in Jamaica and the rest of the Caribbean.

Check your understanding

1. When was radioactivity discovered?
2. What is converted into energy during nuclear fission?
3. Explain what happens during a chain reaction.
4. How is energy production controlled in a nuclear reactor?

3 Development of physics II

Discovery of electricity ▷▷▷

Around 600 BCE an Ancient Greek called Thales discovered that when a substance called amber was rubbed with silk, it attracted light objects.

He had discovered static electricity but had no understanding of what it was. The term 'electricity' is derived from the Greek word for amber. Early scientists continued to experiment with static electricity. They knew about electrical force but understood little of the physics involved.

The US politician and scientist Benjamin Franklin was convinced that lightning had something to do with electricity. To prove this in 1752 he flew a kite during an electrical storm. Contrary to popular myth, Franklin's kite is unlikely to have been struck by lightning, because he would probably been electrocuted, but there was sufficient electric charge in the atmosphere for the kite to pick up some charge.

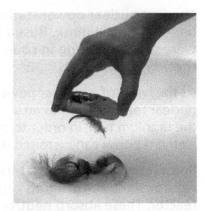

FIG D 0.3.1 Charged amber attracts light objects

Franklin placed a wire on the kite to act as a lightning rod. The bottom of the kite was attached to some wet hemp string, which would conduct electric charge quickly, and to that was attached a length of silk, which was kept dry so it didn't conduct charge. He also had a house key, which he attached to the hemp string.

FIG D 0.3.2 Franklin's experiment

When Franklin placed a finger near the key he felt a spark proving that lightning was related to electric charge in some way. Franklin also had a Leyden jar, which was a device that could store electric charge. He was able to collect charge from the kite string.

In the late 1770s the Italian scientist Luigi Galvani observed that touching the muscles of a dead frog with a metal scalpel caused them to twitch. He incorrectly concluded that the frog's

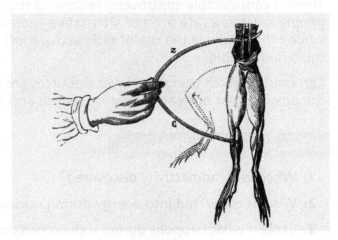

FIG D 0.3.3 Galvani's experiment

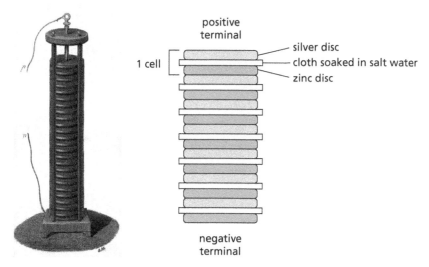

FIG D 0.3.4 Voltaic pile

muscles were producing electricity. What he had in fact done was invent the first electrical cell.

Early in the following century another Italian scientist called Alessandro Volta showed that electricity was created when moisture, from the frog, came between the two different metals.

Volta went on to make the first battery, known as a 'voltaic pile'. He used pure silver and zinc discs separated by cloth which had been soaked in salt solution. Each pair of discs with their connecting piece of cloth was a simple cell. By connecting many cells together Volta paved the way for the study of current electricity.

Activity D 0.3.1

Making a voltaic pile

Here is what you need:

- discs of two different metals (coins and/or washers are ideal)
- discs of felt larger than the metal discs that have been soaked in concentrated sodium chloride solution
- sensitive voltmeter
- connecting wires

Here is what you should do:

1. Make a simple cell by fixing a disc of each metal either side of a piece of soaked felt.

2. Use a voltmeter to measure the voltage across the discs of different metals.

3. Build a pile by adding cells together. Make sure that you put the different metals in the same positions in each cell. Discs of the same metal should not touch each other.

4. Measure the voltage across the ends of your pile as you add more cells.

4 Development of physics II (continued)

We are learning how to:

- understand some important contributions to the development of physics

Integrated circuits »»

You may already be familiar with some of the components we use in simple circuits, like lamps and switches. More complicated circuits may contain other components such as resistors, diodes, capacitors and transistors.

In circuits we describe the components as separate or discrete. Each component can be identified and removed from the circuit if we decide to do so.

While circuits containing discrete components have their uses, the components are bulky and the circuits take up lots of space. As electric circuits evolved, scientists started to look for other ways of building circuits.

During the middle of the last century physicists started to think about how circuits could be made smaller. The first plan was to have miniature components connected together on a ceramic base, but this was superseded by the idea of integrated components on a semi-conductor base.

The first integrated circuit was constructed by Jack Kilby in 1958. This contribution was recognised by the award of the Nobel prize for physics in 2000.

An integrated circuit does not contain miniaturised discrete components. It is a piece of semi-conductor material in which all of the components of an electronic circuit are completely integrated. Different locations on the semi-conductor material are treated in a way that allows them to act in the same way as discrete components.

Kilby's integrated circuit was made using germanium. Shortly after, another physicist called Robert Noyce made an integrated circuit based on the more familiar silicon.

Since the discovery of integrated circuits (ICs), many scientists have contributed to their evolution. ICs have become progressively smaller, while at the same time holding more components. ICs can store huge amounts of data.

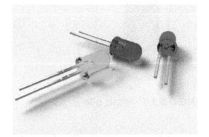
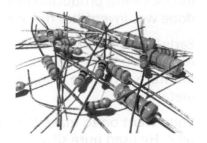

FIG D 0.4.1 Electronic circuits are made up of discrete components

FIG D 0.4.2 Jack Kilby, the inventor of the first integrated circuit

Many of the devices that have become an integral part of everyday life, like cell phones, iPads and laptop computers would not have been possible without the use of ICs.

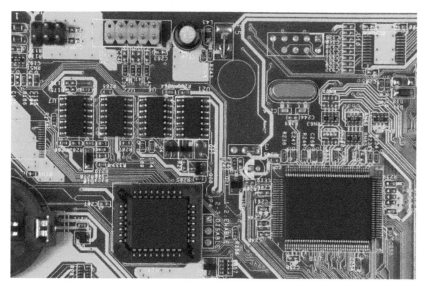

FIG D 0.4.3 Integrated circuits on a computer motherboard

Activity D 0.4.1

Examples of different ICs

There are lots of different ICs. They might look very similar from the outside but they are very different inside and do different jobs. For each of the ICs you have been given:

FIG D 0.4.4 555 – a timer IC

1. Count how many legs it has – these are the way in which it connects with other circuits

2. Check if is has a small piece cut away at one end – what is the purpose of this?

3. Check if it has any numbers printed on it – ICs are numbered so their functions can be identified. For example: 555 is a timer; LM611 is an operational (op) amplifier; LM 311 is a comparator. They may have other numbers and letters to identify the manufacturer.

Check your understanding

1. **a)** Name some discrete components used in circuits.

    b) Explain the advantages of being able to miniaturise circuits.

    c) Name some electronic devices that you think contain integrated circuits.

5 Area and volume

Length ›››

Length is the size of a straight line between one point and another. Length is a measurement in one direction or one dimension.

The SI unit of length is the metre but large values may be measured in kilometres, while small values may be measured in centimetres or millimetres.

The metre is a base unit in the SI system. If we need to measure in two or three dimensions we must derive suitable units based on the units of length.

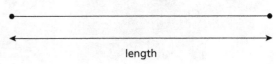

FIG D 1.5.1 Length is a measurement in one dimension

Area ›››

In order to measure the area enclosed by a boundary we need to measure the length in two directions that are perpendicular to each other. We often call these the length and the width.

To work out the area enclosed by a rectangle we multiply the length by the width. The unit in which an area is measured is derived from the unit of length. Area is always expressed as a unit^2. In order to calculate area, the length and width must be expressed in the same unit.

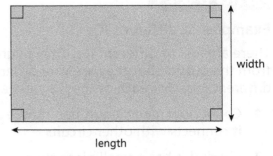

FIG D 1.5.2 Area is a measurement in two dimensions

If the length and width are given in metres the unit of area will be the metre^2, i.e. m × m = m^2.

Notice that the relationship between different units of area is different to the corresponding units of length. For example:

  1 m = 100 cm   but   1 m^2 = 100 cm × 100 cm = 10 000 cm^2

Volume ›››

In order to measure the volume contained by a shape we need to measure the length in three directions that are perpendicular to each other. We often call these the length, width and height.

To find the volume of a cuboid we multiply the length by the width by the height. The unit in which an area is measured is derived from the unit of length. Volume is always expressed as a unit³. In order to calculate volume, the length, width and height must be expressed in the same unit.

If the length, width and height are given in metres the unit of volume will be the metre³, i.e. m × m × m = m³.

Notice again that the relationship between different units of volume is different to the corresponding units of length and area. For example:

1 m = 100 cm but 1 m³ = 100 cm × 100 cm × 100 cm
                          = 1 000 000 cm³

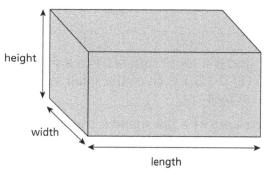

FIG D 1.5.3 Volume is a measurement in three dimensions

Activity D 1.5.1

Here is what you need:

- a metre rule or measure tape

Here is what you should do:

1. Take measurements of lengths, areas and volumes of objects in your classroom.

2. Present your results in a table like the one below.

Object	Length	Width	Height	Area	Volume
Window pole	3.4 m				
Door	2.1 m	1.1 m		2.31 m²	
Chalk box	15 cm	10 cm	10 cm		1500 cm³

TABLE D 1.5.1

Check your understanding

1. State whether each of the following is a unit of length, a unit of area or a unit of volume.

   km   mm³   cm²   m³   cm   km²

2. Carry out the following conversions.

   a) 10 cm expressed in mm

   b) 2 km² expressed in m²

   c) 3 m³ expressed in cm³

Interesting fact

The graphs you draw are a way of displaying data in two dimensions, which we traditionally call the x-axis and the y-axis.

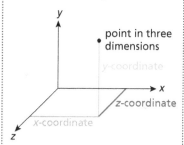

FIG D 1.5.4 Graph in three dimensions

We can also display suitable data as graphs in three dimensions by adding a z-axis but these are not so easy to draw on paper.

6 Area of regular shapes

A grid is a set of squares, like a sheet of graph paper. In Fig D 1.6.1 each of the small squares measures 1 cm by 1 cm.

The **area** of a flat shape is the space contained within its boundaries. The area contained by a square of sides of 1 cm is called a square centimetre or a **centimetre squared**. It has the symbol **cm²**.

The area of a square or a rectangle can be found by putting it on a similar grid and counting how many squares it covers.

A square of sides 4 cm covers 16 squares on the grid. Its area must be 16 cm².

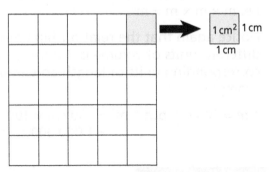

FIG D 1.6.1 A square marked in centimetres

Composite shapes »»

The area of a composite shape can be found by cutting it into pieces and putting those pieces on a 1 cm² grid.

In Fig D 1.6.3 the parts of the letter 'E' form a rectangle 5 cm long by 2 cm wide. The parts cover 10 × 1 cm², so the area of the letter must be 10 cm².

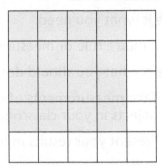

FIG D 1.6.2 Area of a square of sides 4 cm

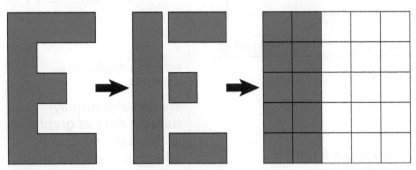

FIG D 1.6.3 The parts of the shape cover 10 × 1 cm²

Finding the area of a shape by putting it on a grid works fine, but is of limited use. How could you use it to find the area of a large shape like a football pitch?

Table D 1.6.1 shows information about the areas of some different shapes. Can you see a pattern between length, width and area?

The area of a square or a rectangle is equal to the product of the sides. In a square the length and width are equal, so:

area of square = length²

The area of a rectangle is equal to the product of the length and the width:

area of rectangle = length × width

Notice that area is always measured in units squared. The unit of area depends on the unit used for the dimensions of the shape. We express small areas in **cm²** and larger areas in **m²**.

Length	Width	Area
1 cm	1 cm	1 cm²
4 cm	4 cm	16 cm²
5 cm	3 cm	15 cm²
5 cm	2 cm	10 cm²

TABLE D 1.6.1

Activity D 1.6.1

Finding the area of surfaces in the classroom

You should work with another student on this activity. Make sure that each of you has an opportunity to measure and to record. Here is what you need:

- metre rule or measure tape

Here is what you should do:

1. Measure the length and width of some square or rectangular surfaces in your classroom. These might be shapes like the top of your desk, the front of your textbook, the chalkboard, etc. Measure small surfaces in centimetres and large surfaces in metres.

2. Record your measurements in a table.

3. Calculate the area of each surface, including the unit.

4. Explain how area can be converted from cm² to m², using one of the surfaces you measured as an example.

Interesting fact

Very large areas, like the area of a country, are expressed in kilometres squared. The area of Jamaica is 10 991 km².

Key terms

area the region bound by the edges of a flat shape

centimetre squared (cm²) and **metre squared (m²)** units of area

Check your understanding

1. Remember to include the correct unit with each of your answers.

   a) Calculate the area of squares that have sides of the following length:

   i) 15 cm   **ii)** 5 m   **iii)** 2.5 cm.

   b) Calculate the area of rectangles that have sides of the following lengths:

   i) 18 cm and 12 cm   **ii)** 5 m and 3.5 m.

2. A house brick has sides of 23 cm, 11 cm and 7.5 cm.

   Calculate the areas of the three sides of the brick you can see in the Fig D 1.6.4.

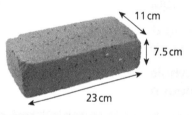

11 cm

7.5 cm

23 cm

FIG D 1.6.4

7 Area of irregular shapes

We are learning how to:
- use appropriate units for area
- estimate the area of irregular shapes

The areas of shapes can be compared by investigating whether the shapes cover each other or not. Fig D 1.7.1 shows a circle, a square and a triangle.

Fig D 1.7.2 shows that the triangle fits inside the circle and the circle fits inside the square.

So the areas of these shapes, from smallest to largest, is triangle, circle, square.

FIG D 1.7.1 Three shapes

FIG D 1.7.2 The triangle fits inside the circle, and the circle fits inside the square

Estimating area ▶▶▶

The area of an **irregular shape** can be **estimated** by counting out how many squares of a 1 cm² grid it covers even when the sides are not whole numbers. The blue rectangle in Fig D 1.7.3 has sides of 4.0 cm and 2.5 cm.

The rectangle covers some whole squares and some half squares. There are:

- 8 squares that are all covered

- 4 squares that are half covered.

The estimated area of this rectangle is 8 + (4 × 0.5) = 10.0 cm². You can compare this with the value obtained using the formula given in lesson D 1.6:

area of rectangle = 4.0 × 2.5 = 10.0 cm²

When an area cannot be calculated using a formula because it is irregular, it has to be estimated. In Fig D 1.7.4 the oval covers the squares of the grid by different amounts.

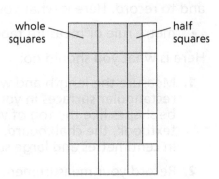

FIG D 1.7.3 Area of a rectangle of sides 4.0 cm and 2.5 cm

The area is estimated by counting up those squares that are at least half covered by the shape. This leads to an over-estimate of the area but this is compensated for by ignoring the squares that are less than half covered.

Using this method, an estimate for the area of the oval is:

8 whole squares covered + 12 squares that are about half covered or more = 20 squares.

Each square represents 1 cm², so this represents an area of 20 cm².

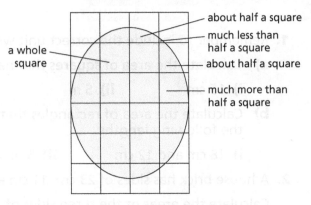

FIG D 1.7.4 Area of an oval shape

Estimating the area of an irregular shape

Here is what you need:

- ruler 30 cm
- sheet of plain paper
- irregular shape cut in card

Here is what you should do:

1. Draw a grid 10 cm by 10 cm on the plain paper using a pencil and ruler.

2. Put the irregular shape on the grid and draw round it.

3. Count the number of squares that are at least half covered by the outline of the shape. You might find it helpful to shade each part as you add it, so that none are missed or counted twice.

4. Write down your estimate of the area of the shape.

Check your understanding

1. A student drew around an irregular shape that had been placed on a 1 cm² grid.

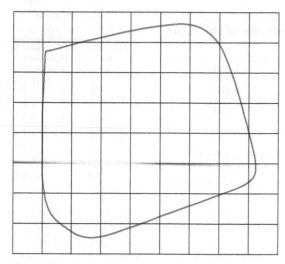

FIG D 1.7.5 The irregular shape

Estimate the area of this shape using the method described above.

Key terms

estimate an approximate amount

irregular shape has sides and angles of different sizes or lacks symmetry

8 Volume of regular shapes

We are learning how to:

- formulate a simple working definition for the term 'volume'
- use appropriate units for volume
- calculate the volume of regular-shaped objects

The **volume** of a solid shape is the amount of space that it occupies. A cube is a regular solid shape that has equal sides; that is, length = width = height.

When the sides of a cube are one centimetre, the cube occupies a space of one **centimetre cubed** or one **cubic centimetre**. This unit of volume is written as **cm³**.

FIG D 1.8.1 A cubic centimetre

Cubes and cuboids ⟩⟩⟩

Most cubes can be broken down into smaller cubes with sides of 1 cm.

Fig D 1.8.2 shows the number of cubes of sides 1 cm in some larger cubes. The volumes of the cubes are given in Table D 1.8.1. Can you see a pattern between the length of the side of a cube and its volume?

Length of side of the cube	Number of cubes of sides 1 cm	Volume of the cube
1 cm	1	1 cm³
2 cm	8	8 cm³
3 cm	27	27 cm³

TABLE D 1.8.1

The volume of a cube is equal to length × width × height.

The same formula can also be used to work out the volume of a cuboid.

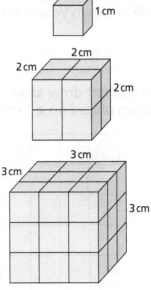

FIG D 1.8.2 How many smaller cubes in each large cube?

Cylinder and sphere ⟩⟩⟩

The volumes of other regular solids can be worked out using suitable formulae.

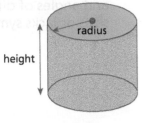

FIG D 1.8.3 Cylinder

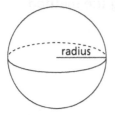

FIG D 1.8.4 Sphere

Volume of a cylinder = base area × height
= $\pi \times radius^2 \times height$

Volume of a sphere = $\frac{4}{3} \times \pi \times radius^3$

The volume of a composite shape can be found by adding the volumes of the smaller shapes from which it is made.

The composite shape in Fig D 1.8.5 can be separated into two cuboids (Fig D 1.8.6).

The volume of the composite shape is the sum of the volume of the cuboids, which is:

$$(7 \times 6 \times 2) + (6 \times 6 \times 4) = 84 + 144 = 228 \text{ cm}^3$$

The volume of large regular solid shapes is measured in exactly the same way but in **cubic metres**. A cubic metre, **m³**, is the volume of a cube that has sides of one metre.

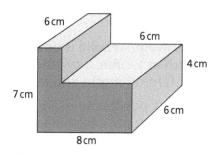

FIG D 1.8.5 A composite solid shape

Activity D 1.8.1

Measuring regular solid shapes and calculating their volumes

You should work with another student on this activity. Make sure that each of you has an opportunity to measure and to record. Here is what you need:

- ruler 30 cm • regular solids shapes labelled A, B, C, etc.

Here is what you should do:

1. Name the solid shape A.

2. Measure the dimensions of A and write them in a table.

3. Calculate the volume of the shape using a suitable formula.

4. Repeat this for all of the solid shapes you have been given

5. Explain how volume can be converted from cm³ to m³, using one of the shapes you measured as an example.

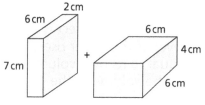

FIG D 1.8.6 Composite shape separated into cuboids

Key terms

volume the space that an object occupies

centimetre cubed/cubic centimetre (cm³) and **metre cubed/cubic metre (m³)** units of volume

1. Count the number of cubes of sides 1 cm in each of the following shapes and use this to give their volume.

a)

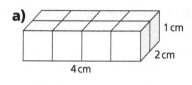

FIG D 1.8.7a

b)

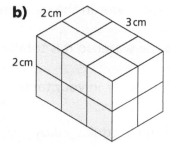

FIG D 1.8.7b

c)

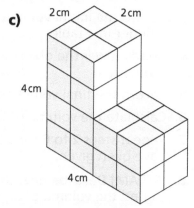

FIG D 1.8.7c

253

9 Volume of irregular shapes

We are learning how to:

- use appropriate units for volume
- determine the volume of irregular-shaped objects

An **irregular solid** is one that doesn't have a standard shape, such as a cube, a cylinder or a sphere. It may have sides of different lengths and it lacks symmetry.

It isn't possible to divide an irregular shape into 1 cm³ cubes, nor to apply a formula to find its volume.

FIG D 1.9.1 An irregular solid

Finding volume by displacement 》》

The volume of an irregular solid must be measured by **displacement**.

When a solid object is submerged in a container of water, the level of the water rises. The object displaces a volume of water equal to its own volume. The new volume is equal to the sum of the volume of the water and the volume of the solid.

volume of shape = volume of water containing the shape
– volume of water

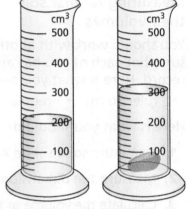

FIG D 1.9.2 Measuring volume by displacement

Activity D 1.9.1

Measuring the volume of an irregular solid by displacement

Here is what you need:

- irregular-shaped objects
- string
- measuring cylinder 250 cm³
- water

Here is what you should do:

1. Half fill the measuring cylinder with water.
2. Tie a piece of string around the first irregular solid. It needs to be long enough to lower the object fully into the measuring cylinder.
3. Record the initial volume of the water in the measuring cylinder in a table.
4. Gently lower the object into the water so it is totally submerged.
5. Record the final volume of the water in your table.
6. Calculate the volume of the object.
7. Repeat steps 2 to 6 for all of the irregular solids you have been given.
8. [STEAM] Describe how this method could be modified to find the volume of an irregular solid that:

   a) floats on water
   b) is soluble in water.

1. The following diagram shows the level of water in a measuring cylinder before and after introducing an irregular solid shape.

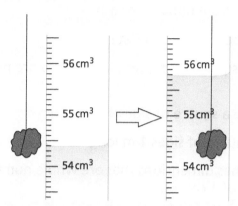

FIG D 1.9.3 Levels of water in a measuring cylinder

a) What was:

   i) the initial volume of water?

   ii) the final volume of water?

   iii) the volume of the irregular solid?

b) Why is it important that all of the solid is submerged in the water?

2. State whether the following shapes are regular or irregular.

a)

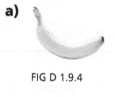

FIG D 1.9.4

b)

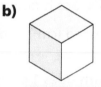

FIG D 1.9.5

c)

FIG D 1.9.6

d)

FIG D 1.9.7

Key terms

irregular solid a solid that doesn't have a regular shape like a cube, a cylinder or a sphere

displacement a solid occupies the space that would be occupied by a liquid

Review of Measuring length and related quantities

- The units of area and volume are derived from units of length.

- Area is the space contained within the boundaries of a flat shape.

- Small areas are measured in centimetres squared (cm^2) and large areas are measured in metres squared (m^2).

- A square centimetre is the area bound by a square of sides 1 cm long.

- A square metre is the area bound by a square of sides 1 m long.

- The area of a square or a rectangle that has dimensions that are whole numbers can be found by putting the shape on a grid of 1 cm squares.

- The area of a regular square or rectangle can be calculated using the equation area = length × width.

- The area of a composite flat shape can be found by calculating the area of each component.

- The relative areas of two or more shapes can be determined by seeing whether the shapes can contain each other or not.

- The area of an irregular shape cannot be calculated and must be estimated.

- To estimate the area of an irregular shape, the shape is put on a grid of 1 cm squares and only those squares that are at least half covered are counted.

- The volume of a solid shape is the amount of space it occupies.

- Small volumes are measured in centimetres cubed (cm^3) and large volumes are measured in metres cubed (m^3).

- A cubic centimetre is the volume of a cube with sides 1 cm long.

- A cubic metre is the volume of a cube with sides 1 m long.

- A cube, a cuboid, a cylinder and a sphere are examples of regular solid shapes.

- The volume of a cube or cuboid can be calculated using the formula volume = length × width × height.

- The volume of a composite solid shape can be found by calculating the volume of each component.

- The volume of a cylinder can be calculated using the formula volume = π × radius of base^2 × height.

- The volume of a sphere can be calculated using the formula $\frac{4}{3}$ × π × radius^3.

- The volume of an irregular solid shape cannot be calculated from a formula and must be measured by displacement.

Review questions on Measuring length and related quantities

Knowledge and understanding

1. Fig D 1.RQ.1 shows a method of measuring volume by displacement.

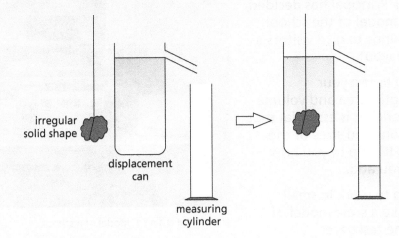

irregular solid shape

displacement can

measuring cylinder

FIG D 1.RQ.1

a) Explain how this method works.

b) Suggest how the method could be modified to find the volume of a piece of cork that floats on water.

Process skills

2. In order to widen a road, a cuboid-shaped block of rock measuring 5 m by 8 m by 3.5 m high has to be removed.

What volume of rock must be removed?

3. A cylindrical-shaped piece of wood has a radius of 10 cm and a height of 40 cm.

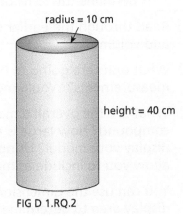

radius = 10 cm

height = 40 cm

a) Is this a regular or an irregular solid shape?

b) What is the volume of this shape?

FIG D 1.RQ.2

4. A football pitch has sides of 105 m and 55 m.

a) What shape is the football pitch?

b) What area is covered by the football pitch?

11 Making a scale model of the school

As part of improving the reception area at your school, the Principal has decided to include a scale model of the school buildings and grounds to give visitors a better idea of its layout.

She has asked you to use your knowledge of length, area and volume to produce the model. It is essential that you get the positions and sizes of the structures correct. It is up to you how much fine detail you add.

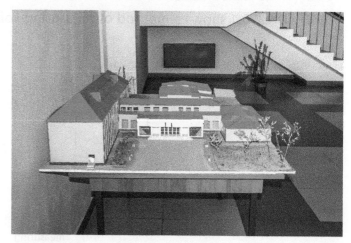

FIG STEAM D 1.11.1 Model of a school

1 You are going to work in small groups to make a scale model of the school. The tasks are:

- to determine a suitable scale for your model

- to obtain all of the measurements you need to make the model

- to determine what materials to use

- to build and paint your model

- to check that your dimensions are correct

- to modify your model as necessary before attaching it permanently to its base.

a) Read through the earlier sections on length, area and volume.

b) What units are going to be most suitable for taking measurements? Would metres provide sufficient detail?

What are the overall dimensions of the school compound? How large is the area where you will display your model? Using all of the display area will allow you to include as much detail as possible.

You can use the dimensions of the school and the display area to determine a suitable scale. For example, if the display area is 2 m long and the school compound is 200 m long and then your scale will be 2 : 200 or 1 : 100. In other words, 1 m on your model will equal 100 m in reality.

c) You will need to determine:

- the positions of individual buildings and other structures within the compound – an aerial photograph or a map of the school would help you to do this if either is available

- the dimensions of individual buildings so they can be made to scale.

d) You will need to determine what materials you intend to use. You might find old cardboard boxes readily available and easy to work with. You are going to need some tools like scissors, and other materials like glue and paints.

e) The group needs to decide who will do what. For example, two students might be responsible for mapping out the positions of roads, buildings etc. on the base, while the remainder of the group can each take on responsibility for the individual structures.

Remember to take some photographs at different stages of your work. Visitors to the school might be interested to see how your model was made.

f) Once the base and all of the structure are complete, lay out the structures in their appropriate positions, but don't fix them permanently to the base. You need to devise some ways of checking that your model is accurate. For example you could:

FIG STEAM D 1.11.2 Aerial photograph of a school

FIG STEAM D 1.11.3 Cardboard is easy to work with

- take some photographs of your model from ground level and then check how these compare to the real thing

- take some measurements at different positions of your model, scale them up using the scale factor, and then compare your answers with the actual values.

g) Once you are satisfied that your model is as accurate as it can be, fix the buildings and other structures permanently to the base.

12 Investigating static electricity

We are learning how to:

- investigate the production of static electricity
- conduct investigations with due regard for safety

The word **static** means standing still. We normally think about electricity as flowing very quickly along metal wires, but under the right conditions electric charge can build up on objects made of materials like glass and plastic.

Charging by friction 》》

You may have noticed that when you use a plastic comb on your hair it sometimes crackles. Static electricity is created by **friction** when you rub your hair with the comb.

If you walk across a nylon carpet and then touch a metal door handle, you may feel a sharp tingle at the end of your fingers. Static charge builds up on your body as a result of friction between the bottoms of your shoes and the carpet. The tingle is a small electric shock as the static electricity is discharged.

FIG D 2.12.1 Lightning is the discharge of static electricity to earth

You might also receive an electric shock when you get out of a car and touch the metal door handle. Static charge builds up on the car due to friction as it moves through the air.

Under certain conditions charge even builds up in the atmosphere. Eventually the charge becomes so great it flows to earth in a massive spark that we call **lightning**.

Charging with static electricity 》》

Any insulator can be charged with static electricity by rubbing it with another insulator. In the laboratory, rods of glass or plastic are charged by rubbing them on fabrics such as wool or silk.

Interesting fact

The Ancient Greeks noticed that rubbing a material called amber on wool gives it unusual properties. It is able to pick up small objects like hairs, threads, pieces of feathers and even dry leaves.

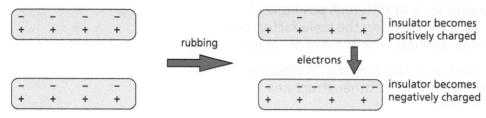

insulator becomes positively charged

insulator becomes negatively charged

FIG D 2.12.2 Charge is the result of the transfer of electrons

When the two insulators are rubbed together, electrons are transferred from one substance to the other. As electrons carry a negative charge, the insulator that loses electrons becomes positively charged while the insulator that gains electrons becomes negatively charged.

Charged objects interact with each other. If you bring two objects that have the same charge, either + or −, towards each other they will repel, but if you bring together two objects that carry opposite charges, that is + and −, they will attract each other.

Key terms

static not moving

friction force that opposes motion

lightning movement of electric charge between the sky and the ground

Activity D 2.12.1

Investigating some effects of static electricity

Here is what you need:

- plastic comb (must be clean and not greasy)
- glass rod
- rubber balloon
- piece of silk
- piece of wool
- small pieces of tissue paper

Here is what you should do:

1. Rub the comb vigorously against your uniform for a short time or until the comb feels warm.
2. Hold the comb near some small pieces of paper.
3. Describe what you observe.
4. Rub a glass rod with a piece of silk.
5. Turn on a tap so there is a very thin column of water flowing.
6. Bring the charged glass rod close to the column of water – but don't touch it.
7. Describe what you observe.
8. Blow up a balloon.
9. Rub the balloon on a piece of wool or a woollen jumper.
10. Hold the rubbed part of the balloon against the wall and then carefully move your hands away.
11. Describe what you observe.
12. The charge on a single electron is $1.60217662 \times 10^{-19}$ coulombs (this is the unit of charge).
    a) Give this value correct to two significant figures.
    b) Explain why is it more convenient to express this value in standard form than to write it out in full.

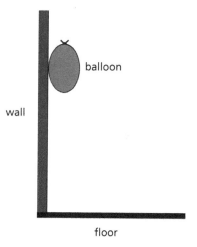

FIG D 2.12.3 The student's experiment

Check your understanding

1. A student rubbed an inflated balloon on her woollen jumper and then held it to a wall. When she took her hands away, the balloon stayed in the same position.
   a) Explain why the balloon becomes negatively charged when it is rubbed on the woollen jumper.
   b) With the help of a diagram, explain why the balloon remains 'fixed' to the wall and does not fall.

13 Uses of static electricity

Uses of electrostatic charge

Electrostatic charging has a number of important applications.

Photocopiers use electrostatic charge to provide a means of copying documents.

Electrostatic charge provides a means of copying documents (Fig D 2.13.1).

When a document is scanned on a photocopier, the image is projected onto a positively charged plate. Where light falls on the plate, the charge leaks away. This leaves a charged area on the plate corresponding to the dark parts of the document.

Negatively charged black (or colour) toner powder is then attracted to those parts of the plate that are still charged. This produces a mirror image of the document on the plate.

original document

physics

the image of the document is projected onto a positively charged copying plate

an exact copy of the document is fixed on paper **physics**

the charge leaks away except on those parts of the plate corresponding to dark areas on the document

paper is placed over the copying plate: toner is transferred to the paper and heated to make it stick

the negatively charged black toner particles are attracted to those parts of the plate that remain positively charged

FIG D 2.13.1 Photocopying

Paper is fed over the plate. The toner is transferred to the paper and is fixed by heating. The result is a perfect copy of the original document.

Electrostatic precipitation

Coal-fired power stations produce a lot of flue-ash. This ash consists of tiny particles of carbon and other materials formed during combustion – this could cause serious atmospheric pollution.

The flue-ash is removed by an electrostatic precipitation unit fitted inside the chimney. Initially the ash particles pass through a negatively charged grid where they become negatively charged.

The ash particles then pass between a pair of positively charged collecting plates. As the particles carry negative charge they are attracted to the plates and attach to them. The ash builds up on the collection plates, so at

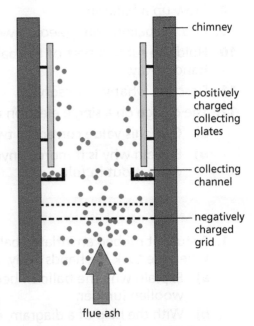

chimney

positively charged collecting plates

collecting channel

negatively charged grid

flue ash

FIG D 2.13.2 Electrostatic precipitation

regular intervals the plates are mechanically shaken and accumulated ash falls into collecting channels. The collected ash is used to make building materials.

Activity D 2.13.1

Making an electrostatic separator

Here is what you need:

- balloon
- duster or woolly jumper
- mixture of salt and finely ground pepper
- open dish or plate

Here is what you should do:

1. Sprinkle the mixture of salt and pepper onto the plate.

2. Blow up the balloon and tie the end.

3. Rub the balloon with a duster or a woolly jumper to charge it.

4. Fix the charged balloon just above, but not touching, the plate.

5. Describe your observations.

6. Explain how the charged balloon is able to separate the salt and pepper.

7. Can you suggest an industrial process in which static electricity may bring about a separation of particles?

Check your understanding

1. Insecticides can be spread over large areas when spread from an aeroplane. The insecticide leaves the aeroplane through charged nozzles.

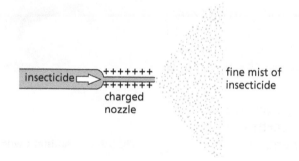

FIG D 2.13.3

a) Describe what happens to the insecticide as it passes through the nozzle.

b) Explain why charging the nozzle allows the insecticide to be used more effectively and more efficiently.

Key term

electrostatic static electrical charge

14 Hazards of static electricity

We are learning how to:

- describe the hazards of static electricity

Electrostatic charges create a number of potential hazards.

Lightning

Under certain weather conditions massive amounts of electrostatic charge may build up in the atmosphere and finally discharge to earth as lightning. Lightning tends to discharge through objects sticking up above the ground such as trees, tall chimneys and towers. That is why standing near these objects in stormy weather is dangerous. **Lightning conductors** are attached to many buildings to prevent or minimise damage in the event of a lightning strike. The conductor is made of thick copper or brass wire that provides the electric charge with an easy passage to earth.

Polythene manufacture

During the manufacturing process, sheets of polythene (and other plastics) pass around various rollers, as a result of which an electrostatic charge builds up on the polythene. The electrostatic charge is removed by fixing a bar containing a **radioactive isotope** across the polythene, just above but not touching it. The isotope causes the air above the polythene to ionise and the charge on the polythene is neutralised.

FIG D 2.14.1 Static electricity builds up on polythene during manufacture

Electronic circuits ⟫⟫

Many of the tiny components used in electronic circuits are very sensitive to electrostatic charge. Even a small amount of charge built up on the hands of a circuit builder, perhaps as a result of rubber-soled shoes rubbing against the ground, is enough to destroy them.

People assembling circuit boards often wear antistatic wristbands. These connect their bodies to earth so that electrostatic charge cannot build up on them.

FIG D 2.14.2 Antistatic wristband

Many industrial processes involve the movement of powders such as coal dust, grain, chocolate powder and flour along pipes. In years gone by it was not appreciated that friction between a powder and a pipe created electrostatic charge.

In a building such as a flour mill, where the air contains combustible particles, the small spark formed when static charge was earthed was sometimes enough to trigger an explosion. In modern factories, pipes are earthed to prevent any build-up of static charge.

Activity D 2.14.1

Assessing risk when transferring fuels

The movement of liquids along pipes results in the build-up of electrostatic charge. This is a particular danger with petrol, diesel or aviation fuel.

Consider the problems created by static electricity when transferring fuels:

- How might electrostatic charge be built up?

- What hazards result from the build-up of electrostatic charge?

- What safety procedures should be used?

Check your understanding

1. During the manufacturing process, artificial fertiliser powder acquires an electrostatic charge. Fig D 2.14.4 shows what happens when bags full of fertiliser powder are sealed.

   a) How does the polythene bag become charged?

   b) Why does the electrostatic charge make it difficult to close the bags?

FIG D 2.14.3 The remains of a flour mill after an explosion and fire

Key terms

lightning conductor metal strip to protect from damage due to lightning

radioactive isotope substance that emits radiation

electrostatic static electrical charge

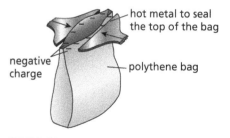

hot metal to seal the top of the bag

negative charge

polythene bag

FIG D 2.14.4

Review of Static electricity

- Static electricity is electric charge built up on an insulator.

- Insulators can be charged by friction.

- Electrostatic charge is the result of electrons being transferred between insulators.

- Insulators that lose electrons become positively charged; insulators that gain electrons become negatively charged.

- Like charges repel and unlike charges attract.

- Electrostatic charge sometimes makes materials behave in unusual ways.

- Static electricity has some important uses including:

  o photocopying

  o electrostatic precipitation of particles in flue gas.

- Static electricity creates some important potential hazards including:

  o damage by lightning strikes

  o build-up of charge during polythene manufacture

  o damage to components in electronic circuits

  o build-up of charge when fluids pass along pipes.

Review questions on Static electricity

Knowledge and understanding

1. Fig D 2.RQ.1 shows a lightning conductor attached to a chimney.

FIG D 2.RQ.1

  a) Suggest a suitable material for making the lightning conductor.

  b) Explain how the lightning conductor protects the roof.

Process skills

2. a) What type of force is there between:

   i) two positive charges?

   ii) two negative charges?

   iii) a positive charge and a negative charge?

Fig D 2.RQ.2 shows how broad-mesh wire netting can be painted.

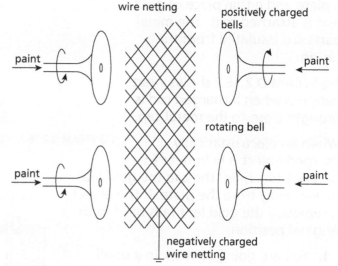

FIG D 2.RQ.2

The paint is delivered through rotating bells. Each bell has a very high positive charge.

  b) Why does charging the paint cause the tiny droplets to separate?

  c) What charge is on the wire netting relative to the paint droplets?

  d) Explain how this method allows the netting to be painted efficiently without wasting paint.

3. Diamonds are electrical insulators. They are found in dirt, which does conduct electricity. Fig D 2.RQ.3 shows an electrostatic method for separating diamonds from dirt.

  a) Explain how the method works.

  b) The particles are closely spaced at W on the conveyor belt. Explain why they are further apart at X.

  c) Explain the curved path of the diamonds between Y and Z.

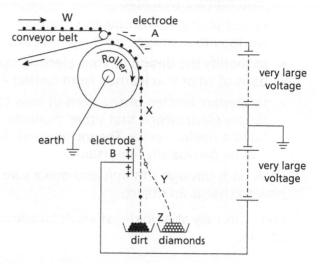

FIG D 2.RQ.3

16 Building an electroscope

A gold-leaf electroscope is a device that scientists use to detect electrostatic charge. It consists of a metal cap attached to a metal rod. The other end of the metal rod is flattened into a plate and a thin piece of gold leaf is attached to it. The metal parts are insulated from the casing.

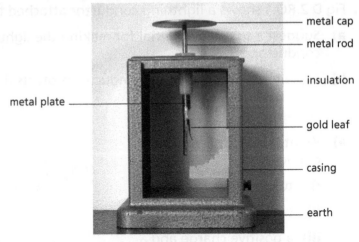

FIG STEAM D 2.16.1 A gold-leaf electroscope

Fig STEAM D 2.16.2 shows what happens when a charged rod is brought close to the metal cap.

When an electrostatically charged object is held near to (but not touching) the cap the gold leaf moves away from the plate. If the object is removed the gold leaf falls back to its original position.

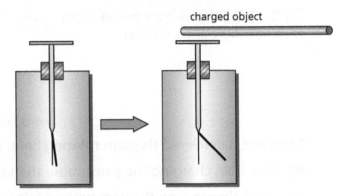

FIG STEAM D 2.16.2 Detecting electrostatic charge

1. You are going to work in a small group to make an electroscope using commonly available objects and materials. The tasks are:

   • to review how to charge an object
   • to examine a gold-leaf electroscope
   • to make an electroscope using whatever objects and materials are available
   • to test your electroscope and compare how well it works with a 'proper' gold-leaf electroscope
   • to modify the design of your electroscope on the basis of what you learned from testing it
   • to prepare written instructions of how to build a simple electroscope that other students can use to build a similar device. The inclusion of illustrations will be particularly important.

   Look back through this unit and make sure you know how to charge an object.

   Look carefully at a gold-leaf electroscope or a photo of one.

a) Think about how you could build an electroscope from everyday objects and materials. For example:

- You won't have any gold foil, but maybe aluminium cooking foil would work if it isn't too thick?

- You won't have a metal case with glass sides but maybe any empty glass jar with a plastic lid would work?

- You won't have a metal cap and rod but maybe a big nail would work? How are you going to get the end flat?

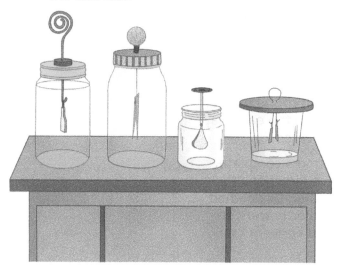

FIG STEAM D 2.16.3 Some home-made electroscopes

Don't forget to take some photographs during construction. These will be useful when you come to write the instructions on how you built your device.

b) When you have completed your electroscope try it out with some different charged objects. Compare how well it performs against a gold-leaf electroscope. You will need to analyse your design.

c) Modify the design of your electroscope by incorporating those features that you have identified as a result of testing. Carry out more tests until you are satisfied your electroscope is as good as it can be.

d) Write a series of instructions to enable another student to build a device like yours.

Instructions are often supported by lots of diagrams and other illustrations. People often find these easier to follow than written instructions alone.

When you have completed your instructions you might be asked by your teacher to describe the construction of your electroscope to the class.

17 Electric current

In the previous unit you learned how electric charge can build up on materials like plastics. This is described as static electricity because it remains in one place and doesn't flow anywhere. An electric current arises when electrical charge flows along a conductor such as a wire.

Conventional current and actual current

We now know that electric charge is carried round a circuit by tiny particles called electrons. However, in the early days of electricity, electrons had not been discovered.

Physicists knew that electricity flowed round a complete circuit but were unable to decide in which direction. It was agreed by convention that current would be deemed to flow from the positive terminal of a cell or battery, to the negative terminal. This was later called **conventional current**.

After the discovery of the electron, physicists realised they had chosen the wrong direction. Electrons carry a negative charge and therefore flow from the negative terminal to the positive terminal. The correct direction was called the **actual current**.

Ampere

The unit of electric current is the **ampere** but this is often abbreviated to amp, and it has the symbol A.

The currents measured in circuits in the laboratory are often smaller than one ampere. In order to avoid using fractions of an ampere, two prefixes are used to create smaller units of electric current.

- A **milliampere**, mA, is $^1/_{1000}$ th of an ampere so
  1000 mA = 1 A

- A **microampere**, µA, is $^1/_{1\,000\,000}$ th of an ampere so
  1000000 µA = 1 A

FIG D 3.17.1 Ammeters

Measuring current >>>

Electric current is measured by an **ammeter**. There are two types in common use.

An analogue ammeter has a moving pointer and the current is read from a scale where the pointer stops. A digital ammeter gives a direct numerical readout. It may be part of a multimeter which has many different uses.

An ammeter must be connected in series to measure the current flowing through a component.

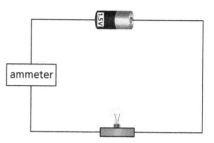

FIG D 3.17.2 An ammeter used in a circuit

Activity D 3.17.1

Measuring the current at different points in a circuit

Here is what you need:

- a battery containing two cells
- bulbs × 3
- ammeter
- connecting wires

Here is what you should do:

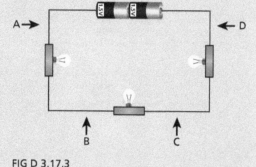

FIG D 3.17.3

1. Construct the circuit shown in Fig D 3.17.3

2. Connect the ammeter at point A in the circuit and record the current.

3. Repeat this at points B, C and D, recording the current each time.

4. What evidence is there that the current is not used up in a circuit?

Key terms

conventional current agreed direction of current before discovery of the electron

actual current direction of flow of electrons

ampere (A) unit of electrical current

milliampere thousandth of an ampere

microampere millionth of an ampere

ammeter instrument for measuring current

Check your understanding

1. **a)** Explain the difference between conventional current and actual current.

   b) State whether each of the following is 'used up' in a circuit.

   i) Current   **ii)** Charge   **iii)** Electrical energy

2. In each of the following give the symbol for the appropriate unit in your answer.

   a) How many amperes are equal to 450 mA?

   b) How many amperes are equal to 750 μA?

   c) How many milliamperes are in 2.5 A?

18 Conductors and insulators

We are learning how to:

- distinguish between electrical insulators and conductors
- relate flow of current to conduction

Electricity is a form of energy. It can flow easily through some materials but not others.

- Materials that allow an electric current to flow through them are called electrical **conductors**.

- Materials that prevent the flow of an electric current are called electrical **insulators**.

Activity D 3.18.1

Conductors and insulators

Here is what you need:

- battery of three cells
- lamp
- two crocodile clips
- connecting wires
- samples of materials – for example, aluminium, copper, plastic, rubber, wood

Here is what you should do:

1. Connect the components of the circuit together as shown in Fig D 3.18.1.

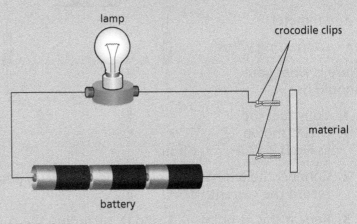

FIG D 3.18.1

2. Before testing the sample materials, test the circuit by touching the crocodile clips together. If the circuit is complete the lamp should light up. If the lamp does not light up check all the connections.

3. Take the first sample of material and clip the crocodile clips to each end of it. If the lamp lights, the material is a conductor. If the bulb does not light, the material is an insulator.

4. Present your observations in the form of a table. On one side write the names of the conducting materials, and on the other write the names of the insulating materials.

5. [STEAM] Describe how this activity could be modified to investigate whether heating a wire affects the amount of current it carries.

Metallic structure »»

All metals are excellent conductors of electricity. To understand why we need to consider **metallic structure**. Metals consist of a matrix of particles surrounded by a 'sea' of negatively charged **electrons**. These electrons are delocalised and free to move about.

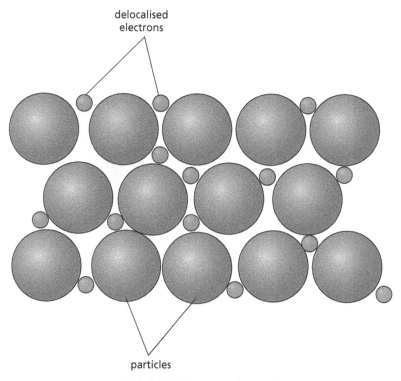

delocalised electrons

particles

FIG D 3.18.2 Structure of a metal

Key terms

conductors materials that allow an electric current to flow through them

insulators materials that prevent the flow of an electric current

metallic structure a matrix of particles surrounded by a 'sea' of negatively charged electrons

electrons negatively charged particles

When a conductor, such as a metal wire, is connected to a battery electrons flow through the conductor carrying electric charge. Electricity is a flow of electrons.

Insulators, such as plastics and glass, do not have delocalised electrons so they are unable to conduct electricity.

Check your understanding

1. Arrange the following materials into two lists: conductors and insulators.

aluminium	copper	glass	iron
plastic	rubber	steel	wood

19 Complete circuits

We are learning how to:
- construct simple electric circuits
- identify a complete circuit

We use mains electricity to power most appliances in our homes but it is far too dangerous for working with circuits in the laboratory. Instead we use a **cell** or a **battery**. They provide much less electrical energy than the mains supply.

You might use the words 'cell' and 'battery' to mean the same thing in everyday language but in science these terms have particular meanings. A cell is what is often incorrectly called a battery, and a battery is a combination of two or more cells.

FIG D 3.19.1 This is a single cell

Activity D 3.19.1

Building simple circuits

Here is what you need:

- cell in holder
- lamp
- connecting wires

Here is what you should do:

1. Make the circuit shown in Fig D 3.19.3.

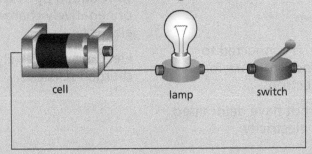

cell   lamp   switch

FIG D 3.19.3

FIG D 3.19.2 When two or more cells are used together to power an electrical device, they are called a battery

2. Draw the circuit and, alongside, write whether the lamp lit up or not when the switch was closed.

3. Make up five more different circuits.

4. Draw each circuit and write whether the lamp lights or not when the switch is closed.

5. Look at the circuits you made in which the lamp lit up. Can you see anything similar about them?

A **circuit** is a complete pathway around which an electric current can flow. The pathway must be made of a conductor such as a metal wire.

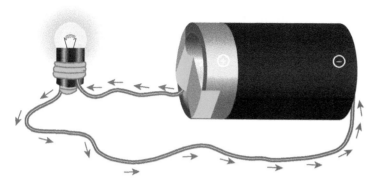

FIG D 3.19.4 Direction of conventional current

A cell has a positive (+) terminal and a negative (–) terminal. Conventionally, the direction of the electric current is taken to flow from the positive terminal to the negative terminal. This is called **conventional current flow.**

In reality the current is the result of a flow of electrons. Since electrons carry a negative charge, they actually flow from the negative terminal (where there are a lot of negative charges) to the positive terminal of the cell (where there are fewer negative charges). This is called **electron flow** and is in the opposite direction to the conventional current.

Check your understanding

1.

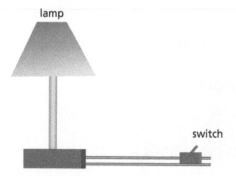

FIG D 3.19.6 A lamp connected to the mains electricity supply

Explain, in terms of flow of current, how the switch can control the current in the lamp circuit in Fig D 3.19.6.

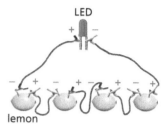
Key terms

cell electrical power source often incorrectly called a battery

battery a combination of two or more cells

circuit a complete pathway around which an electric current can flow

conventional current flow current taken to flow from the positive terminal to the negative terminal of a cell

electron flow electrons flow from the negative terminal to the positive terminal of a cell

20 Cells and lamps

We are learning how to:
• construct simple electric circuits
• observe the effect of using different numbers of cells and lamps in a circuit

When additional components are added to a circuit, they can often be added in different ways, with different results.

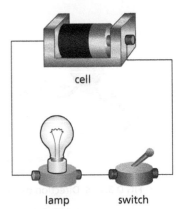

cell

lamp   switch

FIG D 3.20.1 A simple lighting circuit might consist of a cell, a lamp and a switch

Activity D 3.20.1

Making circuits with cells, lamps and switches

Here is what you need:

• battery containing two cells
• two lamps
• switch
• connecting wires

circuit 1

circuit 2

circuit 3

FIG D 3.20.2

Here is what you should do:

1. Build circuit 1 in Fig D 3.20.2.

2. Reverse the direction of one of the cells in circuit 1. Does the lamp still light up?

3. Build circuit 2 and make a note of how brightly the lamps glow.

4. Build circuit 3.

5. Do the lamps in circuit 3 glow less brightly, as brightly or more brightly than in circuit 2?

6. Include a switch at some different places in circuit 3. Do the lamps turn on and off differently according to the position of the switch?

There is a difference in potential energy (**potential difference**) between the terminals of a cell. This is measured in **volts (V)**. A single cell has a potential difference of 1.5 V, which is usually written on its side.

a)

1.5 V + 1.5 V = 3.0 V

b)

1.5 V – 1.5 V = 0.0 V

FIG 3.20.3 Cells can be arranged pointing (a) the same way, or (b) in opposite directions

When two cells are arranged so that their terminals point in the same direction (Fig D 3.20.3a), the overall potential difference of the battery is the sum of the potential differences of the cells, i.e. 3.0 V

When cells are arranged so that their terminals point in opposite directions (Fig D 3.20.3b), the overall potential difference of the battery is the difference between the potential differences of the cells, i.e. 0 V

lamps in series

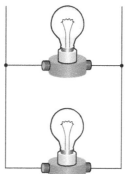

lamps in parallel

FIG D 3.20.4 Two lamps can be connected in a circuit in two different ways

Key terms

potential difference difference in potential energy between two points

volts (V) unit of potential difference

Check your understanding

1. Draw a circuit containing two cells, two lamps and one switch so that both lamps are on when the switch is closed, and one lamp remains on when the switch is open.

277

21 Circuit symbols

We are learning how to:

- represent simple circuits using diagrams
- identify components in an electric circuit from their symbols

It would be possible to graphically draw all of the **components** in an electric circuit diagram but this would be time-consuming. It is much easier to draw circuits using **symbols** to represent each of the components.

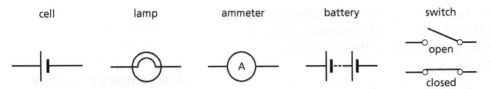

FIG D 3.21.1 These symbols for components are used and understood by scientists all over the world

Notice that the symbol for a cell has two vertical lines. The long, thin line represents the positive (+) terminal and the shorter, thicker line represents the negative (–) terminal. It is important that you draw the symbol in the correct direction in a circuit **diagram**.

Circuit diagrams ⟫

To draw a **circuit diagram**, we draw the appropriate symbols and then connect them together by lines to represent connecting wires.

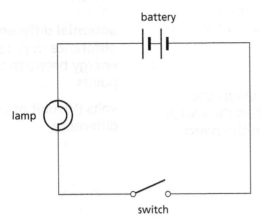

FIG D 3.21.2 A circuit diagram for a circuit containing a battery, a lamp and a switch all connected in series

Notice that if a battery is composed of several cells, repeating the symbol for a cell can be tedious. It is much easier to join the symbols for two cells by a dashed line.

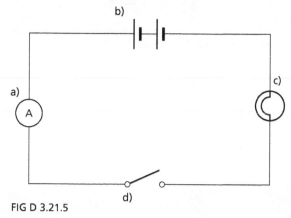

FIG D 3.21.3 How to represent a 9 V battery composed of six cells

Activity D 3.21.1

Drawing circuit diagrams

You will not need any equipment or materials for this activity.

Here is what you should do:

1. Look back at Figs D 3.20.1 and D 3.20.2 and redraw the circuits using suitable symbols.

2. Would you say that it is easier to draw circuits using symbols than drawing the components?

3. Would you say that circuits drawn in symbols are easier to understand than circuits in which the components are drawn?

Check your understanding

1. Name the components in this electrical circuit.

FIG D 3.21.5

2. Draw a circuit diagram containing a battery of three cells, two lamps and a switch connected in series.

Interesting fact

There are two symbols commonly used to represent lamps in circuit diagrams.

lamp as a source of light   lamp as an indicator

FIG D 3.21.4 Symbols for lamps

One symbol is used when the lamp is a source of light, such as in a torch circuit. The other is used when the lamp is an indicator of some kind, such as a light that comes on when an appliance is in use.

Key terms

components parts of a circuit

symbols signs used to represent something

circuit diagram diagram showing how components in a circuit are connected

22 Constructing circuits from circuit diagrams

Drawing circuit diagrams 》》》

To build a given circuit, we need to examine a circuit diagram (Fig D 3.22.1) in order to:

- identify the electrical components needed

- determine how the components are connected together.

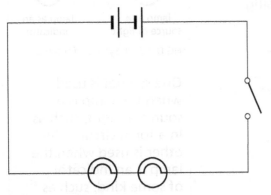

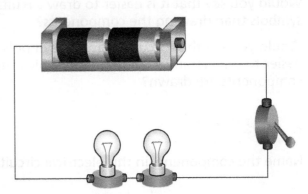

FIG D 3.22.1 The symbols show that the circuit contains: two cells, two lamps and one switch all connected in series

FIG D 3.22.2 The information from the circuit diagram allows us to build the actual circuit

Activity D 3.22.1

Building circuits from circuit diagrams

Here is what you need:

- three cells
- two lamps
- two switches
- ammeter
- connecting wires

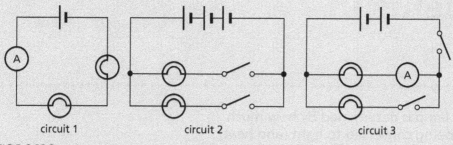

circuit 1   circuit 2   circuit 3

FIG D 3.22.3

1. Select the components you will need to build circuit 1 and connect them together as shown in the diagram.

2. Check your circuit against the circuit diagram to make sure they are the same.

3. Repeat this for circuit 2 and then circuit 3.

Check your understanding

1. Fig D 3.22.4 is a circuit diagram.

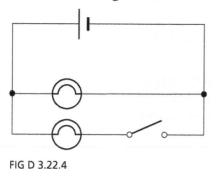

FIG D 3.22.4

   What components are needed to build this circuit (not including connecting wires)?

2. List the components you will need to build a circuit with three lamps in it, where each lamp can be switched on and off independently of the other two. Draw the circuit diagram and then build it.

> **Interesting fact**
>
> Sometimes wires may cross over each other in a circuit but may not actually join together.
>
> wires cross   wires join
>
> FIG D 3.22.5 In order to show the difference between wires that cross and wires that join in a circuit diagram, draw a dot where wires join

23 Connecting components in series

We are learning how to:
- represent simple circuits using diagrams
- connect components in series in a circuit

The brightness of a lamp is determined by how much electrical energy is being converted to light (and heat) energy. The brightness is therefore a good indicator of the amount of current flowing.

Activity D 3.23.1

Investigating bulbs connected in series

Here is what you need:

- battery containing three cells
- ammeter
- four lamps
- connecting wires

Here is what you should do:

1. Connect a single lamp in series with an ammeter in a circuit.

2. Note the brightness of the lamp and the reading on the ammeter.

3. Repeat this for two, three and four lamps connected in series and, in addition, find out what happens when one lamp is partially unscrewed from its holder so it goes out.

4. Record your observations in a table.

5. Comment on how the brightness of the lamps changes as the number of lamps increases.

6. Comment on how the current changes as the number of lamps increases.

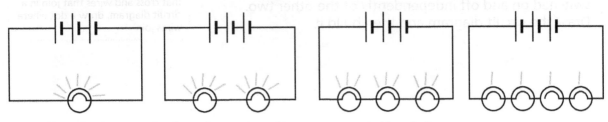

FIG D 3.23.1 What happens when increasing numbers of lamps are connected in series?

As more lamps are added to the circuit, the lamps shine less brightly. If an ammeter is included in each circuit, it will show that the current decreases as the number of lamps increases.

Lamps in **series** are connected in a single circuit (Fig D 3.23.2). If there is a break in the circuit, such as will occur if one of the lamps burns out or is removed, then the circuit is no longer complete and all the lamps will go out.

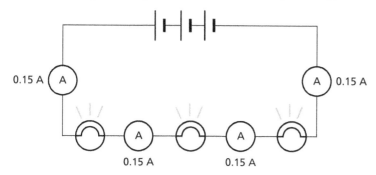

FIG D 3.23.2 When lamps are connected in series, it does not matter where the ammeter is positioned because the current through the circuit is the same at all points

Check your understanding

1. Fig D 3.23.3 shows a circuit in which three lamps are connected in series. The reading on the ammeter is 0.12 A.

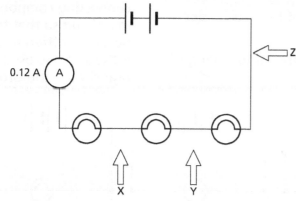

FIG D 3.23.3

a) How would the brightness of the lamps change, if at all, if another lamp was added in series?

b) At which of the points X, Y and Z in the circuit would the current be 0.12 A?

c) What would be the reading on the ammeter if one of the lamps burned out? Explain your answer.

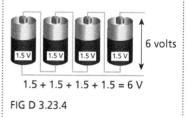
Key term

series way of connecting components so that they are in one loop in a circuit

24 Connecting components in parallel

We are learning how to:

- represent simple circuits using diagrams
- connect components in parallel in a circuit

An electric current only flows through a complete circuit. When two components are connected in **parallel**, there are effectively two circuits along with a part that is common to both components.

Activity D 3.24.1

Investigating lamps connected in parallel

Here is what you need:

- battery containing three cells
- four lamps
- connecting wires

Here is what you should do:

1. Connect a single lamp in a circuit.

2. Note the brightness of the lamp.

3. Repeat this for two, three and four lamps connected in parallel and, in addition, find out what happens when one lamp is partially unscrewed from its holder so it goes out.

4. Comment on how the brightness of the lamps changes as the number increases.

Key term

parallel way of connecting components in a circuit so that the potential difference is the same across all branches of the circuit

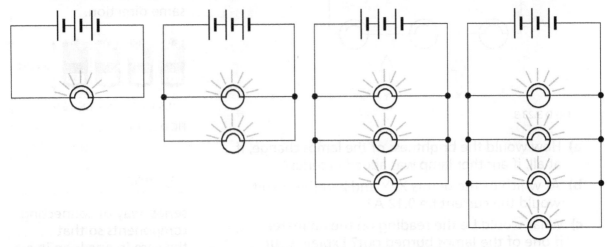

FIG D 3.24.1 What happens when increasing numbers of lamps are connected in parallel?

Lamps in parallel ▶▶▶

Adding lamps in parallel does not alter their brightness. However, it is not possible to keep on adding more and more lamps without end. There will come a time when the battery is unable to provide sufficient electrical energy.

When two lamps are connected in parallel they are brighter than they would be if they were connected in series, but they draw twice as much current from the battery. This means that the battery will be exhausted more quickly. Two lamps connected in series will shine less brightly but will continue to shine for longer because the battery will last for longer.

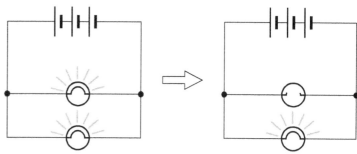

FIG D 3.24.2 When lamps are connected in parallel, if one breaks, the circuit containing the second lamp remains complete and so the second lamp remains lit

1.

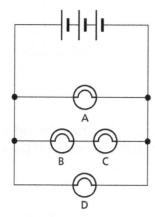

FIG D 3.24.4 Four identical lamps connected to a battery

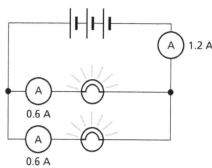

FIG D 3.24.3 If ammeters are at different positions in the same circuit, the total current flowing from the battery is equal to the sum of the currents flowing through each lamp, so here the values are: 0.6 A + 0.6 A = 1.2 A

Copy and complete Table D 3.24.1 to show which lamps would remain on and which would go off when each of the lamps burns out.

Lamp that is burned out	Lamp goes out or remains on			
	A	B	C	D
A	off			
B		off		
C			off	
D				off

TABLE D 3.24.1

Interesting fact

When identical cells are connected in parallel, the potential difference across them is the same as the potential difference across one cell provided they are connected in the same direction.

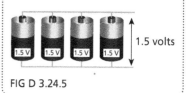

1.5 volts

FIG D 3.24.5

25 Electrical hazards

We are learning how to:

- use electricity safely

Electricity and safety ⟫⟫

Electricity is potentially dangerous so we must learn how to use it safely.

Some plugs have two pins and some have three. Sockets may have caps to prevent children poking things into them.

FIG D 3.25.1 An electrical appliance is connected to the mains electricity supply by a plug, which fits into a socket

Activity D 3.25.1

Examining a plug and socket

Here is what you need:

- plug
- socket

 SAFETY
Even though plugs and sockets are made of plastic, they should never be touched with wet hands. There is a danger that wetness will pass into the plug or socket and this can result in an electric shock.

Here is what you should do:

1. Look carefully at the plug and observe where the wires from the appliance will be connected.
2. Notice that when the plug is pushed fully into a socket there are no exposed metal parts.
3. Look carefully at the socket and where the wires from the supply will be connected.
4. Notice that the holes for the pins of the plug are very small, which prevents people accidentally pushing something in.
5. Notice also that the plug pins must be fully into the socket before they connect with the electricity supply. This means that no parts of the plug pins are exposed.
6. From what type of material are the bodies of the plug and socket made?

Two wires are needed in a plug to make a circuit. Some plugs have three pins and three wires. The third wire is called the **earth wire**. It protects the user should a fault develop in the appliance.

If the wires in a metal table lamp came loose and touched the metal body, anyone touching it would receive an electric shock. The earth wire is connected to the metal body of the table lamp. Most of the current will flow through it so the user would get a small shock and not come to any harm.

An electric appliance that has a plastic body does not need to be earthed because plastic is an insulator. Such appliances are described as **double insulated**.

FIG D 3.25.2 Metal-bodied appliances should be earthed

FIG D 3.25.3 Plastic-bodied appliances do not need to be earthed

Check your understanding

1.

FIG D 3.25.4 Gabriella's hairdryer

a) How does Gabriella connect her hairdryer to the power supply?

b) Why should Gabriella not use her hairdryer when her hands are wet?

c) What is the outer casing made of?

d) Will Gabriella's hairdryer have a 2-pin or a 3-pin plug? Explain your answer.

Key terms

earth wire wire in a plug that is connected to the metal body of the appliance to protect the user in the event of a fault

double insulated an appliance that has a body made of an insulating material

26 Safety devices

We are learning how to:

- explain the importance of fuses
- describe the action of circuit breakers

Fuses 》》》

When an electric current flows along a wire it has a heating effect.

The larger the current the hotter the wire becomes. If it gets hot enough the wire will melt and break the circuit. We can use this effect to limit the amount of current flowing in a circuit.

Cartridge **fuses** are found in some types of domestic plugs. They contain a single wire but this is often contained within an opaque ceramic tube. The thickness of the wire depends on the amount of current intended to be carried in the circuit.

In the past domestic wiring was also protected by fuses. Each circuit had its own fuse. If there was a fault in a particular circuit the fuse wire would melt and current would no longer flow. When the fault was rectified a new length of fuse wire was fitted into the fuse.

FIG D 3.26.1 Heating effect of an electric current

FIG D 3.26.2 Cartridge fuses protect appliances

Circuit breakers 》》》

In many countries traditional domestic fuse boxes have been replaced by consumer units. These are no longer fuse boxes because they do not contain fuses but **circuit breakers**.

Each circuit has its own circuit breaker. In the event of a fault a circuit breaker will trip, switching off the current in the circuit. When the fault is rectified the circuit breaker can be reset simply by pushing a switch.

FIG D 3.26.3 Traditional domestic fuse box

Activity D 3.26.1

Investigating the action of a fuse

Here is what you need:

- battery of two cells
- lamp
- variable resistor
- fuse wire of different thicknesses
- bench board
- crocodile clips
- connecting wires

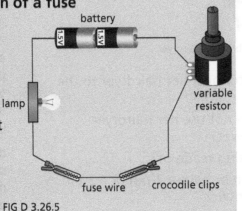

FIG D 3.26.5

FIG D 3.26.4 Modern consumer unit

Here is what you should do:

1. Build the circuit shown in Fig D 3.26.5.

2. The variable resistor will allow you to alter the amount of current flowing in the circuit. The higher the current the more brightly the lamp will shine.

3. Make sure that the knob on the variable resistor is turned fully clockwise. This will ensure the maximum resistance and the smallest current.

4. Place a length of fuse wire between the crocodile clips and put these onto a bench board.

5. Slowly turn the knob on the variable resistor anticlockwise. Observe the brightness of the lamp when the fuse melts and the current ceases to flow.

6. Leave the circuit for a few minutes for the melted fuse wire to cool before removing it.

7. Repeat steps 3 to 6 for fuse wires of different thicknesses.

8. Comment on any pattern between the thickness of the fuse wire and the brightness of the lamp before the wire melts.

FIG D 3.26.6 Residual current circuit breaker

Residual current circuit breakers

A **residual current circuit breaker (RCCB)** is a device that can be connected between the electricity supply and an appliance in order to protect the user from injury. These are often built into modern consumer units.

An RCCB compares the current in the part of the circuit leading away from the electricity supply to the current in the part leading back. If they are not equal, such as will be the case if a fault develops, a switch trips and the current is turned off.

Check your understanding

1. a) What is the purpose of a fuse?

   b) Why are the wires in cartridge fuses different thicknesses?

2. a) What is a circuit breaker?

   b) How would a residual current circuit breaker protect someone cutting a lawn with an electric lawn mower in the event that they mowed over the cable?

Interesting fact

In the event of a fault, an RCCB turns off the current in around 40 milliseconds, which is 0.04 s.

Key terms

fuse wire that melts in the event of excess current

circuit breaker device that trips in the event of excess current

residual current circuit breaker device that protects a user from electric shock when using electrical appliances

27 Resistance

We are learning how to:

- identify fixed and variable resistors
- describe the effect of resistance on the flow of an electric current

All materials resist the flow of an electric current in a circuit. Materials that are good conductors, like metals, have a very low resistance, while materials that are insulators, like plastics and glass, have a very high resistance.

Components called resistors are used in electric circuits to control the flow of current. They are conductors that have particular resistance values. The unit of resistance is the **ohm**, which has the symbol Ω.

There are two kinds of resistors:

- **fixed value resistors** – the value cannot be altered

- **variable resistors** – the value can be changed from zero to an upper limit.

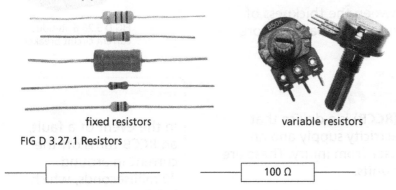

fixed resistors   variable resistors

FIG D 3.27.1 Resistors

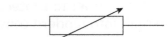

FIG D 3.27.2 Symbol for a fixed resistor

FIG D 3.27.3 Symbol for a variable resistor

The values of fixed resistors are shown as a series of different coloured bands. You might have noticed them on the circuit board of an electrical device.

Fig D 3.27.2 shows the symbol used to represent a fixed resistor in a circuit diagram. The value of the resistor is sometimes written in or under the component.

The value of a variable resistor can be changed within its given range. Variable resistors are sometimes called potentiometers and are commonly used as volume controllers and other controls on devices such as radios and televisions.

Resistors provide a way of controlling the amount of current flowing in a circuit, or in part of a circuit.

In the circuit in Fig D 3.27.4, lamps A and B are identical. The current flowing through lamp A is reduced by the fixed resistor. As a result, lamp A shines less brightly than lamp B.

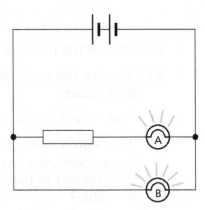

FIG D 3.27.4 Resistors control current in a circuit

Effect of resistance on the brightness of a lamp

D 3.27

Here is what you need:

- fixed resistors of different values – for example, 5, 10, 15, 20, 25, 30 Ω
- variable resistor – range 0–100 Ω
- battery of two 1.5 V cells
- lamp
- connecting wires
- two resistors of equal value

Here is what you should do:

1. Connect a lamp to a battery consisting of two 1.5 V cells and note its brightness.

2. Connect the lowest value fixed resistor in series with the lamp and observe the effect this has on the brightness of the lamp.

3. Repeat step 2 using fixed resistors with progressively higher values.

4. Connect a variable resistor in series with the lamp and observe the effect that altering the value of the resistor has on the brightness of the lamp.

5. Use your observations to describe the effect of resistance on the brightness of a lamp in a circuit.

6. [STEAM] Investigate the total resistance of two resistors of equal value, when they are connected:

   a) in series   b) in parallel.

Interesting fact

The resistors used in practical circuits generally have values of thousands or even millions of ohms. As with all SI units, the prefixes 'k' and 'M' are used, i.e. 1 kΩ = 1000 Ω and 1 MΩ = 1 000 000 Ω.

Key terms

ohm unit of electrical resistance, which has the symbol Ω

fixed resistor resistor whose value cannot be changed

variable resistor resistor whose value can be changed within given limits

Check your understanding

1. **a)** Draw a circuit diagram to show a fixed resistor and a lamp connected in series to a 1.5 V cell.

   b) Draw a circuit diagram to show a variable resistor and a lamp connected in series to a 1.5 V cell.

2. How does a resistor control the amount of current flowing in a circuit?

28 Voltage and current in a circuit

In an electric cell there is a **potential difference**, or a difference in energy levels between the two terminals. This potential difference is applied to any circuit to which the cell is connected. It is measured in volts (V) and for that reason is sometimes called the **voltage**.

Measuring voltage

Voltage is measured by a **voltmeter**. As was the case with ammeters, voltmeters may be analogue or digital.

A digital voltmeter may be part of a multimeter that can also be used as an ammeter depending on which function is selected.

FIG D 3.28.1 Voltmeters

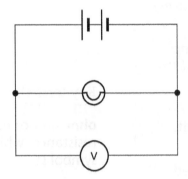

FIG D 3.28.2 A voltmeter used in a circuit

Voltmeters are connected in parallel to a component to measure the voltage across it. When several components are connected in series in a circuit, the sum of the voltages across each component is equal to the supply voltage.

Current and voltage

Current and voltage are two different characteristics of the electrical energy passing around a circuit. An electric current only flows around a circuit if there is a voltage difference between the two terminals of the cell or other power source.

> ### Interesting fact
>
>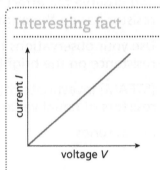
>
> FIG D 3.28.3 *I* / *V* graph for a metallic conductor
>
> The sizes of the current and voltage in a circuit are linked. If you change one, the other will also change. A current/voltage graph for a metallic conductor, like a wire, is a straight line.

Investigating voltage and current in a circuit

Here is what you need:

- battery containing two cells
- lamp
- variable resistor
- ammeter
- voltmeter
- connecting wires

Here is what you should do:

1. Connect the components to build the circuit shown in Fig D 3.28.4.

2. Copy Table D 3.28.1.

Voltage across the lamp	Current in the lamp	Brightness of the lamp

TABLE D 3.28.1

3. Start by setting the value of the resistor to zero and record the voltage, current through and brightness of the lamp.

4. Increase the value of the variable resistance to about one quarter, one half, three quarters and all of its maximum value. Each time record the voltage, current and brightness of the lamp.

5. Comment on your observations.

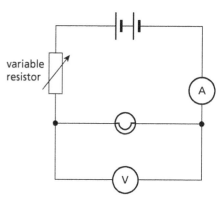

FIG D 3.28.4

Check your understanding

1. Draw a circuit diagram in which there is:

    - a single lamp connected to a battery containing three cells
    - an ammeter to measure the current in the lamp
    - a voltmeter to measure the voltage across the lamp.

2. Four identical lamps were connected in series in a circuit as in Fig D 3.28.5. Comment on the size of:

    a) the voltage across each individual lamp

    b) the total voltage across the lamps.

Key terms

potential difference the difference in energy levels at different points in an electrical circuit

voltage alternative name for potential difference

voltmeter device for measuring voltage

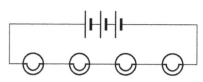

FIG D 3.28.5

Review of Current electricity

- Conventional current is the direction an electric current is deemed to flow in while actual current is the direction of the flow of electrons in a circuit.

- Electric current is measured in amperes, milliamperes and microamperes.

- An ammeter is used to measure electric current.

- Materials that conduct an electric current are called electrical conductors.

- Materials that do not conduct an electric current are called electrical insulators.

- Metals are good conductors because they contain delocalised electrons. Their particles carry electric charge through the metal. Insulating materials do not contain delocalised electrons.

- Electric appliances with metal bodies are connected to an earth wire. This provides a pathway for current in the event of wires coming loose and somebody touching the metal body, which protects the user from a severe electric shock. Electric appliances with plastic bodies do not require an earth wire and are said to be double insulated.

- A cell is a means of providing a small and safe amount of energy. A battery is formed when two or more cells are joined together.

- A cell has a positive (+) terminal and a negative (−) terminal. When cells are connected together to form a battery, they must all be pointing in the same electrical direction.

- In order to flow, an electric current must have a complete circuit.

- An electric current can be measured using an ammeter. The unit of current is the ampere, A, or for smaller currents the milliampere, mA. There are 1000 milliamperes in 1 ampere.

- A circuit diagram is a method of representing an electric circuit by a series of connected symbols. Each symbol represents a component in the circuit.

- Components in a circuit might be connected in series or in parallel.

- When lamps are connected in series, the more lamps there are the dimmer they are because less current flows in the circuit.

- When lamps are connected in parallel, they shine with the brightness of a single lamp up to the point where the cell or battery cannot provide any more electrical energy.

- Lamps connected in parallel are brighter than lamps connected in series, but they draw more current from the battery.

- Resistance is measured in ohms and has the symbol Ω.

- Resistors can be used to control the flow of current in a circuit.

- There is a difference in potential energy or voltage between the terminals of a cell and this is expressed in volts, V.

- Voltage is measured using a voltmeter.

- When the voltage across a circuit changes, the current in it will also change.

Review questions on Current electricity

1. Redraw the circuit in Fig D 3.RQ.1 as a circuit diagram, using appropriate symbols for the components.

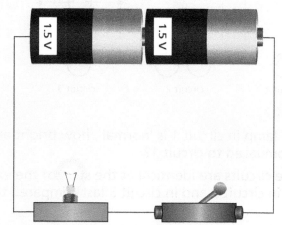

FIG D 3.RQ.1

2. Dante used the circuit shown in Fig D 3.RQ.2 to test if different materials conduct electricity.

material   FIG D 3.RQ.2

   a) How was Dante able to decide whether or not each material conducted electricity?

   b) Before testing the materials, Dante connected the two crocodile clips together. Why did he do this?

   c) Here is a list of the materials Dante tested. Arrange them in groups according to whether or not they conduct electricity.

copper	cardboard	plastic	iron
wood	glass	steel	lead

   d) What name is given to a material that does not conduct electricity?

   e) Give one common feature of all of the materials that conduct electricity.

3. Fig D 3.RQ.3 shows an experiment using some circuits containing identical lamps.

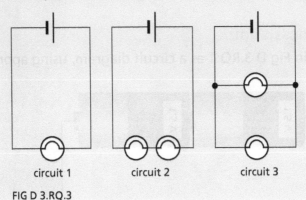

circuit 1   circuit 2   circuit 3

FIG D 3.RQ.3

a) If the brightness of the lamp in circuit 1 is 'normal', how bright are the lamps in circuit 2 and circuit 3 compared to circuit 1?

b) If the cells used in these circuits are identical at the start of the experiment, how long will the cells in circuit 2 and in circuit 3 last compared to the cell in circuit 1?

c) Explain what will happen if one of the lamps burns out in:

   i) circuit 2   ii) circuit 3.

4. Fig D 3.RQ.4 shows a cell and two lamps connected in different ways.

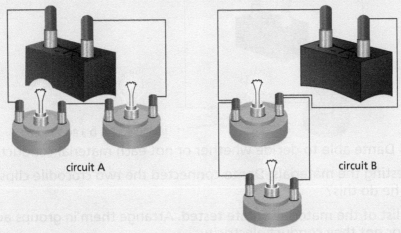

circuit A   circuit B

FIG D 3.RQ.4

a) Redraw the circuits as circuit diagrams.

b) Compared to the brightness of a single lamp connected to a cell, describe the brightness of:

   i) the lamps in circuit A

   ii) the lamps in circuit B.

c) What would happen to the second lamp if one lamp were to break in:

   i) circuit A?

   ii) circuit B?

5. Fareed wants to make a circuit containing two cells, a lamp and a switch so that the lamp lights up when the switch is closed, but he is having problems.

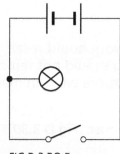

FIG D 3.RQ.5

a) There are three problems with Fareed's circuit. Explain what they are.

b) Redraw the circuit showing the components drawn correctly.

6. In Fig D 3.RQ.6, lamps P, Q and R are identical and components X are identical.

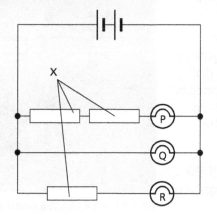

FIG D 3.RQ.6

a) What is the name of component X?

b) Write down the order of brightness of the lamps starting with the brightest.

30 Lighting system for a model house

Before you start work on this activity, you should recall that mains electricity is dangerous. You should not remove the tops from lamps and switches or expose wires in mains lighting circuits.

Mr Livingston is making a model doll house (Fig D 3.30.1) as a surprise for his daughter's birthday.

He wants to make it extra special by having a light in the ceiling of each room and a switch by the door that can turn the light on and off, but he doesn't know anything about electricity.

FIG STEAM D 3.30.1 The model doll house Mr Livingston is making

1. You are going to work in a small group to design a lighting system for Mr Livingston's doll house, to make the components and to make a model to show how your system works. The tasks are:

   - to research house lighting
   - to design a suitable lighting circuit
   - to design and make lamps and switches to a suitable scale for a doll house
   - to build a model of a doll house using cardboard
   - to install your lighting system in your model
   - to test your lighting system
   - to consider how your lighting system might be modified or extended.

   a) Take a look at how the lighting is arranged in your home.

   In each room the switch only controls the light for that room.

   Use your knowledge of series and parallel circuits to design a suitable lighting circuit for a doll house that contains four rooms.

FIG STEAM D 3.30.2 Room light and switch

b) Even small torch bulbs are too big for a doll house. You need to find lights that are smaller than these.

One possibility is light-emitting diodes. These are not bulbs but components that shine when a current flows through them. Red LEDs are often used on electrical equipment to show that something is switched on. They come in three sizes – 3 mm, 5 mm and 10 mm – so you will need to choose which is appropriate for the scale of your model.

If you use LEDs there are two important things you must take into account:

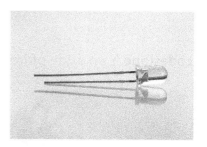

FIG STEAM D 3.30.3 Light-emitting diode or LED

- LEDs cannot be connected directly to cells or they will burn out instantly. They must be wired in series with a resistor. You will need to carry out research to determine the size of the resistor needed.
- LEDs must be connected in a circuit so that the longer pin is connected to the positive side of the cell or battery. Otherwise they will not work.

Similarly, household switches are far too large for a doll house so you will have to design and make your own.

The two examples of homemade switches in Fig STEAM D 3.30.4 might give you some ideas. You will need to make a switch for each room of the model doll house.

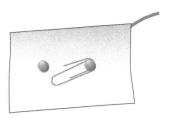

c) Build a model of a doll house using a cardboard box and cardboard dividers for the walls.

Your model doesn't have to be very detailed because you are only going to use it to demonstrate your lighting system.

FIG STEAM D 3.30.4 'Homemade' switches

d) Install your lighting system into your model and test it to make sure the light in each room turns on and off without affecting the lights in the other rooms. Use a battery to power your lights.

e) Consider how you might modify or extend your lighting system. For example:

- You might install two switches in one room so that the light could be controlled from either switch. This is the sort of arrangement that you see in hallways and staircases.
- You might install two lights in one room controlled by only one switch.

f) Prepare a presentation in which you will describe your lighting circuit, explain how you made lights and switches, and demonstrate the lighting circuit installed on your model. You should also be ready to discuss how your lighting circuit could be modified to provide different arrangements of lights and switches.

FIG STEAM D 3.30.5 Model doll house

31 Magnetic and non-magnetic materials

We are learning how to:
- demonstrate the effects of magnetic forces
- determine whether a material is magnetic or not

Lodestone is an oxide of iron and is also called magnetite.

FIG D 4.31.1 Lodestone, a type of rock, attracts objects made of iron, such as tacks, nails and bolts

Activity D 4.31.1

Magnetic and non-magnetic materials

Here is what you need:

- magnet
- objects made of different materials – for example, nail, paper clip, plastic ruler, eraser

Here is what you should do:

1. Hold one end of the magnet near an object and find out if the material is attracted to it.

2. Materials that are attracted by a magnet are described as magnetic materials.

3. Test each object in turn with the magnet.

4. Display your observations in a table. On one side of the table list the magnetic materials and on the other side list the non-magnetic materials.

Materials such as iron and steel that are attracted to a magnet are described as **magnetic**, while materials such as brass, copper and aluminium that are not attracted to a magnet are described as **non-magnetic**.

Permanent magnets

Materials that keep their magnetism for a long time are called permanent magnets.

Materials that have permanent magnetism are iron, mild steel, cobalt and nickel. Modern magnets are often made of special alloys containing these metals, such as alnico and alcomax.

Ceramic or ferrite magnets are made by baking iron oxide and other metal oxides in a ceramic matrix.

FIG D 4.31.3 The element neodymium forms alloys with iron and boron that are used to make powerful permanent magnets

FIG D 4.31.2 Ceramic magnets can be made in any shape but have the disadvantage that they are brittle, so if they are dropped on a hard surface they will break into pieces

Interesting fact

An alloy is a mixture of a metallic element with one or more other elements that may be metals or non-metals. Steel is an alloy of iron and carbon.

Some alloys have more useful properties than the elements from which they are formed. For example, alnico is an alloy of aluminium, nickel and cobalt. It makes more powerful magnets than the pure metals.

Check your understanding

1. Arrange the following metals into two groups: those that are magnetic and those that are not magnetic.

cobalt	copper	gold	iron
magnesium	nickel	steel	zinc

Key terms

magnetic materials such as iron and steel that are attracted to a magnet

non-magnetic materials such as brass, copper and aluminium that are not attracted to a magnet

32 Laws of magnetic poles

We are learning how to:

- demonstrate the effects of magnetic forces
- predict whether two magnetic poles will attract or repel each other

Poles on a magnet »

A magnet has two **poles** – a north pole and a south pole. These are usually represented by the letters 'N' and 'S'.

Forces exist between magnets and are concentrated at the poles. The interaction between two magnets depends on the nature of the poles that are brought together.

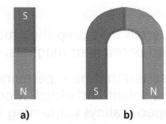

a)   b)

FIG D 4.32.1 **a)** Bar magnets are commonly used in the laboratory **b)** A horseshoe magnet is simply a bar magnet that has been bent into the shape of a horseshoe

Activity D 4.32.1

Law of magnetic poles

Here is what you need:

- two loops of cotton
- two bar magnets
- pencil
- heavy book

Here is what you should do:

1. Put a heavy book on top of a pencil so that the pencil is sticking out from the table.

2. Suspend a bar magnet from the pencil using loops of cotton so that it can turn freely.

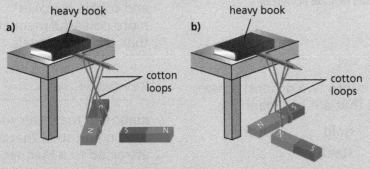

FIG D 4.32.2 **a)** unlike poles **b)** like poles

3. Move the N pole of the second magnet towards the N pole of the suspended magnet and record what happens.

4. Move the N pole of the second magnet towards the S pole of the suspended magnet and record what happens.

5. Repeat steps 3 and 4 using the S pole of the second magnet.

6. What deductions can you make about magnets from your observations?

If one magnet is suspended so it is free to rotate and a second magnet is brought near it:

- If they are **unlike poles**, that is N and S or S and N, the magnets will attract (move towards each other).

- If they are **like poles**, that is N and N or S and S, the magnets will repel (move away from each other).

Interesting fact

It is impossible to say if an iron bar is magnetic or not on the basis of whether or not it is attracted by a magnet.

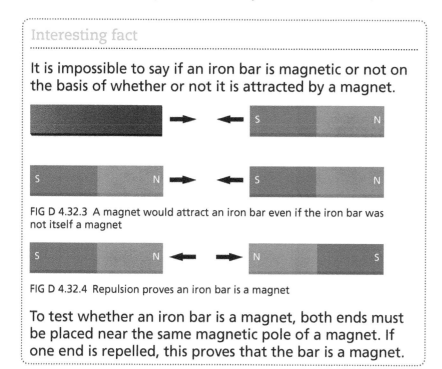

FIG D 4.32.3 A magnet would attract an iron bar even if the iron bar was not itself a magnet

FIG D 4.32.4 Repulsion proves an iron bar is a magnet

To test whether an iron bar is a magnet, both ends must be placed near the same magnetic pole of a magnet. If one end is repelled, this proves that the bar is a magnet.

Key terms

pole the end of a magnet

unlike poles two poles that are different – north and south

like poles two poles that are the same – e.g. north and north

---

Check your understanding

1. A compass needle is a magnet. The north pole of the compass always points towards the Earth's magnetic North Pole, and the south pole of the compass points towards the Earth's magnetic South Pole.

What is the polarity of each of the Earth's magnetic poles? Explain your answer.

FIG D 4.32.5 Compass

33 Magnetic effect of an electric current

When a compass needle is close to a wire, and a current flows through the wire, the compass needle is deflected.

This is called the **magnetic effect of a current**.

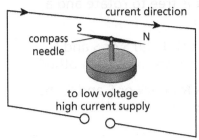

FIG D 4.33.1 The magnetic effect of an electric current

Activity D 4.33.1

Magnetic field around a wire carrying a current

Here is what you need:

- two thick resistance wires
- plotting compass
- plain card
- two DC power sources

Here is what you should do:

1. Make a small hole in the middle of a piece of card and push the wire through it.

2. Connect the wire to a DC power source. This has a positive (+) terminal and a negative (–) terminal.

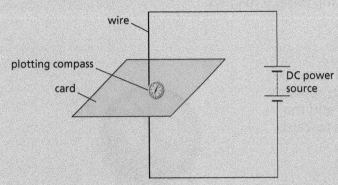

FIG D 4.33.2

3. Move a plotting compass near the wire and show the direction that the compass points by drawing an arrow.

4. Repeat this, moving the plotting compass to different positions until you have built up a map of the field lines around the wire.

5. Reverse the direction of the current through the wire by connecting the wire to the opposite terminals of the power source.

6. See if this affects the shape of the magnetic field lines around the wire and the direction of the magnetic field.

7. [STEAM] Modify your set up to investigate the magnetic field around a pair of wires 2 cm apart when the current is passing through them:

   a) in the same direction   **b)** in opposite directions.

Changing the direction of the current flowing through a wire doesn't alter the shape of the magnetic field it creates but it does alter the polarity of the magnetic field.

This effect is more obvious if we make the wire into a coil. The magnetic fields formed around each individual turn on the coil combine to produce a magnetic field similar to a bar magnet. The coil of wire is now called a **solenoid**.

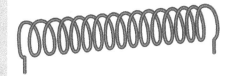

a)   when no current flows the coil is not a magnet

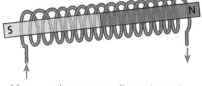

b)   when current flows the coil has a magnetic field like a bar magnet

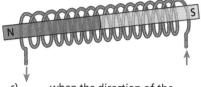

c)   when the direction of the current is reversed the polarity of the magnet is reversed

D 4.33.3 Magnetic field around a coil of wire

Check your understanding

1. Fig D 4.33.4 shows the observations made by a student experimenting with a coil of wire, a compass and a battery.

a)

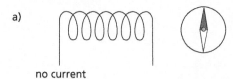

no current

b)

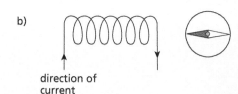

direction of current

c)

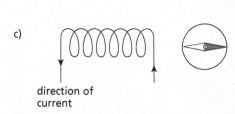

direction of current

FIG D 4.33.4

Key terms

magnetic effect of a current a compass needle is deflected when it is close to a wire carrying an electric current

solenoid coil of wire that becomes a magnet when carrying an electric current

Explain these observations as fully as you can.

34 Making an electromagnet

We are learning how to:
• describe the magnetic effect of a current
• make an electromagnet

To make an **electromagnet** with a useful strength, you need to combine the magnetic fields around many turns of wire by making a coil or solenoid.

The coils of wire on their own are magnetic. However, if they are wrapped around a steel nail they make an even stronger magnet.

Activity D 4.34.1

Making an electromagnet

Here is what you need:

- steel nail
- plastic-coated wire
- DC power source
- paper clips
- plotting compass

Here is what you should do:

1. Get a length of wire that is coated in plastic insulation and wind it round a steel nail.

2. Make between 15 and 20 coils of wire round the nail, depending on the length of the wire.

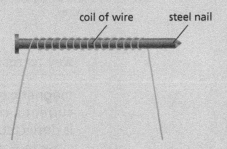

coil of wire   steel nail

FIG D 4.34.1 Coils of wire around a nail

3. Connect your coil to a DC power source.

4. Check that you have made an electromagnet by seeing if metal paper clips are attracted to it.

5. Hold a plotting compass at different points around your electromagnet and use the directions the compass points to to draw a diagram of the magnetic field lines around your electromagnet.

Electromagnetism is sometimes described as temporary magnetism. An electromagnet is only magnetic while a current flows through it. If the current is turned off, the electromagnet ceases to be magnetic.

FIG D 4.34.2 A practical electromagnet

Interesting fact

William Sturgeon made the first electromagnet in 1824.

FIG D 4.34.3 William Sturgeon's first electromagnet consisted of about 18 turns of varnished wire wrapped around a piece of iron in the shape of a horseshoe

Key term

electromagnet a magnet produced when a current flows through a wire or coil of wire

Electromagnets used in devices such as electric bells consist of many coils of thin copper wire. At first glance the wire might not appear to be insulated, but it is. The wire is covered in a layer of lacquer, which is far less bulky than a plastic coating.

Check your understanding

1. Explain why a coil of wire can only attract paper clips when an electric current is flowing through it.

35 Strength of an electromagnet

We are learning how to:

- describe the magnetic effect of a current
- compare the strengths of different electromagnets

An electromagnet is a coil of wire through which an electric current flows. What determines the strength of an electromagnet?

- Would wrapping the coil round a piece of wooden dowel be just as good as wrapping it round a steel nail?

- Does it matter how many turns of wire are in the coil?

- Does it matter how much current flows through the coil?

Activity D 4.35.1

Investigating the strength of electromagnets

Here is what you need:

- steel nail
- wooden dowel
- plastic-coated wire
- DC power source
- paper clips

Here is what you should do:

1. Take a length of wire that is coated in plastic insulation and coil it round a steel nail.

2. Make 20 coils of wire round the nail.

3. Connect your electromagnet to a DC power supply and count how many paper clips it will lift off the desk.

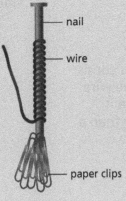

— nail

— wire

— paper clips

FIG D 4.35.1

4. Repeat steps 1 to 3 but use a wooden dowel instead of a steel nail.

5. Now make 10 coils of wire round a steel nail.

6. Connect your electromagnet to a DC power supply and count how many paper clips it will lift off the desk.

7. Repeat steps 2 to 6, but this time use only half of the current used previously.

8. From your observations, deduce what factors determine the strength of an electromagnet.

Increasing the strength of an electromagnet

The strength of an electromagnet is increased by:

* wrapping the coils of wire round a core of a magnetic metal such as iron or steel

* increasing the number of turns of wire in the coil

* increasing the current flowing through the coil.

Check your understanding

1. Say whether each of the following statements is true or false.

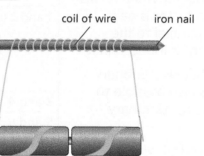

coil of wire   iron nail

FIG D 4.35.2 An electromagnet made by wrapping wire around an iron nail and connecting it to a battery

a) Reversing the battery will reduce the strength of the electromagnet.

b) The iron nail would still be a strong magnet even if the battery was removed.

c) Decreasing the number of turns of wire on the coil would reduce the strength of the electromagnet.

d) The electromagnet would be stronger if the iron nail was removed.

e) Wrapping the wire around two iron nails would make the electromagnet twice as strong.

f) Connecting the coil to a battery with a higher voltage would make the electromagnet stronger.

36 Induced current

Not only does an electric current create a magnetic field, but when a conductor such as a wire is moved through a magnetic field, an **electromotive force** (e.m.f.) is induced in the wire. If the wire forms part of a circuit, an electric current flows in the circuit.

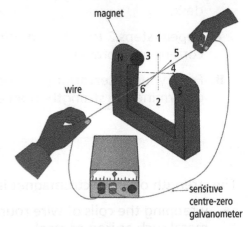

FIG D 4.36.1 Inducing a current in a wire

Detecting small currents with a galvanometer

A galvanometer is a very sensitive ammeter that can detect very small currents. The zero point is at the centre of the scale so that currents flowing in either direction through a conductor, like a wire, can be detected.

In Fig D 4.36.1 a wire has been connected to a galvanometer and held so that a straight section is exactly between the poles of a C-shaped magnet.

Moving the wire in different directions produces different responses on the galvanometer (see Table D 4.36.1).

A current is only induced in a conductor when it cuts across magnetic field lines. If a conductor is held still in a magnetic field, or moves parallel to the magnetic field lines, then no current is induced in it.

In this example, the magnetic field was stationary and the wire was moved in it. It is also possible to induce a current by keeping the wire stationary and moving the magnetic field.

When a magnet is pushed into a coil of wire connected to a galvanometer, the galvanometer deflects in one direction. When the magnet is pulled out the galvanometer deflects in the opposite direction. There is no deflection when the magnet is at rest, even if it is inside the coil, nor when the magnet is moved about inside the coil.

Direction	Response on the galvanometer
1 and 2 (up and down)	The galvanometer deflects in one direction and then in the opposite direction
3 and 4	None
5 and 6	None
Wire stationary	None

TABLE D 4.36.1

Activity D 4.36.1

Inducing a current in a coil

Your teacher will demonstrate this activity. You should observe carefully.

Here is what you need:

• centre-zero galvanometer
• bar magnet
• coil of wire

Here is what you should do:

1. Connect the coil to the galvanometer.

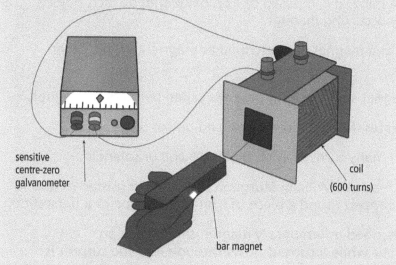

FIG D 4.36.2 Inducing a current in a coil

2. Push the magnet into the coil, hold it stationary and then pull it out. Observe what happens to the galvanometer as you do this.

3. Experiment by putting the magnet in the coil and then moving it up and down, and side to side. Observe the galvanometer as you do this.

4. Experiment by varying the speed of the magnet into and out of the coil. Observe the galvanometer as you do this.

Key term

electromotive force
difference in potential energy that produces a current

Check your understanding

1. Fig D 4.36.3 shows a bicycle dynamo. The cylindrical magnet rotates as the driving wheel rubs against the moving cycle wheel. It is used to provide an electric current to power cycle lights.

a) Explain how the dynamo works.

b) Explain why a light connected to the dynamo glows more brightly when the cycle moves faster.

c) Predict and explain what will happen to the size of the induced current when the cycle stops moving.

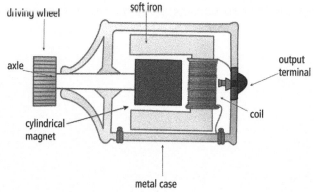

FIG D 4.36.3 A bicycle dynamo

Review of Magnetism

- Lodestone, or magnetite, is a mineral composed of iron oxide that attracts objects made of iron. It is a naturally occurring magnet.

- Materials that are attracted to a magnet are described as magnetic, while other materials are non-magnetic.

- Materials that keep their magnetism for a long time are called permanent magnets.

- The law of magnetic poles states that like poles repel and unlike poles attract.

- An electromagnet consists of many turns of wire, making a coil or solenoid.

- The first electromagnet was made by William Sturgeon in 1824. It consisted of about 18 turns of varnished wire wrapped round a piece of iron in the shape of a horseshoe.

- Electromagnetism can be described as temporary magnetism because an electromagnet is only magnetic while a current flows through it. If the current is turned off, the electromagnetic ceases to be magnetic.

- The strength of an electromagnet is increased by:
  - wrapping the coils of wire round a core of a magnetic metal like iron or steel
  - increasing the number of turns of wire in the coil
  - increasing the current flowing through the coil.

- An electric bell, a relay and a circuit breaker are all common devices that contain an electromagnet.

- An electromagnet can be used to separate iron and steel from other metals in a scrap yard or recycling plant.

- A current is induced in a conductor, such as a wire, when the conductor is moved in such a way as to cut across magnetic field lines.

Review questions on Magnetism

1. A bar magnet was broken into two pieces.

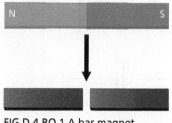

FIG D 4.RQ.1 A bar magnet
broken into two pieces

a) Copy the lower part of the diagram and show the polarity of the new ends formed.

b) Without using any other apparatus or materials, explain how you could show that both parts of the broken bar magnet have themselves become magnets.

2. Johanna was given four magnets. Her task was to compare how strong they were by counting how many small nails each could lift. Her results are shown in table D 4.RQ.1.

Magnet	Number of nails
bar magnet	3
C-shaped magnet	6
electromagnet	4
horseshoe magnet	7

TABLE D 4.RQ.1

a) Which magnet was the strongest?

b) i) Which magnet could be described as a temporary magnet?

ii) Explain why.

3. Say whether each of the following will make the electromagnet stronger, weaker or have no effect.

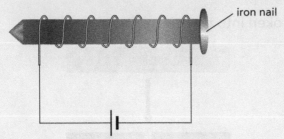

FIG D 4.RQ.2 An electromagnet

   a) Increasing the number of turns of wire.

   b) Decreasing the current flowing through the wire.

   c) Putting the nail into the coil from the opposite direction.

   d) Replacing the nail with a wooden dowel.

   e) Removing the nail so there is nothing inside the coil.

4 Here are some statements about magnets and magnetism. State whether each statement is true or false.

   a) All magnets have a north pole and a south pole.

   b) Lodestone is a form of copper oxide that attracts objects made of iron.

   c) The north pole of a magnet is always stronger than its south pole.

   d) Only iron wire can be used to make an electromagnet.

   e) If a magnet is broken in half, the two ends formed by the break will either both be north poles or both be south poles.

   f) Magnetism is a contact force.

   g) Compass needles always point to magnetic north.

Process skills

5. A student is given three iron bars. The ends of the bars are marked A to F.

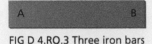  

FIG D 4.RQ.3 Three iron bars

Two of the bars are known to be magnets but the third is not. Explain how the student can identify which bar is not a magnet using only the three bars.

6. Fig D 4.RQ.4 shows an electromagnet in a circuit with three bulbs: X, Y and Z.

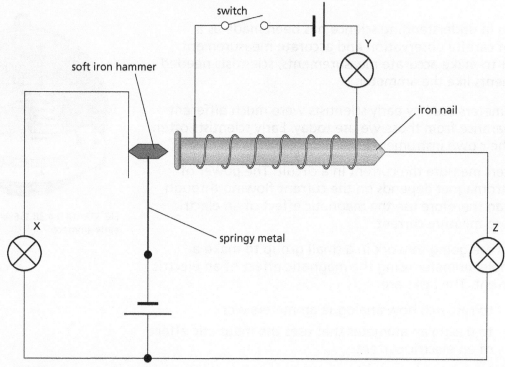

FIG D 4.RQ.4 Electromagnet in a circuit

a) Copy and complete the table by indicating whether each bulb is 'off' or 'on' when the switch is open and when it is closed.

Switch	Bulb X	Bulb Y	Bulb Z
open			
closed			

TABLE D 4.RQ.2

b) Suppose that the iron nail in the circuit is replaced by a length of wooden dowel of the same diameter. State whether each of the three bulbs will be on or off when the switch is closed. Explain your answer.

7. Design a magnetic door lock that allows a door to be normally locked but can be opened when required. You design should indicate what type of magnet would be used and any other parts that would be needed, and also show where the lock would be fitted to the door.

38 Building an ammeter

Progress in understanding science has been made as a result of careful observation and accurate measurement. In order to make accurate measurements, scientists needed instruments like the ammeter.

The ammeters used by early scientists were much different in appearance from those we use today. Early scientists often made their own instruments.

Ammeters measure the current in a circuit. The power of an electromagnet depends on the current flowing through it. We can therefore use the magnetic effect of an electric current to measure current.

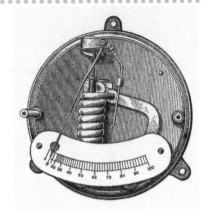

FIG STEAM D 4.38.1 Example of an early ammeter

1. You are going to work in a small group to make a simple ammeter using the magnetic effect of an electric current. The tasks are:

   - to research how analogue ammeters work
   - to design an ammeter that uses the magnetic effect of an electric current
   - to construct your ammeter
   - to calibrate your ammeter
   - to check the accuracy of your ammeter against a laboratory ammeter.

   a) Research in books and on the Internet how analogue ammeters work. In particular look up:

   - moving coil ammeter
   - moving iron ammeter.

   Don't be concerned about the structure of the ammeters but focus on the principles by which they operate. Increasing the current flowing in a coil increases the power of the magnetic field produced by the coil.

   b) Apply what you know about electromagnetism and ammeters to design an ammeter. You will not be able to build anything as sophisticated as a laboratory ammeter. Keep your design simple. Here are a couple of ideas that you might be able to use or modify.

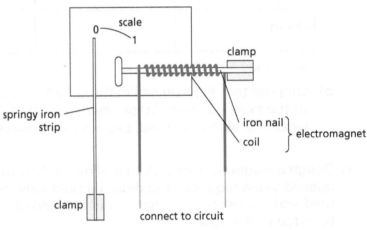

FIG STEAM D 4.38.2 Design A for an ammeter

In design A (Fig STEAM D 4.38.2) the springy iron strip is attracted by the electromagnet and will bend. The higher the current the stronger the electromagnet, and the more the strip will bend. The iron needs to be springy so that when the current is turned off the strip will return to zero on the scale.

In design B (Fig STEAM D 4.38.3) when a current flows through the coil it becomes an electromagnet and the iron rod is pulled towards it. The higher the current the stronger the magnetic field around the coil, and the stronger the pulling force on the iron rod. The iron rod is suspended on a spring so that when the current is turned off the pointer will return to zero.

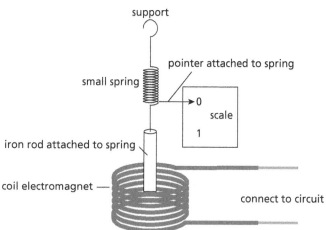

FIG STEAM D 4.38.3 Design B for an ammeter

c) When you are satisfied with your design you should make your ammeter. You might find that during manufacture you need to modify the original design or perhaps incorporate some last-minute ideas. Take some photographs of your ammeter at different stages of manufacture.

d) The scale on your ammeter will need to be calibrated using a laboratory ammeter. Your teacher will show you how the laboratory ammeter works. Connect your ammeter and a laboratory ammeter in series in a circuit. The circuit should contain a variable resistor so you can alter the current to obtain different values. Use the readings on the laboratory ammeter to draw a scale for your ammeter.

e) Once your ammeter is calibrated, investigate how accurate it is by measuring the current in different circuits and comparing the values you obtain with values obtained using a laboratory ammeter.

f) Prepare an illustrated presentation. You should be prepared to describe how you built your ammeter and to discuss the physics involved. You should demonstrate the operation of your ammeter by measuring the current in a circuit. You should also talk about the practicalities of using your ammeter. For example, would it be easy to move from place to place? Can it be easily packed away in a box and brought out when needed?

39 Nature of matter

Three states of matter

All materials exist in one of three states under normal conditions – solid, liquid and gas. The state of a substance depends on temperature and pressure.

We think of water as a liquid because that is the state in which we see it most often. This is because at the ambient temperature where we live water is liquid.

At the South Pole the average temperature, even in the summer, is below the melting point of ice. If we lived there we would think of water as a solid.

On the surface of the planet Mercury the temperature is well above the boiling point of water, so water only exists as a gas.

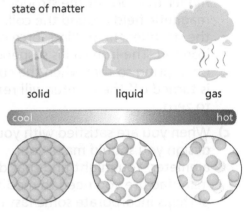

state of matter

solid   liquid   gas

cool   hot

FIG D 5.39.1 Three states of water

Arrangement of particles and heat transfer

Although ice, liquid water and steam are chemically identical, the arrangement of their particles is very different. The result is that the solid, liquid and gas states have different physical properties including the way in which they transfer heat energy.

In a solid the particles are held in fixed positions and their only movement is vibration about fixed points.

Kinetic energy is the form of energy we associate with movement. When a solid is heated the particles gain kinetic energy. Even though they cannot change position, the particles bump into adjacent particles and kinetic energy is transferred. This process of heat transfer is called **conduction**.

The particles in a liquid are a little further apart than in a solid. They both vibrate and can move position. The extra distance

FIG D 5.39.2 The South Pole

FIG D 5.39.3 Surface of the planet Mercury

between the particles and their freedom to change position makes it difficult for particles to transfer kinetic energy to adjacent particles. Only limited conduction takes place in liquids.

Although the particles in a gas have lots of kinetic energy they are too far apart for effective conduction to take place.

FIG D 5.39.4 Particles in a solid vibrate

When a **fluid** is heated the particles gain kinetic energy and move further apart. The volume of the fluid increases. Since density = mass ÷ volume, it follows that if volume increases, the density will decrease.

The less dense heated fluid rises and is replaced by more dense cooler fluid. This process of heat transfer is called **convection**. It applies to liquids and gases but not to solids because the particles in a solid are in fixed positions.

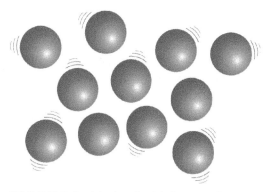

FIG D 5.39.5 Particles in a liquid vibrate and move

Activity D 5.39.1

You should work in a group of about nine students for this activity.

1. Stand in a square with three students on each side, as close as you can to each other.

2. Move your body around without moving your feet.

3. Notice how often you collide with the students next to you, like vibrating particles in a solid.

4. Repeat steps 2 and 3 but each time move a little further away from other students so that your square slowly gets bigger.

5. As the square gets bigger, what effect does this have on the number of collisions you have with fellow students?

6. If you were a particle in a solid how easy would it be for you to transfer energy to adjacent particles as the square gets bigger?

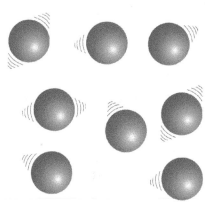

FIG D 5.39.6 Particles in a gas vibrate and move very quickly

Key terms

kinetic energy another term for movement energy

conduction main process by which heat passes through solids

fluid liquid or gas

convection main process by which heat passes through liquids and gases

Check your understanding

1. In terms of the position and motion of particles explain why:

   a) heat cannot transfer through a gas by conduction

   b) heat cannot transfer through a solid by convection.

40 Heat and temperature

We are learning how to:
- distinguish between temperature and heat
- use different scales to measure temperature

Thermal energy is often called heat energy or heat. The terms **heat** and **temperature** are connected but they do not mean the same thing.

Heat is a form of energy. Like all energy, it is measured in joules. Heat energy flows from a hot body to a colder body.

Temperature is a measure of how hot or how cold something is. When a body gains heat energy, its temperature rises and when it loses heat energy, its temperature falls.

FIG D 5.40.1 Temperature is expressed in degrees Celsius (symbol °C) and is measured using a thermometer

Activity D 5.40.1

Heat transfer

Here is what you need:

- two beakers
- hot water but not too hot to put your finger in
- iced water

Here is what you should do:

1. Three-quarters fill a beaker with hot water.

2. Three-quarters fill the other beaker with iced water.

3. Dip your finger in each beaker in turn and feel that the water is hot in one and cold in the other.

4. Leave the beakers to stand on the table throughout the lesson.

5. Near the end of the lesson, dip your finger in each beaker in turn.

6. Is the difference between hot and cold as big as it was at the start of the lesson?

7. What has happened to the water in each of the beakers?

When objects are at different temperatures, there is a temperature gradient between them. Heat energy is lost by the hotter object and absorbed by the colder object until their temperatures are equal.

Celsius scale

Temperature is measured using a **thermometer**. The units of temperature most commonly used are degrees **Celsius**. This has the symbol °C.

The Celsius scale is also sometimes called the **centigrade** scale. The Celsius scale was devised by the Swedish astronomer, Anders Celsius, in the 18th century.

Kelvin scale

Although the Celsius scale is widely used in science, it has one drawback. The melting point and boiling point of some substances are below 0 °C and therefore must be written as negative values.

In order to avoid this problem, a new scale was devised by Lord Kelvin. This scale started at the lowest possible temperature, which is –273.16 °C. This is absolute zero. To make conversion between the two scales easier, the start of the **Kelvin** scale, which is 0 K, is taken to be –273 °C.

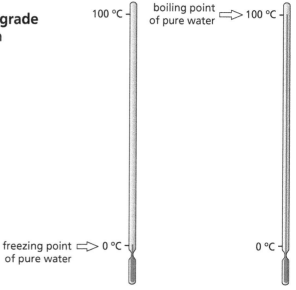

FIG D 5.40.2 On the Celsius scale, pure water freezes at 0 °C and it boils at 100 °C, at normal atmospheric pressure (these two temperatures are sometimes called fixed points)

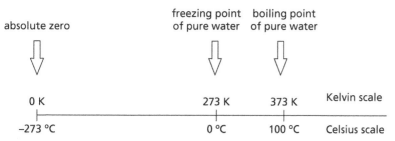

FIG D 5.40.3 Kelvin and Celsius scales

Notice that the unit is the Kelvin and not the degree Kelvin, and it is written as K and not °K. The Kelvin is the SI unit of temperature.

Check your understanding

Use the words 'heat' or 'temperature' to complete each of the following sentences.

1. When a body receives .... energy its .... increases.

2. .... is a form of energy while .... is a measure of how hot or cold a body is.

3. When an object is cooled its .... falls because it loses ....

4. The .... of a pond increases during the day because it receives .... from the Sun.

Key terms

thermal energy a form of energy

heat a form of energy

temperature a measure of how hot or how cold something is

thermometer an instrument used to measure temperature

Celsius a unit of temperature

centigrade an alternative name for Celsius

Kelvin a unit of temperature

41 Thermometers

We are learning how to:

- distinguish between temperature and heat
- use a thermometer to measure temperature

Measuring temperature ⟩⟩⟩

The thermometers most commonly used in the laboratory, and elsewhere, are called liquid-in-glass thermometers. They consist of a sealed length of capillary tube with a bulb at one end.

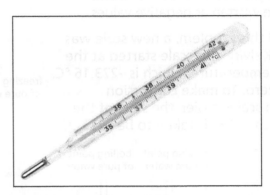

FIG D 5.41.1 There are two liquids commonly used in these thermometers: alcohol (ethanol), which is often dyed red, and mercury, which is silver in colour

Care must be taken when reading liquid-in-glass thermometers to obtain accurate readings.

When a liquid is placed in a narrow tube, the surface or **meniscus** is not flat but curved.

The reading on an alcohol thermometer (Fig D 5.41.2) is always taken from the position of the bottom of the meniscus.

The reading on a mercury thermometer (Fig D 5.41.3) is always taken from the position of the top of the meniscus.

Notice that when you read a thermometer, your eye should be level with the top of the liquid.

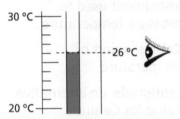

FIG D 5.41.2 The meniscus formed by a thread of alcohol is lower at the centre than at the sides

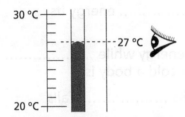

FIG D 5.41.3 The meniscus formed by a thread of mercury is higher at the centre than at the sides

Reading a thermometer accurately

Here is what you need:

- thermometer
- five beakers containing water at different temperatures

 SAFETY

Take care when using hot water. Follow local regulations.

Here is what you should do:

1. Put the thermometer in one of the beakers containing water.

2. Leave it for a few minutes.

3. Record the temperature on the thermometer.

4. Repeat steps 1 to 3 for beakers containing water at different temperatures.

5. **a)** Write an equation that will convert temperature on the Celsius scale to temperature on the Kelvin scale.

   b) Use your equation to express in Kelvin the water temperatures that you recorded.

6. [STEAM] Research how the temperature inside a furnace might be measured, given that it would be impossible to take measurements using a liquid-in-glass thermometer, because the glass would melt.

A thermocolour thermometer consists of a strip of a special type of substance called a liquid crystal. Some liquid crystals change colour with temperature and are described as thermochromic.

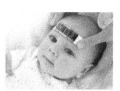

FIG D 5.41.5 A simple thermocolour thermometer can be used to show the temperature in a room or in a device such as a refrigerator, or it can be placed on the forehead of a person to measure body temperature

Check your understanding

1. What is the reading on each of the following thermometers to the nearest half of a degree Celsius?

FIG D 5.41.4

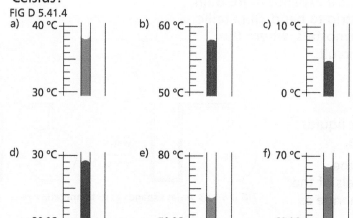

Key term

meniscus surface of a liquid

42 Physical properties that vary with temperature

We are learning how to:
- investigate physical properties that vary with temperature

In general all solids, liquids and gases **expand** when heated, but not to the same extent.

Expanding solids

Both metallic and non-metallic solids expand when heated. The expansion of metals can be demonstrated using the ball and hoop apparatus in Fig D 5.42.1. The metal ball does not fit through the hoop when it is cold, but when the hoop is heated it expands sufficiently for the ball to fall through.

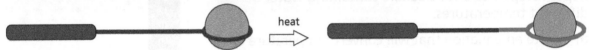

FIG D 5.42.1 Metals expand when heated

Large metal structures like bridges expand in hot weather. One end of the bridge is fixed while the other sits on rollers so the bridge can expand without **buckling**. Similarly, railway lines expand in hot weather, so a small gap is left between sections of line to allow for expansion.

FIG D 5.42.2 Bimetallic strip

A bimetallic strip is a strip composed of thinner strips of two metals bonded together. One metal expands more than the other when heated causing the strip to bend. Bimetallic strips are used in fire alarms and thermostats, where the bending strip completes an electric circuit.

Expanding gases

Gases expand far more than solids or liquids for the same increase in temperature.

If a flask of air is connected to a U-tube containing a coloured liquid, the levels of the liquid in the two arms of the tube change as the air is heated.

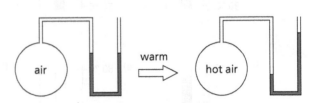

FIG D 5.42.3 A gas expands as its temperature rises

Activity D 5.42.1

Investigating heat and expansion

Here is what you need:

- balloon
- iced water
- plastic basin
- metre rule
- heat source

Here is what you should do:

1. Blow up the balloon and seal it by tying a knot.

2. Using a metre rule, measure the balloon's diameter.

3. Rub the balloon on your jumper or with your hands to warm the air in the balloon and measure the diameter of the balloon again.

4. Hold the balloon in a basin of iced water for several minutes to cool the air in the balloon and measure the diameter of the balloon again.

5. How did the diameter of the balloon change when it was heated and cooled?

Check your understanding

1. Explain what would happen if the air in the round-bottomed flask in Fig D 5.42.3 was cooled by placing a flask of iced water around it.

2. Table D 5.42.1 shows by how much 1 m lengths of different metals will increase in length per 1 °C rise in temperature.

Metal	Increase in the size of 1 m length of metal per 1 °C rise in temperature (m)
Aluminium	0.000 023
Copper	0.000 017
Iron	0.000 012

TABLE D 5.42.1

a) By how much will a 1 m length of copper increase if its temperature increases by 5 °C?

b) By how much will a 50 m railway line made of iron increase in length if its temperature increases by 20 °C?

Key terms

expand get bigger

buckling bending and twisting

43 Heat transfer – conduction

We are learning how to:

- compare types of heat transfer
- describe conduction as the process by which heat is transferred through solids

Heat transfer ⟫

For heat to be transferred, there needs to be a difference in temperature between two points. There are three different methods of **heat transfer**:

- **conduction** – this is the main process by which heat is transferred through solids

- **convection** – this is the main process by which heat is transferred through liquids and gases

- **radiation** – this is the process by which heat can be transferred across open spaces, including the vacuum of outer space.

In real situations heat is often transferred by a combination of these processes.

FIG D 5.43.1 A log fire heats a room by convection and radiation

Conduction

In solids the particles are held in fixed positions. They cannot move position but they do vibrate.

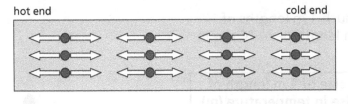

FIG D 5.43.2 Conduction in a solid

When a solid is heated the particles vibrate more energetically. The particles jostle neighbouring particles and in this way movement energy is passed through the solid. This process is called conduction. All solids conduct heat to some extent but some solids are much better **heat conductors** than others.

Do all solids conduct heat energy at the same rate?

Here is what you need:

- rods of metals and non-metals (such as copper, iron, glass, wood)
- candle wax
- boiling water
- large beaker
- cardboard
- small beaker

> ⚠️ **SAFETY**
> Take care when heating.
> Follow local regulations.

Here is what you should do:

1. Melt some candle wax in a small beaker using an electric heater.

2. Dip one end of each rod in the wax so that it is covered in the wax.

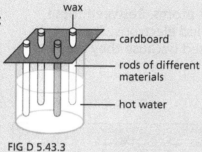
FIG D 5.43.3

3. Make holes in a square of cardboard. Make the holes just big enough to push the rods through.

4. Put the rods in the water so the wax-coated ends are out of the water.

5. On which rod did the wax melt first?

6. On which rod did the wax melt last?

7. Which material is the best conductor of heat?

8. Which material is the poorest conductor of heat?

All metals are good conductors of heat and most non-metals are poor conductors. Poor conductors of heat are called **thermal insulators** and include glass, plastics, wood, water and air.

Check your understanding

1. Explain why a toasting fork is made of metal but has a wooden handle.

FIG D 5.43.5 Toasting fork

Although diamonds are non-metals, they are the best heat-conducting solids known.

FIG D 5.43.4 Diamond conducts heat five times better than copper

Key terms

heat transfer transfer of heat from one place to another

conduction the main process by which heat is transferred through solids

convection the main process by which heat is transferred through liquids and gases

radiation the main process by which heat is transferred through a vacuum such as space

heat conductors objects that transfer heat energy easily

thermal insulators objects that do not transfer heat energy easily

44 Metals as conductors of heat

We are learning how to:
- compare types of heat transfer
- explain why metals are good heat conductors in terms of their structure

Why are metals good conductors?

The reason why **metals** are good conductors of heat can be explained by considering their structure.

A metal consists of a framework of atoms. Between these there are even smaller particles called electrons. These electrons are described as delocalised because they are not held in one place.

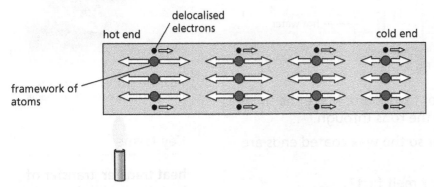

FIG D 5.44.1 Metals have mobile electrons

When a metal is heated, the particles vibrate more energetically, just like the particles of any solid, but in addition to this, heating increases the movement energy of the delocalised electrons. These move quickly and are able to transfer energy through the metal very quickly.

Activity D 5.44.1

Do all metals conduct heat energy equally well?

Here is what you need:
- conduction wheel (Fig D 5.44.2) or strips of four different metals of equal length
- tripod
- beaker
- candle wax
- four paper clips
- heat source

⚠️ **SAFETY**

Take care when heating. Follow local regulations.

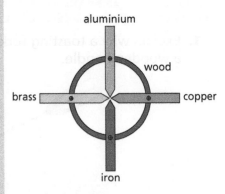

FIG D 5.44.2

Here is what you should do:

1. Melt some candle wax in a small beaker.

2. Put a small amount of molten candle wax on the end of the underside of each metal strip in turn, and hold a paper clip to it until the wax hardens.

3. When the metal strip is placed the right way up, the paper clip should hang down from it.

4. Put the wheel on a tripod and heat the wheel at the centre.

5. Record the time taken for the paper clip to fall from each metal strip. Write your answers in a table.

Metal	Time taken for paper clip to fall (s)

TABLE D 5.44.1

6. State the order in which the metals conduct heat, starting with the best conductor.

metal strip

candle wax

paper clip

FIG D 5.44.3

Check your understanding

1. Some results for the activity described above are given in Table D 5.44.2.

Metal	Time taken for paper clip to fall (s)
Aluminium	45
Brass	83
Copper	26
Iron	125

TABLE D 5.44.2

a) How can you decide which of these metals is the best conductor?

b) State the order in which these metals conduct heat, starting with the best conductor.

c) Chromium is a better conductor than iron but not as good as brass. Suggest the time it would have taken for a paper clip attached by wax to fall from a strip of chromium.

Key term

metal a type of material with delocalised electrons

45 Heat transfer – convection

We are learning how to:

- compare types of heat transfer
- describe convection as the main process by which heat is transferred through liquids and gases

Convection »»

The particles in liquids and gases are too far apart for conduction to take place effectively. Heat is mainly transferred through liquids and gases by another process called convection.

When the particles in a liquid or a gas are heated they move about more quickly. The particles spread out so they are further apart from each other. The volume of a liquid increases a small amount and the volume of a gas increases by a large amount.

Since the density of a substance is equal to its mass divided by its volume, it follows that when the volume of a liquid or gas increases, its density decreases. This decrease in density is the cause of convection. The less dense substance rises above the more dense substance.

Convection in liquids

It is possible to observe convection taking place in water by introducing a coloured chemical or dye to it.

Activity D 5.45.1

Convection in water

Here is what you need:

- beaker
- tripod
- drinking straw
- small crystal of potassium manganate(VII) or dye
- small candle or other heat source

 SAFETY

Take care when heating. Do not touch potassium manganate(VII) with bare hands. Follow local regulations.

cold water

crystal of potassium manganate(VII)

FIG D 5.45.1

Here is what you should do:

1. Pour cold water into the beaker until it is almost full and put it on a tripod.

2. Stand the drinking straw near the edge of the beaker and carefully drop a small crystal of potassium manganate(VII) down the straw so it lies in the corner of the beaker.

3. Gently warm the water around the crystal of potassium manganate(VII) and observe how the purple colour of this substance moves through the water.

4. Continue careful heating until all the water is purple.

5. Draw a diagram to show how the colour moves through the water in the beaker.

The particles responsible for the colour are carried by the water as it moves.

When the water around a coloured crystal at the bottom of the beaker is heated (Fig D 5.45.2), it becomes less dense and rises, carrying some of the coloured particles with it. Cooler water from the top of the beaker falls down to replace it. Overall the water rises as it gets warm and falls as it cools. This movement is called a **convection current**.

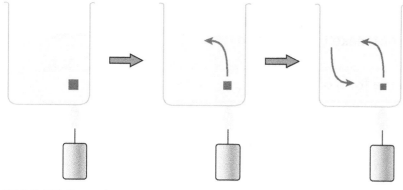

FIG D 5.45.2 Convection currents in water

Interesting fact

Convection currents occur on a massive scale in the oceans and in the atmosphere, and are an important factor in determining climate. Differences in temperature at different places in the oceans and the atmosphere result in the formation of convection currents.

In the oceans, convection currents help to circulate nutrients from the ocean floor into shallow water where they promote the growth of organisms.

Check your understanding

1. With the help of a suitable diagram, explain how heat is transferred through water in a heated pan.

2. Describe what convection currents you would expect to operate in the air in a kitchen when there is a hot cooking hob at one side of the kitchen.

Key term

convection current
movement of particles of a liquid or gas as a result of convection

46 Convection in gases

We are learning how to:
- compare types of heat transfer
- explain convection in gases in terms of changes in density

 Hot air 》》》

Convection takes place in gases in exactly the same way as in liquids.

Birds of prey know all about convection currents. They spread their wings and rise up on air that has been warmed by the land.

FIG D 5.46.1 Birds of prey can rise to great heights without having to use much energy

Activity D 5.46.1

To show that warm air rises

Here is what you need:
- square of thin card
- scissors
- needle
- cotton
- small candle

⚠ **SAFETY**
Take care when heating. Follow local regulations.

Here is what you should do:

1. Draw a snake on a piece of card by drawing a spiral line out from the centre. Do not make the snake too thin.

2. Cut out your snake so it is in the form of a spiral.

3. Thread a piece of cotton through the head of your snake. Tie a big knot at one end to stop the cotton falling through the hole and tie the other end to the end of a pencil.

4. Hold your snake above a small candle flame.

⚠ **SAFETY**
Do not place the snake too near the flame or it will catch alight and burn.

5. Describe and explain what happens to your snake.

6. [STEAM] Research the role of convection currents in creating breezes that blow from the sea towards the land during the day and from the land towards the sea at night.

FIG D 5.46.2

It is important to appreciate that during convection it is not heat energy that is rising but the heated liquid or gas. The heat energy increases the movement energy of the particles in the liquid or gas. As the movement energy increases, the density decreases and the least dense substance moves above the more dense substance.

In the atmosphere, convection currents are responsible for winds. The Sun does not heat the atmosphere directly. It heats the surface of the Earth and this, in turn, heats the air above it. When the air above the Earth's surface is heated it expands, its density decreases and it rises, creating an area of low pressure. Cooler, denser air moves in from surrounding areas of higher pressure to replace the rising air.

FIG D 5.46.3 You can see convection in a gas by observing a fire: smoke particles from the fire rise because they are carried upwards by the hot air

Check your understanding

1. A smoke box consists of a box with two chimneys. A candle is burned under one chimney while smoke from smouldering wooden splints is introduced at the other. The smoke box has a glass front so the movement of smoke can be observed.

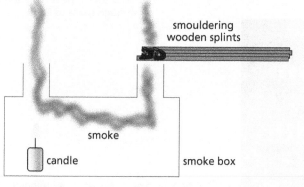

smouldering wooden splints

smoke

candle

smoke box

FIG D 5.46.4

a) Explain why smoke from the smouldering wooden splints is drawn into the box.

b) Would the same thing happen if the candle was not burning? Explain your answer.

Interesting fact

Convection currents help to keep rooms cool in the summer.

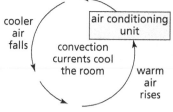

cooler air falls

air conditioning unit

convection currents cool the room

warm air rises

FIG D 5.46.5

Warm air rises and passes through the air conditioning unit. The cooler air falls, pushing the warm air upwards.

47 Heat transfer – radiation

We are learning how to:

- compare types of heat transfer
- describe radiation as the process by which heat is transferred across a vacuum

Radiation

The Earth and the other planets are separated from the Sun by the vacuum of space. A vacuum contains nothing – no solids, liquids or gases. How does heat travel from the Sun to the Earth and the other planets? There is a third way in which thermal energy can be transferred, called radiation.

Heat radiation consists of infrared waves that can travel through a vacuum in the same way as visible light. Heat radiation is not limited to space. There are many examples of devices on Earth that emit heat radiation.

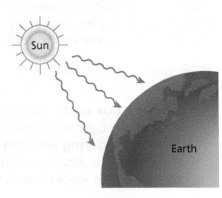

FIG D 5.47.1 Heat radiation travels through space to Earth

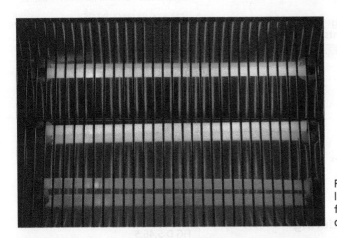

FIG D 5.47.2 An electric fire emits a combination of visible light, which you can see, and heat radiation, which you can feel (the shiny reflector behind the heating element helps to direct the heat radiation into a room)

FIG D 5.47.3 Houses in places that get lots of sunshine are often painted with bright colours (the bright colours reflect more of the sunlight than dark colours so the inside of the house is kept cooler)

Tinted glass contains particles of iron that absorb heat radiation. This reduces the amount of heat radiation passing through the window so the inside of the car stays cooler.

FIG D 5.47.4 Many cars have tinted windows

Activity D 5.47.1

Reducing heat radiation

You will not need any equipment or materials for this activity.

Some different ways of reducing the effect of heat radiation are described in the lesson.

Here is what you should do:

1. Carry out research into some other ways of reducing the effects of heat radiation.

2. Makes some notes and be prepared to share what you have found out in a class discussion.

Check your understanding

1. How do you know that heat does not travel from the Sun to the Earth by conduction or convection?

2. In what form is heat radiation transferred?

3. Why does an electric fire have a shiny metal plate behind the heating element?

4. How can the human body detect heat radiation?

Interesting fact

When it is dark, you cannot see the reflected light from objects, but thermal imaging binoculars detect the heat radiation that they emit.

FIG D 5.47.5 'Seeing' in the dark

48 Radiation and absorption of different surfaces

We are learning how to:

- compare types of heat transfer
- identify good and poor radiators of heat

Emitting and absorbing radiation »

Objects can both **emit** and **absorb** heat radiation.

FIG D 5.48.1 The heat radiation that is continually emitted by a person makes it possible to 'see' them in the dark using a device that detects heat

FIG D 5.48.2 The water in a swimming pool warms up when the Sun shines on it for a few hours

Activity D 5.48.1

Investigate if different surfaces absorb heat radiation equally well

Here is what you need:

- two cans of equal size: one shiny and the other painted matte black

- measuring cylinder

- two thermometers

Here is what you should do:

1. Using a measuring cylinder, fill the two cans with equal amounts of cold water from the same source.

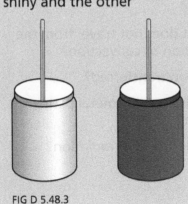

FIG D 5.48.3

2. Put a thermometer in each can and measure the temperature of the water it contains.

3. Write the temperatures in a table.

4. Put the cans in a location somewhere sunny, such as a window ledge.

5. Measure the temperature of the water in each can after 5, 10 and 15 minutes.

6. Write the temperatures in the table each time.

7. Which can was the better reflector of heat radiation?

8. How do you know this?

9. Which can was the better absorber of heat radiation?

10. How do you know this?

11. [STEAM] Describe how the results of this activity might be useful to designers who wish to create suitable clothing for people to wear in warm climates like the Caribbean.

Different surfaces do not emit and absorb heat radiation to the same extent.

- Surfaces that are matte (dull and dark) are the best absorbers and the best emitters.

- Surfaces that are light and shiny are the poorest absorbers and the poorest emitters.

Check your understanding

1. Fig D 5.48.4 shows details of a solar panel used for heating water.

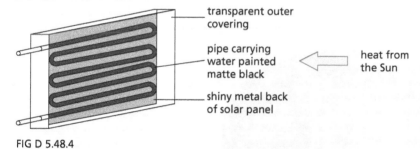

- transparent outer covering
- pipe carrying water painted matte black
- heat from the Sun
- shiny metal back of solar panel

FIG D 5.48.4

Explain each of the following features.

a) The panel has a transparent outer covering rather than a wooden outer covering.

b) The pipe is made of copper and not plastic.

c) The pipe is painted matte black.

d) The back of the panel is shiny metal.

2. The Sun releases 384 600 000 000 000 000 000 000 000 joules of energy each second. Write this value in standard form.

Interesting fact

A refrigerator pumps heat from inside to the air outside. The heat is lost through a coil at the back of the refrigerator.

C- PENTANE
C- PENTAN

FIG D 5.48.5 The coil on the back of a refrigerator is painted matt black so that the maximum amount of heat radiation will be emitted. Heat is also lost from the coil by convection through the air

Key terms

emit give out

absorb take in

49 Thermal insulators and conductors

We are learning how to:

- distinguish between thermal insulators and thermal conductors
- appreciate how thermal conductors and insulators are used

Identifying thermal insulators and conductors

A **thermal insulator** is a material that is a poor conductor of heat. Thermal insulators include wood, plastics, ceramics and glass. A **thermal conductor** is a material that conducts heat well. Most metals are good thermal conductors. Most cooking pans are made from metal so that the heat from the hob is conducted quickly to the food.

FIG D 5.49.1 Many pans have handles made of wood or plastic so that they can be held while food is being cooked

FIG D 5.49.2 Glass is such a poor conductor of heat that a glass blower can hold both ends of a glass tube while heating the middle

FIG D 5.49.3 Food stays hot for a long time in a ceramic dish because ceramics are good thermal insulators

Activity D 5.49.1

To compare how quickly heat travels through metal and plastic

Here is what you need:

- plastic teaspoon
- metal teaspoon
- cup of hot water
- stopwatch

 SAFETY

Take care when using hot water. Follow local regulations.

Here is what you should do:

1. Start the stopwatch.

2. Put the teaspoons in the hot water at the same time and hold them there, one in each hand.

metal teaspoon   plastic teaspoon

FIG D 5.49.4

3. After two minutes, can you feel a difference in the temperature of the two spoons? Which teaspoon was a better thermal conductor? Which teaspoon was a better thermal insulator?

Check your understanding

1. In an experiment, a strip of white paper was wound round a rod. One half of the rod was brass and the other half was wood.

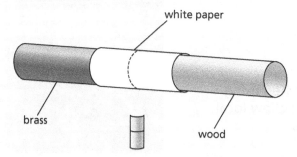
white paper

brass

wood

FIG D 5.49.5

When the paper was passed over a flame several times, the part wrapped round the wood was scorched but the part wrapped round the brass was not. Explain why.

Key terms

thermal insulator a material that is a poor conductor of heat

thermal conductor a material that conducts heat well

50 Air as a heat insulator

We are learning how to:

- distinguish between thermal insulators and thermal conductors
- explain the importance of air as a thermal insulator

Trapped air ≫

Heat is conducted through materials as a result of movement energy being passed from one particle to the next. The particles in a gas are much further away from each other than in a solid or a liquid. Gases are therefore poor conductors of heat.

Trapped air can be used as an **insulator**.

Wool keeps animals that live in a cold climate, such as sheep, warm in the winter. The wool can be shorn off the sheep and used to knit woollen jumpers to keep people warm.

Fibreglass consists of many layers of glass fibres. Small pockets of air are trapped between the fibres, giving this material excellent insulating properties.

Bird feathers are sometimes used to stuff duvets because of their insulating properties.

FIG D 5.50.1 Wool is a natural fibre that can trap air

FIG D 5.50.2 Fibreglass is often used to insulate the roof space of buildings to reduce heat loss

Activity D 5.50.1

Which material is the best insulator?

Here is what you need:

- four beakers
- four thermometers
- four types of insulating material
- cardboard
- scissors
- hot water
- measuring cylinder

 SAFETY
Take care when using hot water. Follow local regulations.

Here is what you should do:

1. Cover the bottom and sides of four beakers, each with a different insulating material.

FIG D 5.50.3 In cold weather, birds can fluff their feathers out to trap air between the feathers and reduce the loss of heat from the body

2. Cut out four cardboard lids for your beakers. Mark the lids A, B, C and D.

3. Make a small hole in the centre of each lid large enough to push a thermometer through.

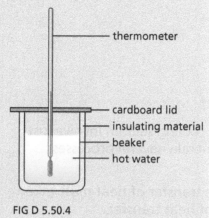

FIG D 5.50.4

4. Using a measuring cylinder, pour an equal volume of hot water into each of the beakers.

5. Put the lids on the beakers and record the initial temperature of the hot water.

6. Measure the temperature of the water in each beaker every two minutes.

7. Record your values in a table.

8. Use your data to draw a graph of temperature against time for each insulating material on the same grid.

9. From your graphs decide which material is the best insulator and which is the poorest.

Check your understanding

1. In some countries, buildings have outer and inner walls. A building can be insulated by filling the cavity with plastic foam containing bubbles of air.

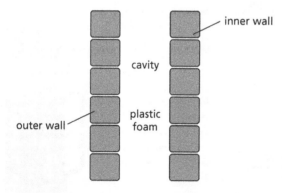

FIG D 5.50.5

a) Explain how heat could be lost from the inner wall to the outer wall across the cavity.

b) Explain why filling the cavity with plastic reduces heat loss.

Interesting fact

Hollow synthetic fibres are used in duvets and sleeping bags. The fibres trap air between them but there is also air inside each fibre.

FIG D 5.50.6 Hollow fibres are very efficient insulators

Key term

insulator material that reduces heat transfer

51 Total heat transfer

We are learning how to:

- distinguish between thermal insulators and thermal conductors
- appreciate the contribution of different processes to total heat transfer

Everyday examples of heating or cooling seldom involve just one method of heat transfer. Generally several processes occur together.

A device designed to control the transfer of heat must take into account all three methods of heat transfer.

Vacuum flask ⟩⟩⟩

A vacuum flask is designed to keep liquids hot on a cold day or cold on a hot day. To do this it must reduce heat transfer by conduction, convection and radiation.

The vacuum flask (Fig D 5.51.2) contains a glass vessel that has an inner and an outer wall. The air is removed from between the walls to leave a vacuum. The inner surfaces of the vessel are silvered. The flask is sealed by a cork stopper and plastic cap. Table D 5.51.1 shows how these features of the vacuum flask reduce heat transfer.

FIG D 5.51.1 In a wood-burning stove, heat is transferred through the metal of the stove by conduction, the air in the room is heated by convection and the fire also gives out heat radiation

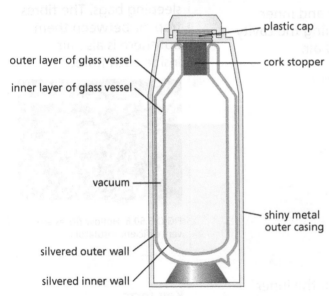

plastic cap

outer layer of glass vessel

inner layer of glass vessel

cork stopper

vacuum

shiny metal outer casing

silvered outer wall

silvered inner wall

FIG D 5.51.2 Inside a vacuum flask

FIG D 5.51.3 A vacuum flask keeps liquids hot on a cold day or cold on a hot day

Method of transfer	Feature of the vacuum flask
Conduction	The vessel is made of glass, which is a poor conductor. The stopper is made of cork and plastic, which are also poor conductors.
Convection	The vacuum between the inner and outer walls of the vessel prevents heat loss from the vessel by convection. Convection currents cannot form where there is no air.
Radiation	The inner surfaces of the vessel are silvered. The inner wall reflects heat radiation back into the vessel. This will prevent heat radiation leaving the flask, therefore keeping the contents hot. The outer wall reflects heat radiation from outside the flask. This will prevent heat radiation entering the flask, so keeping the contents cold.

TABLE D 5.51.1

Activity D 5.51.1

Examining a vacuum flask

Here is what you need:

- vacuum flask

Here is what you should do:

1. Carefully examine the vacuum flask and identify the structures discussed in the lesson.
2. Note the different materials used to make the vacuum flask and consider whether they are thermal conductors or thermal insulators.
3. Look at the mirrored surfaces and consider how reflecting heat radiation reduces the transfer of heat.

Interesting fact

Cool bags are designed to reduce heat transfer by conduction and radiation.

FIG D 5.51.4

Check your understanding

1. Fig D 5.51.5 is a diagram of a refrigerator.

   a) Explain why the refrigerator walls contain insulating material.

   b) Suggest a suitable material for insulating the refrigerator walls.

   c) Name the process by which heat is transferred:

   i) from the fluid through the metal tube

   ii) from the cooling fins into the room.

   d) Explain why the tube is made of metal and not plastic.

   e) Explain why there are fins on the heat exchanger.

   f) Explain why the cooling fins are painted matte black.

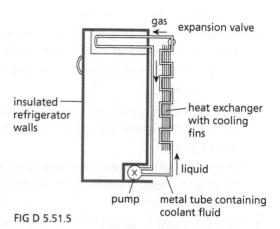

FIG D 5.51.5

343

Review of Thermal physics

- The particles in a solid are in fixed positions and close to each other.
- Kinetic energy can be transferred between adjacent particles in a solid.
- The particles in a liquid are able to move and are close together.
- The particles in a gas move very quickly and are far apart.
- Conduction takes place in solids, and to a much lesser extent in liquids.
- Convection takes place in liquids and gases.
- Heat is a form of energy and is measured in joules.
- The temperature of an object is a measure of the amount of heat energy it contains.
- When two objects with different temperatures are placed together, heat energy passes from the hotter object to the cooler object until both objects are at the same temperature.
- Temperature is measured using a thermometer. The most common type of thermometer used in laboratories is called a liquid-in-glass thermometer. The liquid is usually alcohol (ethanol) (containing a dye to make it easier to see) or mercury.
- The top of a column of liquid is called the meniscus and it is not flat.
- Temperature is most often measured in degrees Centigrade or Celsius. The symbol for this is °C.
- On the centigrade scale pure water freezes at 0 °C and boils at 100 °C at normal atmospheric pressure.
- The Kelvin scale is sometimes used in science.
- Solids, liquids and gases expand when heated.
- There are three different processes by which heat can be transferred – conduction, convection and radiation.
- Conduction is the way in which heat is transferred through solids. Heat increases the kinetic energy of the particles in a solid and this is passed to surrounding particles. Metals are good heat conductors, and non-metals are generally poor heat conductors.
- Convection is the main way in which heat is transferred through liquids and gases. When a liquid or gas is heated its volume increases. As its volume increases its density decreases. It rises away from the heat source to be replaced by cooler liquid or gas. This results in the formation of convection currents.
- Radiation is the way in which heat is transferred across a vacuum. Heat radiation is sometimes called infrared radiation.
- Materials that are poor conductors of heat energy are called thermal insulators, or just insulators.
- Air and other gases are poor conductors of heat. Many materials used as insulators, such as fibre glass, rock wool and expanded polystyrene, have pockets of gas trapped inside them.
- In real situations heat transfer is seldom limited to just conduction, convection or radiation. Heat transfer is more often a combination of two or even all three of these processes.
- Devices used to prevent the movement of heat energy, such as the vacuum flask, must be designed to reduce conduction, convection and radiation.

Review questions on Thermal physics

1. Fig D 5.RQ.1 shows how the particles in water are arranged in three different states.

a) Which state is represented by each diagram?

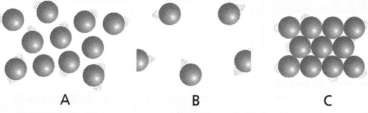

A   B   C

FIG D 5.RQ.1

b) In which state(s) is heat transferred mostly by:

   i) convection?   **ii)** conduction?

2. Fig D 5.RQ.2 shows a mercury thermometer.

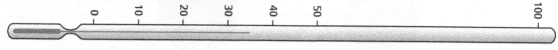

FIG D 5.RQ.2

a) Copy Fig D 5.RQ.2 and use a ruler to complete the scale between 0 and 100 °C.

b) Cyclohexane is a substance that melts at 7 °C and boils at 81 °C. Mark these temperatures on your thermometer using 'M' for melts and 'B' for boils.

c) In what state is cyclohexane at room temperature?

d) Apart from being a liquid, state two other properties of mercury that make it suitable for use in a thermometer.

3. Fig D 5.RQ.3 shows a frying pan. It is composed of two materials, X and Y.

FIG D 5.RQ.3

a) i) Suggest what material X could be.

  ii) Explain your answer.

b) i) Suggest what material Y could be.

  ii) Explain your answer.

4. A student filled a thin-walled flask with cold, coloured water and connected a capillary tube to it.

She then held the flask bulb in her hands for ten minutes.

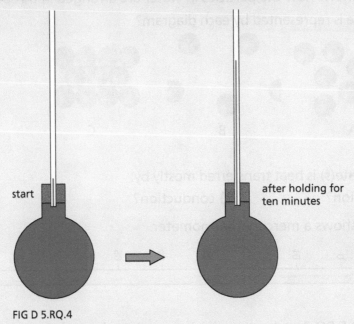

start

after holding for ten minutes

FIG D 5.RQ.4

a) What change was there to the apparatus?

b) Explain this change.

5. Fig D 5.RQ.5 shows ice cubes being heated in test tubes A and B.

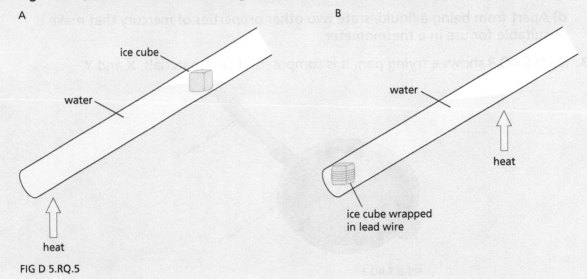

A

B

ice cube

water

heat

water

heat

ice cube wrapped in lead wire

FIG D 5.RQ.5

a) In which test tube will the ice cube melt more quickly?

b) Explain your answer to a).

6. An electric heater was placed exactly between two cans holding equal volumes of water. The cans were identical except that one was shiny silver (can A) and the other had been painted matte black (can B).

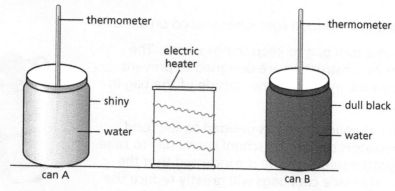

FIG D 5.RQ.6

The temperature of the water in each can was measured every minute for a quarter of an hour. The data collected is given in the table.

Time (minutes)	Temperature of water in can A (°C)	Temperature of water in can B (°C)	Time (minutes)	Temperature of water in can A (°C)	Temperature of water in can B (°C)
0	20.0	20.0	8	24.0	25.5
1	20.5	20.5	9	25.0	26.5
2	20.5	21.0	10	25.5	28.0
3	21.0	21.5	11	26.5	29.0
4	21.5	22.5	12	27.5	30.5
5	22.0	23.0	13	28.5	31.5
6	23.0	24.0	14	29.5	33.0
7	23.5	25.0	15	31.0	34.5

TABLE D 5.RQ.1

a) State three things that were kept the same to ensure that a fair comparison was made between the cans in this activity.

b) Name the main process by which heat energy is transferred from the electric heater to the two cans.

c) Plot graphs of temperature, on the y-axis, against time, on the x-axis, for can A and can B on the same grid.

d) Explain any difference in the graphs for the two cans.

53 Making a cool box

Cool bags are used to keep food cool when you go on a picnic.

You could also use a cool bag to keep things warm. The materials used in its construction are designed to prevent heat flow between the inside and the outside of the bag in either direction.

The Head Teacher at your school has decided to sell food and drinks to spectators during the school sports day to raise funds for new sports equipment. He is concerned that the cost of buying ready-made cool bags will greatly reduce the profits made on selling refreshments so he has turned to his science students for help.

FIG STEAM D 5.53.1 A cool bag

1. You are going to work in a small group to make a cool box using readily available materials. The tasks are:

   - to research the design of cool bags currently for sale in your community
   - to identify readily available materials that you think could be used in the construction of a cool box
   - to devise a method of manufacturing the cool box from the available materials
   - to compare how efficiently your cool box keeps food and drinks cool compared to a commercially available cool bag
   - to modify the design of your cool box to improve its efficiency
   - to compile a report, which is to be accompanied by a PowerPoint presentation. This should include photographs and/or a video sequence showing the construction of your cool box, and data showing how efficiently it performs.

   a) Refresh your memory by looking back through lessons 5.3, 5.5 and 5.7 on how heat is transferred and through lesson 5.9 on thermal insulators and conductors.

   b) Look at the different cool bags for sale in your local market or supermarket. What materials have been used in their manufacture? Do the sides feel padded? Can you guess by feeling them what the padding might be? How do these materials relate to what you know about insulators and conductors?

   c) What materials are readily available, either for free or at low cost that you could use to make a cool box? Can you obtain cardboard boxes from the local supermarket or perhaps the school office?

What about the materials to fit inside your cool box?
For example:

o Can aluminium foil be used to reflect heat radiation?

o Cotton wool and fibreglass as good insulators
but may not be readily available. What about
waste paper from a shredder? Would that provide
sufficient insulation?

Are there any other issues to be taken into
consideration? For example, your cool box needs to be
light enough to carry when it is filled with food and
drinks. It would be inappropriate to use materials that
might taint the food or drink in any way.

d) Make your cool box.

Draw up a plan of what materials you are
going to use and how you will use them.

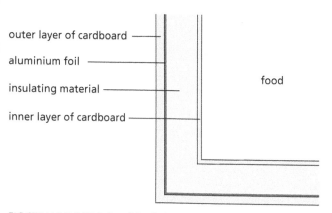

Fig STEAM D 5.53.2 shows one possible
structure for a cool box. For this design
you might consider questions like:

- How thick should the layer of
  insulation be?

- What insulating material should
  be used?

- Is there any advantage in having
  a second layer of aluminium foil attached
  to the inner layer of cardboard?

FIG STEAM D 5.53.2 Possible design for a cool box

Take some photographs at different stages of
the construction.

e) Devise a way to compare the efficiency of your cool box
with that of a commercially available cool bag. You could
place a beaker of iced water in each and monitor how
much the temperature rises during one hour.

Use the results of your test to modify your construction
and retest your cool box until you are happy with its
performance.

Prepare a PowerPoint presentation of the work you have
done. You should be prepared to explain your design and
your choice of materials, and illustrate your method of
construction with suitable photographs or a video sequence.
You should use the data collected to describe how your cool
box performed compared to a commercially available cool
bag and say how you modified your design to improve its
performance.

Index

Note: Page numbers followed by f or t represents figures or tables respectively.

Index

Acknowledgements

The publishers wish to thank the following for permission to reproduce photographs. Every effort has been made to trace copyright holders and to obtain their permission for the use of copyright materials. The publishers will gladly receive any information enabling them to rectify any error or omission at the first opportunity.

(t = top, c = centre, b = bottom, l = left, r = right)

Cover Blew_s/Shutterstock, p6t Monkey Business Images/Shutterstock, p6c Yuri Korchmar/ Shutterstock, p6b Monkey Business Images/Shutterstock, p8t Artic_photo/Shutterstock, p9 endeavour/Shutterstock, p10t Antonio Guillem/Shutterstock, p10c hafakot/Shutterstock, p10b Marmaduke St. John/Alamy Stock Photo, p12c Vlad61/Shutterstock, p15t Adisa/Shutterstock, p15c Pelham James Mitchinson/Shutterstock, p15b New Africa/Shutterstock, p16t Sumire8/ Shutterstock, p16tl Mindscape studio/Shutterstock, p16tr Chromatos/Shutterstock, p16l Martin Shields/Alamy Stock Photo, p16c Vereshchagin Dmitry/Shutterstock, p16bl BALOOM/ Shutterstock, p16br Chromatos/Shutterstock, p16b FoodStocker/Shutterstock, p17t Jakye/ Shutterstock, p18t MilanB/Shutterstock, p18c PRILL/Shutterstock, p18b Tim Knight/ Shutterstock, p28t Studiovin/Shutterstock, p29tl Gjermund/Shutterstock, p29tr StockPhotosArt/ Shutterstock, p29bl Gloverk/Shutterstock, p29br Urfin/Shutterstock, p32b Matveev Aleksandr/ Shutterstock, p33t DENNIS KUNKEL MICROSCOPY/SCIENCE PHOTO LIBRARY, p33b Lukasz Pawel Szczepanski/Shutterstock, p34t Nicku/Shutterstock, p34c Jess Kraft/Shutterstock, p34b Chronicle/Alamy Stock Photo, p35tl Crystyna Szulecka Photography/Alamy Stock Photo, p35tr Dane Jorgensen/Shutterstock, p35c Rolf Richardson/Alamy Stock Photo, p35bl Jess Kraft/ Shutterstock, p35br Radius Images/Alamy Stock Photo, p36t Science History Images/Alamy Stock Photo, p36c Science History Images/Alamy Stock Photo, p36b Vecton/Shutterstock, p38b with thanks to the Sickle Cell Support Foundation of Jamaica, p42t Onchan/Shutterstock, p46t ALEXANDRE DOTTA/SCIENCE PHOTO LIBRARY, p48t Gresei/Shutterstock, p52t Elena Schweitzer/Shutterstock, p54t Debbie Ann Powell/Shutterstock, p54c Gorodenkoff/Shutterstock, p55t Lightspring/Shutterstock, p55b gritsalak karalak/Shutterstock, p56l Lebendkulturen.de/ Shutterstock, p56c Lebendkulturen.de/Shutterstock, p56r Ye.Maltsev/Shutterstock, p57t Sumruay Rattanataipob/Shutterstock, p57b vsop/Shutterstock, p58 Leszek Glasner/Shutterstock, p59 mimagephotography/Shutterstock, p66b Monkey Business Images/Shutterstock, p70ct Dr. Norbert Lange/Shutterstock, p70cb Elisa Manzati/Shutterstock, p71t Sruilk/Shutterstock, p71bl Juris Sturainis/Shutterstock, p71br Mega Pixel/Shutterstock, p73cb Kazakova Maryia/ Shutterstock, p76c Emilio Ereza/Alamy Stock Photo, p76b Daniel Fung/Shutterstock, p80tl Krzysztof Skalny/Shutterstock, p80tc Artem evdokimov/Shutterstock, p85b David Smart/ Shutterstock, p86l CORDELIA MOLLOY/SCIENCE PHOTO LIBRARY, p86b Mary Lane/ Shutterstock, p90 Ashley Cooper/Alamy Stock Photo, p91 Rigamondis/Shutterstock, p92t Kuttelvaserova Stuchelova/Shutterstock, p92c Anest/Shutterstock, p92b wavebreakmedia/ Shutterstock, p93t Brent Hofacker/Shutterstock, p93b PhotoSunny/Shutterstock, p94c wavebreakmedia/Shutterstock, p95t Migstock/Alamy Stock Photo, p96cl Dan Kosmayer/ Shutterstock, p96cr PhotoMediaGroup/Shutterstock, p96bl BERNATSKAYA OXANA/Shutterstock, p96br Andrey_Popov/Shutterstock, p97t Matthias G. Ziegler/Shutterstock, p98br CREATISTA/ Shutterstock, p98bl Blend Images/Shutterstock, p99t Rob Bayer/Shutterstock, p100t Monkey Business Images/Shutterstock, p100c Pressmaster/Shutterstock, p102r DIBYANGSHU SARKAR/ Getty Images, p102l THOMAS COEX/AFP/Getty Images, p106 Mauricio Graiki/Shutterstock, p108t Romanova Nitali/Shutterstock, p108b Inozemtsev Konstantin/Shutterstock, p112 Jacob Lund/Shutterstock, p115t G Allen Penton/Shutterstock, p121l Crystal Eye Studio/Shutterstock, p121r John T Takai/Shutterstock, p127t Crabgarden/Shutterstock, p128t GagliardiImages/ Shutterstock, p128c Paul Doyle/Alamy Stock Photo, p128b BSIP SA/Alamy Stock Photo, p132t

Acknowledgements

BlueRingMedia/Shutterstock, p241b curraheeshutter/Shutterstock, p242t Dorling Kindersley ltd/ Alamy Stock Photo, p242c Everett Historical/Shutterstock, p242b age fotostock/Alamy Stock Photo, p243l PRISMA ARCHIVO/Alamy Stock Photo, p244t Jan Babak/Shutterstock, p244ct Pitipong Boonbanlu/Shutterstock, p244cb Cristian Storto/Shutterstock, p244b AFP/Stringer/Getty Images, p245t Unkas Photo/Shutterstock, p245b Leonard Whistler/Shutterstock, p249 Windu/ Shutterstock, p254t Yauhenka/Shutterstock, p255l Nataliia K/Shutterstock, p255b maxim ibragimov/Shutterstock, p258 Ruslan Harutyunov/Shutterstock, p259t Efanov Aleksey Anatolievich/Shutterstock, p259b Saami Ansari/Shutterstock, p260t Panksvatouny/Shutterstock, p264b Dmitr1ch/Shutterstock, p265t Keystone Pictures USA/Alamy Stock Photo, p267t Peter38/ Shutterstock, p268t charistoone-images/Alamy Stock Photo, p270t Andrei Nekrassov/ Shutterstock, p270b MA8/Shutterstock, p274br Volodymyr Krasyuk/Shutterstock, p286l PhotoSerg/Shutterstock, p286r PhotoSerg/Shutterstock, p287tl John Kasawa/Shutterstock, p287tr Krivoshein Igor Alexandrovich/Shutterstock, p287b Sue yassin/Shutterstock, p288t Feng Yu/Shutterstock, p288ct Pakin Praditcharoen/Shutterstock, p288cb BetterTogether/Shutterstock, p288br Romaset/Shutterstock, p289 Luke Thomas/Shutterstock, p290tl Sergiy Kuzmin/ Shutterstock, p290tr Ralph Huijgen/Shutterstock, p292tl Tanasan Sungkaew/Shutterstock, p292tr Jfanchin/Shutterstock, p298t B Christopher/Alamy Stock Photo, p298b Dmitry Bakulov/ Shutterstock, p299t Nor Gal/Shutterstock, p300 Phil Degginger/Alamy Stock Photo, p301t Fedorov Oleksiy/Shutterstock, p301b Peter Sobolev/Shutterstock, p303b Terekhov Igor/ Shutterstock, p307l Anton Kozlovsky/Shutterstock, p307r Science & Society Picture Library/Getty Images, p316t NEW YORK PUBLIC LIBRARY/SCIENCE PHOTO LIBRARY, p318t Chirokung/ Shutterstock, p318c Sean M Smith/Shutterstock, p318b Dotted Yeti/Shutterstock, p319t EDU WATANABE/Shutterstock, p319c EDU WATANABE/Shutterstock, p319b EDU WATANABE/ Shutterstock, p322tl Vova Shevchuk/Shutterstock, p322tr Bart_J/Shutterstock, p323r Science Photo Library/Alamy Stock Photo, p326t Erhan Dayi/Shutterstock, p327r Sararwut Jaimassiri/ Shutterstock, p327b Ffolas/Shutterstock, p329b zhgee/Shutterstock, p332t Anirut Krisanakul/ Shutterstock, p333t yelantsevv/Shutterstock, p334c Natalia Barsukova/Shutterstock, p334b Kovnir Andrii/Shutterstock, p335t Chesh/Alamy Stock Photo, p335b Stocktrek Images, Inc./Alamy Stock Photo, p336tl Dario Sabljak/Alamy Stock Photo, p336tr Romakoma/Shutterstock, p337r sciencephotos/Alamy Stock Photo, p338tl Warren Price Photography/Shutterstock, p338tr Celiafoto/Shutterstock, p338b Sergiy Zavgorodny/Shutterstock, p339r Jorg Hackemann/ Shutterstock, p340t Pete Pahham/Shutterstock, p340c Alena Brozova/Shutterstock, p340b Simon g/Shutterstock, p341r POWER AND SYRED/SCIENCE PHOTO LIBRARY, p342tr ARENA Creative/Shutterstock, p342br MidoSemsem/Shutterstock, p343t Ivonne Wierink/Shutterstock, p345tl EDU WATANABE/Shutterstock, p345tc EDU WATANABE/Shutterstock, p345tr EDU WATANABE/Shutterstock, p348 Ugorenkov Aleksandr/Shutterstock.